CISO D

M000239550

A Practical Guide for CISOs

Volume 1

Bill Bonney

Gary Hayslip

Matt Stamper

CISO DRG Joint Venture Publishing

Praise for
CISO Desk Reference Guide
A Practical Guide for CISOs
Volume 1

"CISO Desk Reference Guide is a one-of-a-kind reference. "

RADM (Ret) Kenneth D. Slaght
Co-Chair and President
Cyber Center Of Excellence

~~~~~

"The best book ever written on the role of a modern day CISO. Ground breaking with insights and advice on every page, The CISO Desk Reference Guide is a major contribution to the industry."

Jane Frankland
Founder of Cyber Security Capital, Board Advisor ClubCISO

~~~~~

"...the book is unique, as the reader gets the opinion on each topic from the three authors independently. For the reader, it's like having a private conversation with experts in the field on the readers' timeline ... in short, when really needed...."

Winnie Callahan, EdD
Director, University of San Diego Center for Cyber Security
Engineering and Technology

~~~~~

"I wholeheartedly recommend the CISO Desk Reference Guide to anyone who is or wants to become a Chief Information Security Officer."

Stephen Cobb, CISSP
Senior Security Researcher, ESET North America

~~~~~

"This is a fantastic resource for every security professional seeking to improve their skills and their careers. ... It's rare to find a treasure trove of knowledge like this. I look forward to Volume 2."

Vickie Miller
Chief Information Security Officer
FICO

~~~~~

"Tremendous value. Insightful and impactful for any organization, any executive and any board. Ties the criticality of managing risk to the need to be a part of the core business in a mature and commonsense way. This should help organizations futureproof their business with concepts and frameworks that are relevant today and for tomorrow."

Mark Wales
Vice President, 30+ year industry veteran and board member of the Workforce Institute

~~~~~

"I recommend this book for experienced CISOs who want fresh thinking on current topics, new CISOs who want to learn from the best, or others in information security and risk management who desire a greater foundation on the complex world of CISOs."

Todd Friedman
Chief Information Security Officer
ResMed

~~~~~

"The CISO Desk Reference Guide is written with a unique tri-perspective of three authors... is powerful in that it demonstrates there is never just one solution to any situation..."

Gabriele Benis
Former Vice President of Internal Audit
Intuit, Inc.

~~~~~

"The field of Information Security and compliance is complex at the very least. Three icons in the cybersecurity community, Bill Bonney, Gary Hayslip, and Matt Stamper through the use of what they call "Tri-Perspective" take on each practical subject matter, and truly make it a "CISO's Desk Reference Guide!" The call to action with the five immediate "Next Steps" will be a great comfort to those new CISOs that walk into the job the first day...And this desk reference book will be a great resource for the CEO, Board and CISO."

David W. Rooker, CISSP
Chief Information Security Officer
Actian Corporation

Copyright © 2016 CISO DRG Joint Venture

ALL RIGHTS RESERVED

CISO DRG Joint Venture Publishing
8895 Towne Centre Drive, Suite 105 #199
San Diego, CA 92122

<www.CISODRG.com>

ISBN 978-0-9977441-1-8

DISCLAIMER: The contents of this book and any additional comments are for informational purposes only and are not intended to be a substitute for professional advice. Your reliance on any information provided by the publisher, its affiliates, content providers, members, employees or comment contributors is solely at your own risk. This publication is sold with the understanding that the publisher is not engaged in rendering professional services. If advice or other expert assistance is required, the services of a competent professional person should be sought.

To contact the authors, write the publisher at the address provided above, "Attention: Author Services."

Cover illustration and original artwork
by Gwendoline Perez

Copy Editing by Nadine Bonney

Contents

Acknowledgements

Bill Bonney: I would like first to thank my wife, Nadine, for her loving support. She has always been my biggest fan and a source of constant strength. I am grateful for the support and camaraderie from my colleagues in the San Diego Information Security community, especially the members of the San Diego CISO Round Table. I sincerely appreciate the space and patience from my colleagues at TechVision Research that gave me the freedom to finish this work. Finally, thank you to my partners Gary Hayslip and Matt Stamper for their friendship and collaboration, it has been a wild ride, gentlemen!

Matt Stamper: I am grateful for all of the support I've received in undertaking this effort. My thanks to my colleagues in ISACA, the CISO Round Table, InfraGard, and my friends in the industry. Sharing insights and best practices with such talented individuals is greatly appreciated. I want to acknowledge and thank my family...especially my wife Lisa and our daughters Lauren and Danielle. Their patience with me cannot be overstated. I am also indebted to my parents for giving me a love of learning. Lastly, my thanks to Bill Bonney and Gary Hayslip. Working on this book together has been a great journey and your collaborative spirit has made this possible.

Gary Hayslip: I would like to tell my wife of 25 years, Sandi, thank you for your patience and calming influence. Your love and support has allowed me to stay focused on this project. You are my best friend and I thank you for putting up with my late night rewrites and rambling debates. I often say that cybersecurity doesn't exist in a vacuum, but it will flourish in a community. I'd like to thank the collaborative San Diego cybersecurity community. I am truly grateful for the support and collaboration I have received over the last 20 years. I especially appreciate my friends and colleagues in Peerlyst, ISACA, ISSA, OWASP, SOeC, CCOE, InfraGard, CyberHive, EvoNexus and the CISO Round Table, each of whom has contributed to the knowledge and passion that I have for our cybersecurity community. I am honored to count you as mentors, friends and peers. Finally, I want to thank my two partners, Bill Bonney and Matt Stamper. I am happy I listened to your idea over fish tacos and beer. This train ride together has been amazing. I am honored to count you as friends and I look forward to continuing this journey.

The authors wish to thank Gwendoline Perez for all her work in creating original cover art, graphical illustrations and design advice. In addition, Nadine Bonney deserves special appreciation as well for painstakingly combing through our run-on sentences, word usage disasters and our collective under-appreciation for the Chicago Manual of Style. We would also like to acknowledge our lawyer, Marinda Neumann, who patiently helped us set up our joint venture to begin creating a body of work we hope will benefit the information security community for years to come.

Finally, the authors wish to thank the following industry and academic leaders who were kind enough to provide thoughtful review comments that have helped make the CISO Desk Reference Guide a reality. As Gary Hayslip is fond of saying, cybersecurity doesn't happen in vacuum, but it flourishes in a community.

Thank you to Jerry Archer, Gabriele Benis, Kip Boyle, Dr. Winnie Callahan, Stephen Cobb, Limor Elbaz, David Hahn, Jane Frankland, Todd Friedman, Peter Gregory, Vickie Miller, David. W. Rooker, RADM (Ret) Kenneth D. Slaght, and Mark Wales for your time to review and provide thoughtful feedback.

Preface

Bill Bonney, Gary Hayslip, and Matt Stamper met in the summer of 2014 as members of the very inclusive and collaborative cybersecurity community of San Diego, California. Besides being the eighth largest city in the U.S. and a very welcoming community, San Diego is home to several pockets of technological innovation. These include very successful biotechnology, life sciences, and mobile technology industries; a plethora of defense contractors and aerospace research companies; a blossoming startup community in the Internet of Things (IoT) and Cybersecurity; and a thriving academic environment. San Diego is also home to the fewest number of "Fortune 500" company headquarters, per capita, in the U. S.

The decision to write this book came from the shared realization by the authors that the dramatic escalation in cyber threats was not going to peak any time soon. Cybercrime would continue to move "down the food chain" as more relative economic value is managed via interconnected computer networks. Mid-sized firms in particular, the kind that make up the local commercial base in San Diego, would come under increasing pressure as targets both for their own value and as the supposed "weaker links" in the supplier ecosystem of larger, multinational companies.

Each of the authors has enjoyed over 30 years of success in the Information Technology field, but they have very different backgrounds. It became obvious as they got to know each other by participating on panels and speaking at industry events that these different backgrounds brought diverse and complementary perspectives to the problems the cybersecurity community currently faces. What started as a panel discussion on the role of the modern CISO sparked such a lively audience discussion that the authors began to consider turning this topic into a book for new CISOs and CISOs at mid-size firms in particular.

But to allow those different perspectives to come through as obviously in print as they did during interactive sessions, they decided to take a unique approach in writing this book. Instead of dividing up topics or co-authoring each chapter, they decided to have each author write a separate essay about each topic from their own unique perspective. While this approach presents minor duplication and an interesting transition in styles from one essay to the next, the authors believe that this tri-perspective take on each topic will provide a number of benefits to the reader.

The book is conceived as a desk reference guide and structured as nine chapters with an introduction, three essays, and a summary for each chapter. The introduction highlights the different perspectives that each author brings to the chapter and sets the tone with the questions that the authors used to frame their thoughts. The summary pulls together five key points and five immediate next steps for the reader and his or her team, making this a very practical guide for CISOs.

The order of the essays within each chapter follows the arc of our authors' differing backgrounds and perspectives. Bill Bonney's essays lead off each chapter and provide a high-level perspective that reflects his background in the finance industry and the structured governance that comes with working in a highly regulated industry. Matt Stamper's essays come next and his perspective on providing services to many customers simultaneously provides insight into a highly programmatic approach. Gary Hayslip's essays finish each chapter and his vast experience in the trenches as a hands-on cyber expert provides the reader with a treasure trove of lists and lessons that they can repeatedly reference.

As a desk reference guide written specifically for CISOs, we hope this book becomes a trusted resource for you, your teams, and your colleagues in the C-suite. The different perspectives can be used as standalone refreshers and the five immediate next steps for each chapter give the reader a robust set of 45 actions based on roughly 100 years of relevant experience that will help you strengthen your cybersecurity programs. In the conclusion of this book we provide contact information and encourage you to join the community of CISOs who use these resources. We also encourage you to provide us with feedback about the guidance and about our tri-perspective approach to this book. We hope you like it.

Introduction

The title "Chief Information Security Officer" (CISO) is relatively new in industry, and because of this, there is a lack of institutionalized support. By that we mean that many organizations are still discovering what exactly a CISO does and how to be good partners to them. Readers of this book are already aware that the demand for talented CISOs is much greater than the supply and that the turnover rate is high. As we become more digitally interconnected companies, indeed whole industries, that didn't believe they needed a strong information security program in the past are now forced to play catch up.

This book, "CISO Desk Reference Guide, Volume 1," is conceived as a practical guide for CISOs. Volume 1 is intended to be foundational and addresses the key elements that new or experienced Chief Information Security Officers need to address when inheriting an immature cybersecurity program or building a new cybersecurity program. Our expectation is that Chief Technology Officers (CTOs) and Chief Information Officers (CIOs), along with their colleagues in the C-suite, can also benefit from reading this book and will become better partners to the CISO as a result.

In this volume, we address where we believe the CISO should report to be most effective, and then provide practical advice on regulatory, compliance, and audit concerns; the importance of knowing what data you have and where it is stored; and the criticality of your third-party risk management program. We then walk the reader through creating a metrics program and communicating with C-suite colleagues and the board. The first volume concludes by looking at risk management, including the emerging requirement to manage cyber liability insurance; approaches to managing the processes and tools in your portfolio; and setting up a security policy framework that will act as the underpinning for your program.

So now, let's turn to the role of the CISO and the fundamental elements of a successful cybersecurity program.

Chapter 1 – The CISO

Introduction

Where and to Whom Should the CISO Report?

We begin our book with one of the most basic and fundamental issues facing cybersecurity today, namely the reporting structure for CISOs. As our authors will note, this reporting structure has a tremendous impact on the efficacy of the organization's security operations. This discussion highlights the differences between traditional, IT-focused views of cybersecurity and those that are evolving to view cybersecurity as a risk-management function.

While there are differences in approach and perspective, our authors collectively emphasize how important it is for the CISO to know their organization's industry, regulatory requirements, and lines of business. This organizational context has important implications for the security operations' staffing levels and budget.

Bill Bonney highlights how organizations are demanding more of their CISOs and the fact that CISOs are expected to expand upon their deep technical knowledge to also include domain expertise in the areas of risk management and business operations. His analysis highlights how the balance between technical skills and business acumen is frequently influenced by the level of maturity of the organization.

Matt Stamper suggests that the reporting relationship for the CISO reflects how the organization views risk. Organizations that take a more expansive view of cybersecurity and risk will likely have a CISO reporting outside of traditional IT, generally reporting to the CEO or CFO. His perspective is that there are also inherent challenges in having a CISO report into IT. Under these scenarios, the CISO is placed in the unenviable position of having to judge the work of their boss, frequently the CIO.

Gary Hayslip offers a pragmatic view of where CISOs should report depending upon the industry context of the organization. What is clearly emphasized, and all the authors agree on this point, is that organizations that have a designated security officer – a CISO – will have better security outcomes than those who have not formalized this role within their organization. Gary highlights how critical it is for the CISO to truly know the organization – its people, its data, its industry, its applications, and its infrastructure. As Gary notes, "cyber doesn't exist in a vacuum."

Some of the questions the authors used to frame their thoughts for this chapter include:

- Who should I (the CISO) report to?
- How and where should the CISO and security program fit within the organization's structure?
- How and why do I see this changing?

Report to and Organizational Structure – Bonney

> "For many organizations, the CISO needs to be the Chief Resilience Officer."

We often think of reporting relationships and organizational structures as fixed. You get hired to do a job, reporting to a particular person in a department, business unit, or functional group that has a certain structure, and you learn to operate within those parameters. But as cybersecurity risks have become high-profile news-generating events, the CISO role has had to evolve. With that higher profile you sometimes get greater latitude to adapt to the changing threats, but you almost always inherit greater expectations that the approach taken by you, the CISO, on any given issue will be appropriate from a C-level perspective, not just technically correct.

What does that mean? It means that organizations are asking more from the CISO. Besides the technical standards and regulatory requirements that you've mastered, you are expected to know the products, the business, your customers, and the market in which your organization competes. You are also expected to act in a way that is best for the organization, placing the needs of the organization before the needs of your career or any other personal outcome. That's called a "fiduciary responsibility." If you need to change the structure of the information security group to meet the organization's needs, do it. If you should be placed in a different part of the organization to best serve its information security needs, it's up to you to determine that and advocate for it.

With that as backdrop, let's look at all three parts of this question: To whom should I report? How should the organization be structured? How should I expect that to change over time? We'll look at each of these questions through the lens of a C-level executive making the determination about what is right for the organization. We'll assume that whether you, the CISO, were hired at the C-level or not, you wish to and are expected to contribute as if you were a C-level executive.

Three Criteria for Deciding

The three criteria I'm going to apply are organizational maturity, business domain, and skill alignment.

By organizational maturity, in this context I mean specifically how experienced is the organization in dealing with the types of risks that threaten the continuity of its lines of business? Does it build in operational resilience to account for disasters and disruptions, develop continuity plans to recover normal operations, and communicate those plans to employees, key partners, and customers? Does it practice responding so that people throughout the organization, including within the customer and partner eco-systems, know what to do when disruption or disaster strikes?

By business domain, in this context I mean specifically what is the nature of its external environment? Does the organization operate in a highly regulated environment? Is the market segment in which it operates subject to numerous security or operational threats? Is it in a highly technical arena?

And finally, by skill alignment, in this context I mean specifically how do the skillsets within the Information Security department align with the expertise in the rest of the organization? Which business units or functional groups are responsible for business continuity? Where does responsibility for risk management lie? Is Information Technology managed centrally, regionally, or within business units? Where do the CIO and CTO report? Given this environment, what is the appropriate balance between technical skills and business acumen for the CISO?

Organizational Maturity

Let's start with organizational maturity. A key factor in your thinking should be that for many organizations, the CISO needs to be the "Chief Resilience Officer." This is especially true for those organizations without significant muscle memory in building and executing continuity plans. If the organization does not have much experience in this area, you should give strong consideration to having the CISO report to the Chief Executive Officer (CEO). In this environment, the organization is more likely to experience a devastating cyber-attack than a physical threat, and it is not likely to be ready for either without your help.

As the CISO, and informally the Chief Resilience Officer, it is your job to help the organization identify the key assets that must be recovered for the organization to continue as a viable entity and determine how to ensure that outcome. You'll drive the creation of action plans that will be executed in the event of a crippling cyber-attack. To do this successfully you'll need the full, active support of the entire executive team. Head nods and lip service are not sufficient. You'll need to answer for yourself "at what reporting level am I likely to get that support?" and advocate for that outcome.

The breadth of impact that a cyber event would have and the number of touch points that cyber-preparedness activity is likely to require throughout such an organization would be substantial. For that reason, it is likely that a CISO would be less effective as a sub-function of either Finance (reporting to the Chief Financial Officer (CFO)) or Information Technology (reporting to the Chief Information Officer (CIO)), even though these leaders typically own risk and technology, respectively. Nor is it likely that a Chief Operating Officer (COO) will have sufficient breadth of responsibility in this case.

If the organization has a mature process for business continuity, then it is imperative that the CISO is closely aligned with whoever owns business continuity. Ideally, you'll work with these key individuals to improve the existing plans to include recovering from a cyber-attack. At a minimum, you will need to share communication and escalation processes. Hopefully this will be a member of the C-suite so you can integrate with the team charged with keeping the company in business while the disaster, attack, or disruption is abated. If continuity planning is assigned but is too far removed from a C-level executive, you'll need to help the organization re-think its position and elevate that function or subsume it into your department.

Finally, if the organization is more mature and has high-functioning, independent business units that tend not to rely on centralized back-office functions, you should consider using more embedded resources to support the business units directly. While you're still likely to have a greater impact by centralizing infrastructure protection, incident response, and governance functions, embedding application security business partners directly into the business' technical and product teams may improve their ability to flex and keep up with changing business requirements.

Serious consideration should be given to ensuring that the CISO has the ability to make the difficult decisions without undo interference and is empowered to take appropriate and deliberate action with the necessary dispatch.

You should identify the issues where your specific leadership is key, such as incident response, enforcement of contract terms, and duties designated by regulatory bodies for your industry, and work with the C-suite to validate escalation paths and decision making authority.

Business Domain

I listed three factors above: the regulatory environment, threat environment, and technical environment. For organizations under significant regulatory oversight, there is likely already significant organizational capability built up around complying with control requirements. Examples include the financial industry and the medical industry. In many cases, corporate governance will be structured to comply with mandatory management oversight. This might include empowering specific committees of the board of directors with key responsibilities, and the designation of specific members of the management team with formal roles in risk management and information security. Guidance from the Federal Financial Institutions Examination Council (FFIEC), the multi-agency bank regulator, requires an organization's board of directors to sign off on information security policy and business continuity planning. It also requires that information security officers report either to the board of directors or to senior management as a safeguard to ensure appropriate separation of duties.

In these cases, the CISO must report at a level sufficient to provide appropriate oversight for key information technology strategy *and* execution. This would usually indicate reporting to the CEO or a C-level executive. While reporting to the CIO in this case can work, this should be approached carefully as the guidance goes on to state: "Typically, the security officers should be risk managers and _not_ a production resource assigned to the information technology department" (FFIEC 2015) (emphasis added).

I look at regulatory requirements as a governance cover charge. They mandate minimum *regulatory* standards of due care. In cases where the threat environment is above average (for instance, the 16 critical infrastructure sectors), due care should have a higher bar. The minimum bar might serve a smaller organization well. But, as the organization grows and becomes more visible, the threat environment will grow with it. The CISO might become a critical partner for the CEO as cyber risks multiply and be an occasional "external face" of the organization. The board of directors may need to elevate the CISO to report to the CEO with a dotted line to the Board to ensure the appropriate amount of oversight for this increasingly critical function.

Additional inputs to this equation may come from the type of business being conducted. If attacking your organization yields a disproportionate reward relative to other organizations, because of name recognition or because of your role in other business' security, you may have to structure your reporting relationship differently. This might be the case because your organization provides armored car services to many merchants, or sells computer security products for which the correct *and secure* function is essential to other organizations' systems operating securely.

In these cases, besides key oversight of Information Technology implementation, the CISO may well be the key escalation point to mobilize senior management, take control over multiple event responses, or even be the primary interaction point for communication channels. Again, the CISO will need well-formed partnerships with key players on the incident response team as he or she might be juggling the primary attack, news about that attack, and impacts to the organization's current assets or customer/partner assets. Given the highly visible role, the CISO in this organization should probably report at the CEO or COO level.

If the organization is in a heavily regulated industry or operates in part of the critical infrastructure, you might consider more centralization of the application security function to create a critical mass in the protective domain while embedding more of the governance functions to localize accountability and timeliness around the detect and repair functions.

Skillset Alignment

To finish this discussion, let's look at how to align the skillsets of the Information Security department, and its leader, with the skillsets in other parts of the organization. Traditionally, the CISO role has either been directly placed in a technology department, reporting to the CIO or the CTO, or evolved internally, from network management or compliance. As the CISO role has continued to grow in stature, CEOs' business unit General Managers (GMs) are expressing the opinion that the CISO needs to develop profoundly greater business acumen. Some place a higher importance on this than on technical depth. The sentiment is understandable. It's hard to imagine a new business initiative that won't have significant technical components.

Chapter 1 Key Point and Action Item 2

The role of the CISO comes with a C-level designation that denotes both the criticality to the organization as well as the responsibility bestowed on the individual hired into that role. Compared to the CIO and CTO, the other C-level technology roles, it is relatively new and still emerging and evolving into its ultimate form. As the CISO, you have the duty to ensure that you integrate into the C-suite through your reporting relationship and though the working relationships you build in your organization.

You should openly explore the options with the leadership team and advocate for the best outcome for your organization.

Business leaders see the CISO as having started later but being on the same maturity path as the CIO. There are obvious similarities between the roles. The role of the CIO emerged from a business need to centralize technology management and add efficiency, reliability, and cost predictability to organizations' rapidly growing and ever more complex technology footprint. The perceived risk being addressed was that complexity, cost, and unreliability were spiraling out of control and creating a drag on the organization's competitiveness and profitability. Business leaders note that the successful CIO is first a business partner. They embrace and champion new delivery models such as cloud SaaS offerings and recognize the opportunity to take advantage of clustered expertise, capability and innovation. They are able to learn and improve from various forms of "shadow IT," incorporate into their portfolio what makes sense for their organization and view all of the IT consumption models as part of their toolkit to enable the business to move with the speed and agility it requires.

Similarly, a C-level role for information security is evolving to allow organizations to bring order from chaos and provide leadership in a highly complex domain that cuts across all functional groups and business units. But many business leaders see the CISO emerging from a compliance-driven, risk-averse environment and want to see evidence that the CISO can properly balance risk versus reward and avoid establishing what they perceive as unnecessary barriers to success. Business leaders bear some responsibility for this perception in that until recently the CISO was often unnoticed until a breach occurred, and then was blamed and fired as a result of the breach. Still, it is important that the CISO take several pages from the CIO playbook to truly learn the business and how to run their organization as a business. The CISO will need credibility with the business units to be given the latitude to implement critical security controls and introduce the rigor needed for successful continuity planning and cyber resilience.

One key caveat, though, is that although a business focus is critical, the CISO role is different from the CIO role in a very important way. Regulatory and contractually mandated security controls often require an individual within the organization to be assigned the authority to respond to a security event by ordering emergency actions to protect the organization and its customers from an imminent loss of information or value. This person is required to have sufficient knowledge, background, and training, as well as an appropriate position within the organization, to enable them to perform these tasks.

Although most of this discussion has been about the CISO personally, the organization will not be able to accomplish its goals without structuring the rest of the information security department to complement the CISO's efforts. In order to allow the CISO to work with the GMs to develop that intimate understanding of the business objectives, the senior leaders in information security must work with their peers to understand and influence the choices of key underlying technologies and development platforms, and should be keenly aware of major milestones and deliverables. All the while, the security engineers must work with their counterparts in the development organizations on threat models and secure coding methods within the development platforms that are in use. Members of the Security Operations Team need to work with network engineers, database administrators, and systems administrators to understand normal and anomalous usage patterns.

In addition to the deep subject matter expertise security engineers are required to have, they must also be excellent team players, capable of explaining security concepts in a way their development and support partners can consume, be well versed in the tools being used by their peers, and most importantly, deeply aware of and supportive of their peers' deliverables. The business alignment of the CISO should cascade all the way down to the Security Operations Team and everyone in the security organization should be focused on both their technical role and the business impact of their actions.

And finally, while these are key attributes to be used as hiring and evaluation criteria, the entire team should think of themselves as risk managers and align themselves with those members of the legal, finance, and operations teams that are responsible for identifying, understanding, and addressing risk throughout the organization.

CISO Reporting Structure – Stamper

> "What's clear is that the role of the CISO as the champion for cybersecurity and risk-mitigating activities has reached a level of importance that heretofore has not been seen within organizations."

We open our book with a fundamental question, "Where should the CISO sit within the organization?" The answer to this simple question can have a significant and material impact on your organization's cybersecurity program. I love the title of Geert Hofstede's book: *Cultures and Organizations: Software of the Mind*. Culture becomes the core software of the organization...structuring decision-making, reporting relationships, and other entity-specific activities. Organizational culture is influenced as much by the organization's structure (specifically reporting relationships) as the organization's structure is influenced by its culture. The two factors cannot be addressed without minimally assessing one or the other. Where the CISO sits within the organization provides insights into organizational dynamics and how the organization views risk management. Indeed, the reporting structure for the CISO can be one of the most important determinants of the effectiveness of this role within the organization.

Throughout my career, I've always spoken about the importance of two key variables: context and structure. I view these as highly interrelated. Structure is foundation. It guides activities, outcomes, and provides flow-enhancing limits to decision-making[1]. Context complements structure. Context is like a pivot table...being able to quickly see relationships between data. Context and structure. Structure and context. We see the importance of context and structure when looking at industries, regulations, markets, and within an organization, the reporting relationships. The absence of structure coupled with limited context can stifle careers, undermine organizational capacities, and introduce risk that could have otherwise been avoided. Another way to look at context and structure is to think about staffing levels and competencies. Do we have the right people in the right roles doing the right work with the

---

[1]. The notion of flow-enhancing limits to decision-making may be counterintuitive but a clear visual is the proverbial kid in a candy store. When confronted with near limitless options, there is a tendency to take pause and assess options. As any parent knows, time breaks the laws of physics and just stops. When processes and procedures are vaguely documented or organizational structures are absent (e.g. who owns this process, what reports are required, who should be informed, how is this measured, etc.), indecision results. Well-structured processes reduce this dynamic.

right tools? Staffing levels and competencies is context and structure in action. Evaluating staffing levels and competencies will surface important detail related to the organization's obligations – be they contractual, regulatory, or the hidden hand of the market.

To whom, then, should the CISO report? This will reflect the industry context and organizational structure of the firm. The answer to this question provides insight into how the organization views cybersecurity. If we boil the options down to two different approaches, we see how the role of the CISO is evolving. One approach, likely the more traditional, is to have the CISO report into IT…likely to the CIO or CTO. This reporting relationship tends to view security from a technical perspective. A separate, growing approach is to have the CISO report directly to the CEO or CFO. This reporting relationship views cybersecurity in broader, risk-focused terms. We are also seeing a new security role emerge…the non-CISO CISO. An individual designated as a security officer given regulatory or industry requirements. As noted above, organizational dynamics will drive one approach over another. Let's take a look at the considerations of each reporting environment.

The "Technical, IT-Focused CISO" Reporting to Traditional IT Leadership

When the CISO reports into a traditional IT structure, there is likely a more technical focus related to cybersecurity activities. The CISO's primary function is to minimize the risks associated with IT services and to provide technical, cyber-related expertise to the CISO's colleagues within IT. This approach could be thought of as the "packet police." It's a dangerous world, and the CISO and his or her staff are there to ensure that only good packets enter (or leave) the organization. Effectively, the CISO's perspective has pivoted down to the bits and bytes that, in the aggregate, become the information used to run the organization. To simplify the distinction, there tends to be a layer 2 / layer 3 bias. Cybersecurity is network centric and core activities in this role center on device and network security. Again, this an overly simplified view of the CISO function to make the distinction more explicit when compared to the empowered CISO role discussed below.

There are important benefits from an IT-centric and technical approach to the CISO role. The cyber threats facing organizations today can be highly sophisticated attacks, advanced persistent threats (APTs) if you will, that require deep technical knowledge to discover and remediate. Specifically, the CISO's team would need to understand packet analysis, network design and topology, and technical indicators of compromise (IOCs) to triage and respond to anomalous behavior within the organization. These skills and competencies are at the center of cybersecurity. An IT-centric CISO becomes a critical member of the IT leadership team validating security configurations and practices.

Of concern with this reporting relationship, however, is the inherent conflict created by the reporting structure. If the CISO's core function is to ensure that IT security practices and configurations are managed correctly, communicating challenges with these practices upward in the organization (e.g. to the CISO's boss) can be problematic. Essentially, the CISO is asked to police his or her boss' work, evaluating the risk considerations created by the boss' selected technologies and their deployment. Such feedback can be career-limiting to say the least. For this structure to work correctly, the CISO and the CISO's boss must be open, professional, and focused on objective outcomes. Managing through the dynamic of questioning the IT leadership's practices, competencies, and policies puts an enormous strain on this role. This is the reason why separation of duties is such an important control.

The CISO may also be forced to react to organizational changes including vendor selection, platform assessment, and architectural design. Depending upon the organizational dynamics at hand, security-by-design may be impossible if the CISO is the downstream recipient of IT decisions made elsewhere or at a different layer within the organization. The CISO is effectively asked to clean up security-related matters that could have been precluded with greater cyber input earlier in the decision-making process.

Other challenges are presented by this organizational structure. The visibility of cybersecurity-related matters is critical to other lines of business, the executive team, and the board of directors. When the CISO reports into traditional IT leadership, there is an opportunity to have the CISO's insights and recommendations tabled or altered before reaching other critical audiences within the organization. This is a risk that is not acceptable from the perspective of the board or the C-suite. Simply stated, the board and the C-suite need to be aware of the cyber threat landscape facing the organization and having this context potentially watered down or omitted from the agenda is too risky. This is the same reason why larger organizations maintain an internal audit function that does not report into the organizational structure they are charged with evaluating.

Where CISOs report organizationally is evolving to reflect these dynamics. Given the existential risks associated with poor cyber outcomes for many companies, the CISO function can no longer be buried two or three layers deep within traditional IT. Boards of directors and certain members of the C-suite have fiduciary requirements to manage their organization's risk. Not having accurate, complete, and timely detail related to cyber risk undermines this fiduciary responsibility. As a consequence, we are seeing a new CISO emerge. This modern CISO is a business partner and, ideally, a welcomed member of the C-suite.

The Empowered CISO

If we view cyber as a risk factor warranting executive attention, a view I strongly support, risk considerations related to cybersecurity must be adequately documented, assessed, and managed by the organization's broader leadership team. To accomplish this, I strongly believe that CISOs today need to be the peers of the CIOs and CTOs of their organizations and that they need to report directly to either the CEO or CFO. It is also highly advisable that the CISO have calendared meetings with the board of directors to ensure that the board is aware of the cybersecurity risks confronting the organization.

Key to this peer-based organizational structure is a broader, more holistic view of cybersecurity practices both within and without (think third parties and partners) the organization. Beyond the critical skills and competencies required to evaluate technical security matters, a CISO reporting outside of the traditional IT structure would also need additional context related to legal and regulatory matters (our next chapter). Indeed, the Securities and Exchange Commission (SEC) began issuing guidance to public companies to evaluate security risks as part of their overall risk management practices. The SEC has even gone so far as to issue guidance on the impairment of goodwill that could result from a breach (*CF Disclosure Guidance: Topic No. 2, Cybersecurity - October 13, 2011*).

The Federal Trade Commission (FTC) has broadened its definition of "unfair and deceptive trade practices" to incorporate inadequate cybersecurity controls. Consent decrees issued by the FTC, let alone potential fines, are frequently measured in 20-year duration biannual audits. Effectively, consent decrees result in a public shaming of the organization at the extreme end, to, minimally, a public acknowledgement that the organization's cybersecurity practices were woefully inadequate. All of these scenarios impact the C-suite and the board of directors. Their oversight of cybersecurity practices (staffing levels and competencies, risk management, tools, third-party providers, etc.) requires unfettered information (more accurately conveyed as the *ground truth*).

The empowered CISO requires skills in combinations that are frankly hard to find and provide a limiting factor on this approach. This is clearly one of the reasons why there is intense competition for highly-qualified CISOs in the market today. The empowered CISO must possess technical acumen across a variety of technologies and platforms and couple this requisite technical knowledge with a deep, organization-wide understanding of risk-management and privacy as well as legal and regulatory obligations.

To be successful, the empowered CISO needs to understand the strategy of the organization, the information and data the organization handles, its lines of business and stakeholders, as well as the organization's overall risk appetite. The empowered CISO must also have solid interpersonal skills to work with colleagues across the organization that may view cybersecurity and associated controls as an impediment to taking action. The CISO becomes the advocate in chief of good cybersecurity practices.

What does this translate to with respect to day-to-day activities? It means that the CISO needs to be seen frequently by non-IT members of the organization. An empowered CISO meets regularly with peers and department heads to understand their practices and the needs of their teams from more than a cyber-specific perspective. As part of this *management by walking around*, the CISO learns about the organization's initiatives, stakeholders' objectives, shadow IT, non-IT sponsored applications, and key vendor relationships. This ground truth will provide important context for the CISO's cybersecurity activities. Equally important, having a highly-visible CISO provides informal, but critical, opportunities for security training. These ad hoc discussions offer a level of knowledge transfer that is rarely matched in more formalized security training efforts within an organization.

Chapter 1 Key Point and Action Item 3

The CISO should be deeply integrated with the C-suite and form strong working relationships with key executives to both advance the cause for better cybersecurity outcomes and gain a comprehensive understanding of the business needs and objectives. At the same time, the CISO's staff must engage at their respective levels with their colleagues for the same fundamental reasons. The CISO cannot influence the changes in behavior needed for good cybersecurity outcomes alone. It takes the entire team teaching, learning, advocating, and speaking with one voice.

You should work with your team to develop a mission statement and a set of clearly articulated objectives that your staff can use to provide consistent guidance to their peers and partners.

The empowered CISO functions in an advisory role within the firm. As such, the empowered CISO will weigh in on critical, potentially non-IT decisions including vendor selection (minimally guidance on vendor-specific due diligence), data classification and treatment, and other activities that could impact the confidentiality, integrity, and availability of key systems supporting the organization. CISOs in this new role need to be highly effective communicators with notable powers of persuasion when formal authority is not fully commensurate with the cybersecurity requirements at hand. Stated differently, the empowered CISO needs to have the respect of colleagues within the organization to influence business decisions in a manner that is consistent with cybersecurity objectives but that do not appear to be undermining, delaying, or interfering with the organization's agility. These *soft* skills and influence usually require time to develop. CISOs must have the time and organizational commitment to grow into their roles.

The Non-CISO CISO

What if a company does not have a CISO? For many smaller organizations, IT may consist of one or two individuals providing network or system administration. Even mid-sized companies often lack a formal head of IT security. Here, cyber risk can be at its highest. A small, non-IT focused organization does not necessarily mean that cybersecurity and privacy obligations are not required of this organization. We see this scenario frequently with professional services firms, notably accountancies and law firms, which handle their clients highly-sensitive information. Risk factors, many of which could be deemed to be existential for the firm, may go undocumented, unassessed, and unmitigated.

How then do smaller organizations address cybersecurity in the absence of a CISO? One simple approach is to formally designate a security officer within the organization (this is something that is mandated by federal law for organizations subject to HIPAA-HITECH – for those so inclined, please reference code: 164.308(a)(2)). This designation functions as an administrative safeguard. Designating someone within the organization to function as the security officer will at least get cybersecurity on the agenda. Ideally, this individual will have a strong operational understanding of the organization – its processes, key vendors, key customers, contractual requirements, types of data processed, and the like. This insight informs a risk-management approach to cybersecurity for the non-CISO CISO.

For the newly-designated security officer, the world of cybersecurity can be daunting. Fortunately, there are approaches that can be undertaken to flatten an otherwise step learning curve.

Cybersecurity risk is a subset of overall risk-management practices. The security officer would be well-served by adopting the practices that are outlined in the empowered CISO section noted above, namely learning the core functions of the organization and the types of information that are processed. A few basic questions can help kick start the process of evaluating cybersecurity practices within the organization.

A non-CISO CISO should ask the following:

- What obligations does the firm have (be they mandated by law or contract) relative to protecting our employees' or customers' data?
- Where does this information live within the firm (e.g. which applications, processes, vendors, or IT systems)?
- What are the current administrative, technical, and physical safeguards in place protecting this information and data?
- What resources will I need to be able to evaluate the current practices?
- Where can I go to get additional support to develop a cybersecurity competency within my organization?

These basic questions will start the process and help newly-designated security officers begin evaluating cyber risk within their organizations.

The role of cybersecurity within an organization, even for those who have previously considered themselves immune to needing IT security, has become central to appropriate risk management practices. The fundamental importance of IT for firms today cannot be underestimated. Knowing the risks related to using IT must be captured and understood by executive management and the board as part of the organization's overall risk-management strategy.

The voice of this analysis comes from the CISO. This necessitates that cybersecurity practices be present on the executive agenda. Specifically, the CISO, regardless of reporting relationships, should provide guidance and expertise on the following:

- Cybersecurity practices, procedures, and metrics
- Data and asset classification from a cybersecurity and risk-perspective (including privacy impacts)
- Vigilance and monitoring of cybersecurity activities and trends
- Oversight of auditing and governance practices including liaising with internal and external audit
- Incident response in collaboration with the organization's counsel
- Security policy design
- Security services implementation
- Security training
- Holistic risk management and risk assessment reporting (including vendor and business processes)

What's clear is that the role of the CISO as the champion for cybersecurity and risk-mitigating activities has reached a level of importance that heretofore has not been seen within organizations. We are, in effect, entering the era of the CISO.

The Role of The CISO – Hayslip

> "...your role of CISO in an organization is what you make of it – cyber doesn't exist in a vacuum. It will thrive when shared and distributed throughout an organization."

The position of Chief Information Security Officer (CISO), though relatively new for many organizations, is one of technical complexity that is not for the faint of heart. This position is the leading cybersecurity expert for a company and in many companies the CISO will receive full repercussions if there is a data-security breach. Incumbents in this position will make decisions that impact all aspects of an organization and its ability to conduct business. Some of these decisions will involve interpreting regulations, establishing new policies, or influencing employee/corporate culture. There are several questions whose answers will help the CISO fully understand if they are positioned to provide value to their organization or if they are on the outside looking in.

As the CISO, having answers to these questions will be fundamental in your ability to provide quality cybersecurity services to your company and its business units.

1. What is my role as CISO in my organization?
2. Who should I, as the CISO, report to in my organization and why is that important?
3. Is my security program sourced correctly, does it fit within my organizational structure?
4. What changes do I see in the future for the role of CISO?

I believe the answers to these questions will provide clarity to the CISO and enable them to partner effectively with their company's stakeholders. This information will also provide the CISO with a fuller understanding of how their organization views cybersecurity. In essence, do they look at the cybersecurity program as the "No, you can't do that!" program, or is it viewed as the company's "Secret Weapon?" In the discussions that follow, I will provide my perspective on these questions and I hope through our discourse you will learn how this knowledge can be applied to your journey as a CISO.

What Is Your Role as CISO?

The formal position of CISO is relatively young. For many years, a good network engineer was expected to fill in and do security as an additional component of their job. However, within the last 10 years or so there has been strong movement in organizations to designate someone solely responsible for information security. Granted, federal law and compliance regimes such as HIPAA-HITECH and PCI have had a hand in moving companies in that direction. It can be said that many organizations hired a Security Director or CISO to meet their auditor's check box.

However, over the last several years, due to the prevalent rise of cybercrime many organizations have come to realize that their ability to reduce cybersecurity risk and defend themselves rests on who they have in the CISO position. In effect, companies are acknowledging that if they lack a CISO, they are increasingly vulnerable. Companies now face a cyber truism, that cybersecurity is not an information technology problem, it is an enterprise-wide risk management problem and you need a CISO to address this risk.

So now we come to the first question, *"What is my role as CISO in my organization?"* As a current CISO, the answer to this question to me is critically important. In this position I have the responsibility to protect an organization's assets (data, networks, applications, people) and, by providing key security services, not interfere with my company's ability to conduct business. This becomes increasingly difficult when, as a CISO, you face disparate risks that include technologies such as "ever-present" mobile devices, the global span of organizations' business operations with network/data boundaries across continents and the constant threat of new cybercrime variants. It is because of this responsibility, and the associated risks that I want to understand the scope and limitations of my position as CISO. Some questions that I believe a CISO would want to fully explore are:

- As CISO, do I have the authority to act in an emergency?
- As CISO, do I have the authority to manage the organization's cybersecurity suite?
  - Do I control my budget?
  - Do I select what devices/applications are installed in my cybersecurity suite?
  - Do I have the authority to change and write policy?
- As CISO, am I a member of the IT leadership team?
- As CISO, am I allowed to present cybersecurity issues to executive management?

The answers to these questions will provide insight into how the role of CISO is viewed by your company. Lacking the authority to manage a security incident will be a major obstacle for you. The job of CISO is like that of a digital firefighter. If you don't have the authority to manage the teams responding to a security incident, you are in effect fighting a fire without a firetruck. Without a firetruck you can still put out the fire, but it takes longer and more damage is done to the structure. In today's age of advanced malware attacks, it is critical that as CISO that you have the authority to marshal the proper resources to quickly stop and remediate a security incident. Otherwise, the organization is exposed to undue risk.

As the CISO of an organization, you will typically inherit a security program that was in place before you accepted your position. As you review your company's security program and its varied components, it's inevitable that you will find changes that you wish to implement. You may want to use an established risk framework such as COBIT, ISO, or NIST to better evaluate your organization's technology risk baseline. You may want to change your SIEM solution to one that provides better data analytic capabilities.

The question here is: do you have the authority to make these changes, or can you only make recommendations and the final decision will be made by someone outside of cybersecurity? Again, if this is the case and as CISO you are unable to directly make changes to your cybersecurity suite, standing policies or budget, it will be extremely difficult for you to upgrade your cybersecurity program and reduce the risk exposure to your organization. Here is what you need to find out if this is a current issue for you:

- Is this lack of authority because previous CISOs were not trusted?
- Is this an organizational business rule not allowing you as CISO to directly manage your cybersecurity program?

The answers to these two questions will help you understand what work is required to make the case that cybersecurity is critical to the organization and you need flexibility to keep it current. I have found that part of getting the trust from an organization to manage its cybersecurity suite is to demonstrate that you have strong technical skills and you are able to define cybersecurity and its value in business terms. You must be able to demonstrate that you understand the current "legacy" issues and have a vision for what the "future" state of cybersecurity in the organization should look like. Remember, you must be able to explain the value your vision will bring to the company.

To do this correctly, it is extremely critical that you are part of the IT leadership team and if possible that you have access to the executive management team. You will need to ensure that your vision of cybersecurity is aligned with the overall strategic view of IT for your organization. As a member of the IT leadership team you must also create and nurture connections with your organization's various business units. You will need their buy-in that cybersecurity is important and this network of stakeholders will be critical for the success of your program. Get these stakeholders involved in reviewing policy with your team, ask them to provide input on ideas for new security projects or request assistance in remediating security issues.

As I finish this question, one last point I want to make is that your role of CISO in an organization is what you make of it – cyber doesn't exist in a vacuum. It will thrive when shared and distributed throughout an organization. You may not be given much freedom in the beginning to make changes, so collaborate with your peers and meet your stakeholders. Understand how your organization conducts business, how the business units use data, and what applications drive revenue for the organization. This knowledge will provide context for the changes you recommend and help your cybersecurity program get the visibility it needs to mature. Your role as CISO is to not only be the "business defender," but to be a valued "business enabler." To do this, get answers to these questions and start to collaborate and build the "value" story of what a mature cybersecurity program delivers to your business.

Understand that your role as the CISO is to enable the business, not just defend the business. It is vitally important that you establish this mindset with your peers and your staff. Your influence will be directly proportional to how your peers assess you in this specific regard.

You should actively work to build and then nurture relationships with your peers based on the foundation of the organization's objectives and needs and seek ways to provide value as a business enabler.

Who Should I Report to as CISO?

The role of CISO exists to provide an organization's executive management team professional advice on matters of cybersecurity and enterprise risk management. For a CISO to be successful in their role they need to be *independent*. This means that the CISO needs to be able to operate without pressure or influence, and they need to be able to focus on protecting the organization and its assets without undue interference. The CISO also needs to be *entrusted*. This means that they must have the ability and authority to make changes to the organization's cybersecurity suite. They are entrusted to make recommendations and changes to deployed protective measures in order to reduce risk to the organization while minimizing business impact. The CISO also needs to be *positioned*, meaning that they need to hold a position within the organization that allows them to intertwine cybersecurity into all aspects of the organization's culture and recommend changes when needed.

With this viewpoint of the CISO's role in mind, let's look at our next question – *"Who should the CISO report to and why is that important?"* In a 2014 security survey conducted by ThreatTrack Security (T. Security 2014), it was found that out of 203 U.S.-based, C-level executives interviewed, 47% of CISOs reported to their CEO, 45% reported to the CIO and the last 8% reported to positions such as the COO, CFO, or Chief Compliance Officer (CCO). Another interesting fact from this survey is that to whom the CISO reports is situational in many organizations – typically based on the business verticals of the company. So with this information as context, I believe the CISO should ideally report to the CEO or another C-level executive such as the organization's CIO or CTO. It is fundamentally important that whomever the CISO reports to understands the unique role this position plays in the organization.

Regardless of whether the CISO reports to a C-level position inside or outside of the department of Information Technology, they should report to someone who supports, understands, and champions the CISO and their cybersecurity program to the executive management team. This arrangement provides the CISO with:

- Independence
- The ability to make recommendations and disagree
- The ability to take a balanced, strategic view in deploying security controls
- Empowerment to build and embed the cybersecurity program within the organization

This arrangement also has its downside for the CISO. If they are outside the department of Information Technology, one of the main issues is that they could lose their critical perspective on IT's long-term strategy for the business. They could also face losing credibility or cooperation to control corporate IT assets if they are outside the department of Information Technology's sphere of influence.

Alternatively, if the CISO reports to the CIO this still doesn't guarantee that he/she will have the authority to fully carry out the requirements of their position. A CIO can be focused on daily operations and service delivery, and cybersecurity could be put on the shelf to be dealt with at a more convenient time. This reporting structure could actually degrade a company's security program and increase its exposure to liability.

In the end, it will typically be the CEO and board of directors that will decide what reporting structure they are comfortable with for the CISO. Here are some of the factors that I believe should be used to determine the reporting structure:

- Is there someone presently available to do security? (Do you need a CISO?)
- Does the executive management team view cybersecurity as a critical service to the company?
- Does the CISO have the education and experience to administer the cybersecurity program from a business perspective?
- Is the C-level executive who manages the CISO knowledgeable about cybersecurity?
- Can the CIO provide the CISO with the business/soft skills necessary for him/her to be successful?

One last point about why I believe where and to whom the CISO reports is important. In 2014 PricewaterhouseCoopers (Cooper 2014) conducted a survey called "Global State of Information Security." Over 9,000 respondents from around the globe answered the survey's myriad questions on cybersecurity. The survey found that in organizations with the CISO to CIO reporting structure, there was 14% more system downtime and financial losses were 46% higher than in organizations with the CISO to CEO reporting structure.

I believe this makes the point that CISOs reporting in the C-suite results in a reduction in conflict between the CIO's objectives and the CISO's objectives. To me, as peers they have more in common and should work together to provide innovative and secure IT services to their organization.

Do I Have the Tools to Be Successful?

As CISO, one of your core assets will be your teams. A critical component for effectively managing them is to know whether or not your security program is appropriately staffed and budgeted. The answer to this question has haunted many a CISO for years.

> So keeping this idea of "cyber as a service" in mind, let's discuss our next question - *"Is my security program sourced correctly?"* Note, as CISO you will find there will be some imbedded corporate issues that will influence the size of your security teams, your suite of tools, and their corresponding budgets. Some of the issues you will inherit as a new CISO are as follows:
> - What is the security team's type and level of work?
>   - Do the teams work in a Security Operations Center (SOC)?
>   - Do the teams conduct security data analytics?
>   - Do the teams provide forensics/penetration testing?
> - Is the responsibility of cybersecurity distributed throughout the organization?
> - What is the level of responsibility and risks managed by the teams?
> - Are there resources available to field a cybersecurity program?

Cybersecurity is viewed as a cost center because it's hard to calculate the value of the reduction in risk to an organization's business operations. There are many CISOs, myself included, who feel that our product of cybersecurity and enterprise risk management is actually a service and we should look at ourselves as a service center to our company's business units.

As you can see from this short list, the security program and its teams will be operating in some unique environments. If, as CISO, you are managing a SOC, you will have costs associated with it whether it's outsourced or on premise. You will have to pay for hardware, software, and labor to manage the SOC, provide daily security operations, and schedule downtime for maintenance and patch remediation.

Another issue that will influence your security program is whether the responsibility of cybersecurity is managed solely by you as the CISO or has been distributed throughout the company's organizational units. I have seen companies that have insourced security to each of their departments to manage individually with the corporate CISO providing overall governance and security recommendations. Obviously, a distributed model provides the CISO with minimal ability to change the security program because budget and staff are not under his/her control. One last issue, and probably one of the most important, is the fiscal reality of the company. Does it have the resources available to field and stand up a cybersecurity program? This honestly will depend on the maturity level of the organization. As the company grows, they will become more cognizant of compliance and federal and state regulations and this will lead to someone being appointed to manage information security for the business.

Now that you understand some of the contributing issues that will influence your cybersecurity program, let's discuss some metrics that you can use to measure its maturity. Some of these metrics will depend on factors determined by the organization, how it approaches risk, and how it conducts business.

In 2014, Gartner (Scholtz and McMillan 2014) published "Tips and Guidelines for Sizing Your Information Security Organization." In this paper, they discussed factors that influenced the staffing levels of security teams. One of the comments I do believe applies is that to get a baseline on staffing levels you should look at organizations of your size, type, and revenue level/user base. With that information in hand, consider the factors listed below to understand what your organization needs.

- What is the risk appetite of the company? (Heavy compliance = low risk appetite)
  - What is the extent of the risks the security team will need to manage?
- How dependent is the company on information?
- To what extent are personnel outside of security performing current security operations?
  - Security patching, firewall rules configuration, and log monitoring?
- What is the organizational structure of the enterprise? (Centralized, decentralized, outsourced?)

Having answers to these questions will paint you a picture of how the organization is structured, how it conducts business, what information is deemed critical and how much risk the company is willing to accept. In the Gartner paper, having these answers allows you to properly size your security team and its budget using these three metrics:

1. Number of corporate users per security full-time equivalent (FTE)
2. Security FTEs as a percentage of Information Technology FTEs
3. Security program budget as a percentage of the Information Technology budget

The first metric, *"Number of corporate users per security full-time equivalent,"* is based on the risk appetite of an organization and its data needs. The Gartner paper used the user base of 500-3,000 users as an adjustable range to measure against for each security FTE. So for example, if you have 3,000 users in your organization and you have a high risk tolerance, you would expect to have at least one security FTE – you would measure full to the right. However, if your company works with critical data which falls under a compliance regime such as PCI or HIPAA-HITECH, your risk appetite will be very low. The lower your risk appetite, the less risk you are willing to be exposed to as an organization. This will result in a measurement that for every 500-3,000 users in your company you will move your FTE calculator to the left, resulting in more security team personnel.

An example of how this would work: I am the CISO for a City of 1.5 million citizens. We are a large organization that cannot risk downtime and our risk appetite is very low, which results in us adjusting this metric to the left. So our metric is *"Every 1,000 users equates to one security full-time equivalent (FTE)."* I have over 10,000 users and I am presently building my team to field 10 security FTEs.

Chapter 1 Key Point and Action Item 5

As CISO, one of your core assets will be your teams. Given the limits on resources that every leader deals with, it is vital that every member of your team be at the appropriate skill level and have the learning agility and interpersonal skills necessary to excel at their job.

You should assess your team, determine strengths and weaknesses, and develop a plan to improve or replace where deficiencies exist.

The risk appetite of the organization again drives the second metric, *"Security FTEs as a percentage of Information Technology FTEs."* The Gartner report stated that the number of security FTEs should be about 5% of the overall Information Technology FTEs. Now, this is a recommendation. In my case, the IT department has over 150 personnel performing IT services in 40 departments. If we did 5% of those numbers, I would be looking at less than 10 security FTEs. This is why you need to understand your organization so you can make the case that with its low risk appetite, more security is warranted.

The third and final metric is, *"Security program budget as a percentage of the overall Information Technology budget."* The above paper stated that the security budget should be about 5% of the overall Information Technology budget. Understand that this budgetary number should only be used as a baseline to measure your program. I have used this number to give myself an idea of where my program, on average, should be based on the size of my organization and the amount of risk we are willing to accept. As you build out your security suite and onboard new security FTEs, you too can use this metric as a tool to measure the maturity of your program and compare it to like-sized organizations for validity.

As CISO, remember that there will be business-related factors that will influence your metrics. It's critical to understand the needs of your organization so you can take these metrics as a baseline and adjust them to properly size your team and its budget. You can use these numbers in comparison to organizations of your size, type, revenue level, or user base to measure the maturity of your program as you grow it to provide quality cybersecurity services to your customers.

Where Do I See My Role in The Future?

For our final discussion, let's talk about how I see the role of the CISO evolving. The future of cybersecurity will mature in parallel with the evolving tactics of cybercriminals and the escalating change of Information Technology. Many of the new technologies such as Cloud (in all its variants), Software-defined Networks (SDN), Mobile Technologies, Internet of Everything (IoE), and Data Analytics will fundamentally impact how networks and security programs are implemented. These technologies will also be leveraged by cybercriminal organizations, resulting in new forms of digital crime not seen today. So now let's discuss our final question, *"What changes do I see in the future for the role of CISO?"*

I believe the aforementioned technologies will substantially transform the role of the CISO. You will see some technologies which typically would be in the network operations portfolio consolidated under the umbrella of cybersecurity. Because of this change, I believe future CISOs will need to possess an extensive knowledge of technology and how it applies to their business operations. They will need to assess risk for new technologies that will be added to disparate "legacy" corporate networks. These corporate networks will become more intertwined with the Internet - sharing, processing, and storing ever-expanding quantities of data. This data itself will evolve as more organizations accept online social media platforms. You will see corporate "professional" data merge with "personal" customer data, resulting in new data privacy requirements.

It is these data privacy requirements, and the accompanying federal/international laws that govern them, that I believe will cause many CISO roles to mature into a Chief Privacy Officer (CPO) type of position. After all, protecting privacy is closely related to protecting data, and many look at privacy as just another form of risk for the CISO to manage. This growing role is critically important, it will impact all CISO's across the globe in one form or another. I would strongly advise new CISO's to educate themselves on this topic if it is new to them. One great resource that could be used for this purpose is the International Association of Privacy Professionals (IAPP) https://iapp.org/

In this future view, I see network security, data privacy, physical security, and operations security merging into the new cybersecurity portfolio. To effectively manage enterprise risk across this new portfolio of technologies, the future CISO will require a cybersecurity suite designed for continuous monitoring, alerting, and quick incident response. Security will become behavior-analytic driven as security teams employ tools that use data and threat analytics to be proactive in remediating security incidents.

I also envision that organizations' perimeters will change. The perimeter will no longer be based on the physical or logical location of network assets but on the location of corporate data. The CISO and his/her security program will become more focused on data – who has access (identity), what they are allowed to access (authorize), where it is stored, and how it is protected. This data-centric view will become the new perimeter for the CISO and his/her teams to defend, and the new mantra for this view of security will be "total verification of identity and access."

In conclusion, the role of CISO will be based on the needs of the company. However, as CISO you must remember that the cybersecurity/cybercrime environments are dynamic and susceptible to fast-moving changes. If you understand the strategic goals of your organization and have built a vibrant stakeholder community, you should have the essentials in place to mitigate any new risks while minimizing impact to business operations.

As I previously stated, the role of CISO is challenging. You will deal with an exceptional amount of risk tied into your company's business rules and technology portfolio. It will be your responsibility to assess the risk exposure of your organization and provide alternatives that will protect your company, its assets, and its data. To do this effectively, educate yourself on new threats and technologies, educate your teams, update your security program and policies, and use your stakeholder network. Remember, cybersecurity is a service that is intertwined in all business operations and it is incumbent upon the CISO to effectively manage this service and make it a valuable resource to their company.

Summary

For Chapter 1, we began our discussion by asking these three questions:

- Who should I (the CISO) report to?
- How and where should the CISO and security program fit within the organization's structure?
- How and why do I see this changing?

Each of our authors provided their point of view, exploring the organization's structure, the appetite for risk, and the business objectives, and emphasized the strongly held belief that the CISO must be empowered, responsible, trusted, and an equal partner to the senior leaders. Yet, in many cases, this is still aspirational.

In closing, we leave you with these five key points and next steps:

1. Serious consideration should be given to ensuring that the CISO has the ability to make the difficult decisions without undo interference and is empowered to take appropriate and deliberate action with the necessary dispatch. **You should identify the issues where your specific leadership is key, such as incident response, enforcement of contract terms, and duties designated by regulatory bodies for your industry, and work with the C-suite to validate escalation paths and decision making authority.**

2. The role of the CISO comes with a C-level designation that denotes both the criticality to the organization as well as the responsibility bestowed on the individual hired into that role. Compared to the CIO and CTO, the other C-level technology roles, it is relatively new and still emerging and evolving into its ultimate form. As the CISO, you have the duty to ensure that you integrate into the C-suite through your reporting relationship and though the working relationships you build in your organization. **You should openly explore the options with the leadership team and advocate for the best outcome for your organization.**

3. The CISO should be deeply integrated with the C-suite and form strong working relationships with key executives to both advance the cause for better cybersecurity outcomes and gain a comprehensive understanding of the business

needs and objectives. At the same time, the CISO's staff must engage at their respective levels with their colleagues for the same fundamental reasons. The CISO cannot influence the changes in behavior needed for good cybersecurity outcomes alone. It takes the entire team teaching, learning, advocating, and speaking with one voice. **You should work with your team to develop a mission statement and a set of clearly articulated objectives that your staff can use to provide consistent guidance to their peers and partners.**

4. Understand that your role as the CISO is to enable the business, not just defend the business. It is vitally important that you establish this mindset with your peers and your staff. Your influence will be directly proportional to how your peers assess you in this specific regard. **You should actively work to build and then nurture relationships with your peers based on the foundation of the organization's objectives and needs and seek ways to provide value as a business enabler.**

5. As CISO, one of your core assets will be your teams. Given the limits on resources that every leader deals with, it is vital that every member of your team be at the appropriate skill level and have the learning agility and interpersonal skills necessary to excel at their job. **You should assess your team, determine strengths and weaknesses, and develop a plan to improve or replace where deficiencies exist.**

Matt Stamper's conclusion for this chapter bears repeating: What's clear is that the role of the CISO as the champion for cybersecurity and risk-mitigating activities has reached a level of importance that heretofore has not been seen within organizations. We are, in effect, entering the era of the CISO.

Chapter 2 – Regulatory, Compliance and Audit

Introduction

How Do Regulations, Frameworks, and Standards Impact Cybersecurity and Audit Practices?

In this chapter, our authors review strategies and techniques to assess and address the seemingly infinite number of regulations and standards that impact cybersecurity practices and the ensuing audits used to validate security controls. Each of our authors touch upon some of the more prevalent regulations we face as CISOs including regulations that impact sectors such as healthcare and financial services as well as critical infrastructure. Our authors collectively emphasize the importance of taking a collaborative approach to regulatory compliance...working with other stakeholders within our respective organizations to understand what is required of the security programs we oversee. Key actors in these processes include the organization's legal counsel, its chief risk officer, and other C-level executives that have a fiduciary responsibility to oversee the governance of the organization.

Bill Bonney begins this chapter with the basic premise that regulations and compliance requirements mandate "minimum standards of due care." Bill's experience working with publicly-traded organizations that are subject to both Sarbanes-Oxley compliance and regulatory audits offers great advice on how to approach an audit as a CISO and how to work with colleagues throughout the organization to prepare for this level of oversight. Bill's guidance also notes how important it is as the CISO to evaluate the organization's contractual obligations. These may be especially impactful for organizations in healthcare that are subject to HIPAA-HITECH.

Matt Stamper continues with an assessment of the regulations that mandate specific security practices and suggests that we've entered an era where security can no longer be ignored by boards of directors and our colleagues in the C-suite. The CISO is effectively charged with advocating legally-defensible security practices. Matt also highlights the special role that the Federal Trade Commission (FTC) has had in establishing minimum security practices with its enforcement of Section 5 of the Federal Trade Commission Act (FCTA), which addresses "unfair and deceptive trade practices."

Gary Hayslip emphasizes how critical it is for the CISO to "meet and greet" fellow executives and stakeholders. This informal discovery leads to actionable guidance related to regulatory compliance and the required controls. Gary's analysis also suggests that the regulatory requirements should inform the type of controls and techniques deployed. Gary warns CISOs not to make controls, processes, and techniques overly complex as this will typically overwhelm the organization and have the opposite of their desired effect. Despite Gary's background with the Navy, the Department of Defense, and municipal government, he brings a refreshing "business perspective" to dealing with regulations and compliance.

The authors would like to pose some important questions to think about as you read this chapter:

- Which regulations apply to my organization?
- What is the status of our current regulatory compliance?
- How efficient is my team in working with auditors and regulators?

Regulatory Requirements and Audit – Bonney

> "Start with your executive peers for a general idea of what requirements you have, but do a deep dive with the procurement team."

In the first chapter, I talk a little about regulatory oversight. I point out, for instance, that in the overall scheme of information security, regulatory requirements are really cover charges. I also noted that typically, in mature organizations with well-known or substantial regulatory requirements, corporate governance would be structured to comply with mandatory management oversight obligations. To be clear, I believe that regulations and compliance requirements mandate *minimum* standards of due care.

The reality is that while regulatory and compliance requirements do not in and of themselves keep your data secure, they are obligatory, with the specifics depending on industry, locale, and organizational structure. But, truth be told, despite the disdain that many hold for compliance activities and requirements, they can often be leveraged as a foundation for a good information security program.

In this chapter, I will expand on some of those thoughts and talk about setting up your program for regulatory success, leveraging that foundation for successful governance, and engaging with your internal and external audit teams as key partners in your governance program. I will take the questions for this chapter in order. What are my regulatory requirements? How do I set up my program for success? And how do I engage my auditors and regulators?

How Do I Know What My Regulatory Requirements Are?

That brings us to the first question I am going to address: how do I know what my regulatory requirements are? I'm going to take an expansive view of this. By expansive, I mean I'll consider a wider range of compliance regimes that aren't all strictly regulatory.

Let's begin with the obvious: if the organization is a publically-traded company listed in the U.S., it is subject to compliance with the Sarbanes-Oxley Act of 2002, which was enacted to ensure reliability in financial reports filed by public companies with the U.S. Securities and Exchange Commission. Check with your Chief Information Officer (CIO), Chief Technology Officer (CTO), Chief Operations Officer (COO), Chief Financial Officer (CFO) or Corporate Controller to understand how these obligations are currently managed and how you should engage with the appropriate teams. In general, you'll be responsible for some subset of the Information Technology General Controls (ITGCs) that your organization has defined to comply with Section 404.

If the organization holds personal data for employees or customers, it is likely subject to privacy regulations from applicable state privacy and breach laws, along with potential international implications depending on the localities involved. Prior to European Union (EU) rules changes in 2015, U.S. multi-nationals complied with the European Safe Harbor rules, but as of this writing, the Safe Harbor protections are being redefined. Check with your Chief Privacy Officer (CPO), Chief Risk Officer (CRO), or Chief Legal Officer (CLO). If your organization doesn't have these leadership positions a good fallback is the CFO, who will often own risk for medium sized firms. Here you'll again have a subset of IT controls.

For good proxies on what is required to meet these controls, you can use the Massachusetts privacy regulations (201 CMR 17.00) for preventative control requirements and Nevada breach notification law (N.R.S. § 603A.010) and the California data breach notification law (SB 1386) for breach notification requirements and, to provide a sober reminder of the reach of some state regulations, review the Texas extreme notification requirements (Texas Medical Records Privacy Act), which are actually more stringent than those found in the federal Health Insurance Portability and Accountability Act (HIPAA).

Of course HIPAA is one of the other major regulatory regimes you'll need to pay attention to if you are a "covered entity," which are generally healthcare clearinghouses, employer sponsored health plans, health insurers, and medical service providers. One of the more interesting features of HIPAA is that covered entities are required to cascade their obligations to Business Partners and Business Associates (look for any business associate agreement (BAA) your organization has signed) to ensure that all third parties that are involved in handling Protected Health Information (PHI) are obligated to safeguard the PHI in their care.

Besides healthcare, there are other industries that have their own regulatory regimes. Some examples:

Federal agencies must comply with FISMA, the Federal Information Security Management Act. DoD contractors are subject to DFARS 252.204-7012, which requires a subset of NIST 800-53 controls and DoD contractors that handle classified information are subject DFARS Rule 78 Fed. Reg. 69273.

Organizations that accept credit cards for payment or process credit cards are subject to the Payment Card Industry Data Security Standards (PCI-DSS) and organizations that use Experian data agree to comply with the Experian Independent Third Party Assessment (EI3PA).

Finally, similar to the contractual requirement of adhering to PCI-DSS controls (these are not regulations, you agree to comply in your contract with the Payment Card Industry), organizations often agree to data handling requirements that usually include security requirements by accepting contact language specifying security and privacy related duties.

To get a picture of all of the contractual security compliance regimes, it is best to start with your executive peers for a general idea of what requirements you have, but do a deep dive with the procurement team or whichever group is responsible for managing contractual compliance. Contractual compliance is something most audit firms will look at while conducting financial audits, which implies some group within the organization will be responsible for tracking the obligations that have been agreed to. If the structure within your organization is not obvious, you can start with the CFO or Controller.

Typically, signed addendums, engagement letters for third-party assessors, and the resulting attestations will list the individuals in the organization who are authorized to represent the organization and that is an excellent place to start to determine what has been committed and who is executing and testing controls.

For banks and certain other financial institutions, there are a host of compliance regimes, including compliance with the Gramm–Leach–Bliley Act (GLBA) and adhering to guidance from the IT Examination handbook of the Federal Financial Institutions Examination Council (FFIEC), the multi-agency bank regulator. Other organizations that provide services to the financial industry are often required to provide third-party attestations about their controls. This used to be called a "Statement on Auditing Standards No. 70" (SAS-70) report, but in 2011, the American Institute of Certified Public Accounts (AICPA) replaced the over-burdened SAS-70 with a new standard called the "Statement on Standards for Attestation Engagements No. 16" (SSAE-16). This was more than a name change.

In addition to creating extra burdens on the organization obtaining the audit (called the "Service Provider") and transferring some responsibility from the auditing firm (called the "Service Auditor") to the Service Provider, the changes also defined and formalized additional types of attestations (SSAE-16 SOC2 and SOC3) based on trust principles, including: Security, Availability, Processing Integrity, Confidentiality, and Privacy. Financial institutions typically have mandated management duties as well, and the CFO or Chief Audit Officer (CAO) can be consulted to start your discovery for these compliance requirements.

What I have covered above is not meant to be 100% complete. An entire book could be dedicated to listing and describing all the compliance regimes touching information (or data) security. Rather, I have laid out several fundamental principles. First, there are some mandatory security regulations for nearly every organization, certainly any organization that would require a full time CISO. Second, compliance obligations come in both mandatory (regulations) and voluntary (contractual) varieties. And third, for each requirement there are logical places to start your discovery about what is required and determine the role you must play.

Chapter 2 Key Point and Action Item 1

It is extremely important that you understand your regulatory and contractual obligations for data handling, breach disclosure, and policy stewardship and enforcement. Key resources include your organization's legal department, the executive team, especially in finance and procurement, and both internal and external auditors. A common theme in the regulatory requirements for cybersecurity is the designation of responsible roles within the organization to establish and be accountable for mandated security programs. In hiring a CISO, your organization is designating you as that accountable individual.

You should schedule time to review with legal, procurement and finance the set of regulatory requirements as well as contractual obligations which apply to your organization.

Setting Up for Success

Now I'd like to turn to setting up your program for success. The underlying assumption of this section is that these elements are not in place and you are setting them up for the first time. If you have stepped into a functioning governance program, you have the pleasure of using this section to assess program completeness.

In Chapter 1, I referenced a number of functions of the Information Security group as I discussed placement of key resources. These functions included infrastructure protection (often referred to infrastructure security, security engineering, data center security), application security, security operations (incident response), governance, project (or program) management, and business partners. Security architecture, governance, project management and business partners may be embedded as shared or dedicated resources into both infrastructure security and application security, or stand alone with their own resources. Smaller and larger companies obviously have some or all of these capabilities in-house and may contract for the remaining services.

Most information security organizations, as they mature, start designating individuals with more focused duties. One of the first positions to receive this treatment is the dedicated security compliance role. Larger organizations typically call this "Governance" or "Security Governance" or "Information Security

Governance." In many organizations, Governance initially applies only to compliance activities and does not address program effectiveness or performance management. However, it usually does include playing both a security compliance subject matter expert (SME) role and a follow up or "Project Management" role to ensure other departments within the organization understand and follow through on their information security compliance duties.

One unpleasant fact of security compliance is that requirements tend to expand over time. There are a lot of reasons for this:

- The organization may become subject to additional requirements when it adds lines of business.
- The organization's baseline standards, frameworks, and control sets might become more rigorous because of increasing risk or expanded regulatory oversight within their industry.
- The scope of the organization's business operations will often grow along with customer acquisition.

A frequent contributor to this expanding security compliance burden is that auditors and regulators hold controls testing and demonstrating compliance to ever-higher standards. Auditors and regulators are becoming more educated about the risks they are tasked with assessing and better trained in the tools and methods for conducting those assessments.

Many organizations struggle under this increasing burden. Three techniques I have used to get on top of the expanding control and compliance landscape are:

- Outsource some or all of the compliance activities. In my experience, this is best used as a short-term solution, unless the compliance activities are part of an overall security service package or for infrequent activities that require little institutional knowledge.

- Add headcount in either Information Security or the business units or functional groups where control execution takes place. Where to add the headcount is determined based on how specialized the skill set is and whether it can be amortized (spread) across the entire organization.

- Purchase a GRC (Governance, Risk, and Compliance) package or service. I believe this to be the most long-term, cost effective way to handle the increasing burden, especially when purchased as a service. In that model, it is easy to scale up and down depending on need and there are little or no upfront capital costs (though you do need to consider set up fees).

An effective strategy for establishing or recovering a security compliance function involves these three steps:

- Engage a services firm for a needs assessment and to perform project management, evidence collection, and (if necessary) security controls testing.

- With the results of this assessment, you can begin defining job requirements and recruiting full-time people to drive this function internally.

- After hiring the right personnel, have them work with the service provider to identify and implement a GRC package suited to your organization's needs.

The value in using a GRC package is that it allows for much greater efficiency in capturing, storing, organizing, and sharing compliance artifacts. These include policy documents, control statements, operational reports that demonstrate compliance, control testing reports and operational items such as project dashboards, compliance calendars, and control execution schedules. The idea is to pull this information out of individual spreadsheets, email folders, and locally-saved project plans, and put it in specialized (and optimized) repositories that can be shared across the organization and with audit personnel as needed. Additionally, most of these packages are connected in some way to the underlying control frameworks (such as ISO 27001, NIST 800-53, and PCI-DSS) used to assess compliance. This approach decreases (but does not eliminate) the need for personnel that are deep subject matter experts in compliance frameworks, and automates the process of staying current with regulations and standards.

A common complaint about GRC packages is that they are expensive, complex to install and configure, and difficult to maintain. As is the case with almost every type of enterprise software, recent offerings that use the Software as a Service (SaaS) model have greatly reduced the cost and complexity of these types of solutions. Firms no longer need to scope million-dollar automation projects to implement solid GRC solutions that require minimal care and feeding.

At the beginning of this chapter I mentioned leveraging the investments in compliance as a foundation for a good information security program. I am a firm believer that there is both an immediate and a long-term value in leveraging the people, processes, and tools that organizations require to comply with mandatory controls. The value adds come in the following forms:

- Most organizations have compliance requirements beyond security controls, including financial system audits, contract audits, and the tracking of other agreements that require repetitive activity and/or retaining evidence of execution. GRC tools often have broad operational capabilities that can help organizations address these needs.

- Computer systems, including networks, compute capacity, and storage, operate more effectively and are more secure when they are managed properly, including life-cycle management, endpoint protection, and basic hygiene, such as updating to current versions, and patching known vulnerabilities. Applying the hygiene that is required for security compliance across all or most of an organization's information technology landscape can make the entire landscape more effective.

- Development, deployment, and maintenance of the business systems deployed on the organization's computer networks experience fewer disruptions when configurations are managed consistently across the entire organization.

This is not meant to be an exhaustive list. it is merely a demonstration that compliance costs do not need to be a sunk cost but can be leveraged to include improvement across a range of operational goals. The IT controls mandated by compliance regimes represent foundational controls that, in my opinion, should be in place anyway.

How to Engage with Your Auditors

The last question for this chapter is about how to engage auditors and regulators. I think it is extremely important to recognize the role that auditors and regulators play.

> Broadly speaking, there are four types of functions involved:
>
> - Internal Audit is a function commissioned by the board of directors to help the Board understand how management is addressing specific types of risk.
>
> - External Audit is a function also commissioned by the board of directors, in this case to provide an independent third-party assessment. CPA firms, including the "Big 4" multi-national firms, as well as other regional firms, usually carry out these audits. Results are typically reported directly to the board of directors.
>
> - Similar to, but distinct from, external audit are third party attestation firms that perform specialized compliance tests, such as adhering to PCI-DSS.
>
> - Finally, regulatory bodies, such as the FFIEC, deploy examiners to review an organization's compliance with its regulatory obligations. In many cases, regulators also rely on reports from independent auditors who assess the target organization's compliance using an agreed-upon test for compliance.

Each of these groups requires a similar but different engagement model. To start, these relationships are all built on timeliness and transparency, and that builds trust. In my experience, organizations get the best audit results (which is not the same as the lowest number of findings) when they engage the audit resources as partners.

Remember that internal audit is empowered by the Board to help them effectively run the company. Your team should be completely upfront with internal audit – not only is it every employee's duty to the Board and the shareholders, but the audit process will often expose ways you can be more effective. This is especially important to the modern CISO. Because of the rapid and wealth-destroying ramp up in cybercrime, boards of directors are demanding of their audit teams a full assessment of where their organizations stand on cyber preparedness. (Deloitte Development, LLC 2015) It is essential that the board have a comprehensive view of the organization's risk profile. That is also your best option to increase funding and management attention on cyber initiatives. Working with internal audit to make sure they completely understand where risk is greatest and how best to address the gaps is a great way to keep the Board informed.

External audit is also empowered by the Board and is another tool for the Board to manage operations. Your stakeholders are still the Board and shareholders, but as mentioned above, regulators also rely on their reports. While there may be a temptation to be a bit guarded, especially when auditors use jargon that might be unfamiliar to technical people, management and the Board take these audits very seriously. And, as of October 2011, public companies are expected to address potentially material cybersecurity risks and cyber incidents in the Management's Discussion and Analysis of Financial Condition and Results of Operations (MD&A) that they file with the SEC on a quarterly basis. It is understandable to limit the scope of audits to manage cost and elapsed time.

However, do not limit scope because of operational shortfalls and do not allow your team to mislead auditors. By building trust with your external audit team, you will be involved in the framing of these issues and that can be critical to reassure shareholders and regulators that your organization has appropriate plans to address any gaps.

Chapter 2 Key Point and Action Item 2

Audit functions, whether commissioned by the board or as a result of partners exercising their right to audit are a valuable tool for maintaining confidence in your organization's ability to discharge its duties pertaining to the safeguarding of the data with which you have been entrusted.

You should review your most recent audit reports across all your regulatory and contractual obligations and schedule time with audit leadership and the leadership of audited functions to review remedial activities.

Third-party assessors for contractual obligations like PCI-DSS are essentially tasked with validating your assertion that you comply with the controls you agreed to take on, for instance, when you contracted with a member of the Payment Card Industry, such as a bank, merchant service, or payment gateway. While they do have a business reason to demonstrate independence and integrity in the eyes of the standards body to maintain their accredited status, they are hired by and are working for your organization. Approach the relationship as a partnership. Where controls are weak, work with the assessor to design compensating controls and a path to strong controls. They don't want to see you fail.

Examiners for regulatory bodies are different in that they are not employed by your organization or hired through any contract with your organization. However, they typically share a fundamental desire to see you succeed. Their job is to protect the systemic integrity of the industry they regulate. Given this responsibility, they have the ability to sanction your organization directly, which can mean civil and criminal penalties, orders to cease operations, and orders to address issues within mandated timeframes. Though the consequences can be severe, the engagement model is not that dissimilar.

Certainly setting scope is extremely important, for example it's not helpful to have non-regulated businesses examined by regulators. It wastes their time, and your time, creates confusion and potential inappropriate jeopardy. From my experience, they are usually pretty patient and respectful of your time. In a certain sense, they work for the entire industry. Here, the best model is to be thoughtful and leverage experience. Avoid assigning junior people to "handle" examiners. A great option is to work with internal audit to coordinate a measured and professional interaction.

In general, I don't believe that employees need to be "coached" to work with auditors. In my experience, being straightforward and transparent about work processes and the ability to document assertions is the best approach. What does help is to prepare employees so they know what to expect from their audit partners and what management expects of them.

It's important to remember that auditors are subject matter experts first in the audit or examination process, and second, sometimes to a much lesser extent, in the business process they are assessing, and then third, especially if they are not employees of your company, in knowledge of how your internal processes work and the relationships between internal parties.

Fixing The Relationship with Your Auditor

As I mentioned above, these are trust relationships that are built on timeliness and transparency. I have listened to and overheard a lot of skepticism, distrust, and outright fear from individual contributors to senior executives about how to interact with auditors. Some are worried they will get in trouble for doing something wrong. Some view the time spent with auditors as wasted time and the time that is spent gathering evidence and providing documentation as busy work. This causes behaviors that, purposely or not, obstruct the assessment process. In some cases, the auditors are assigned "handlers" to choreograph activity and process owners are coached to provide guarded answers and escalate every question that they don't have a coached response for. I have also seen the opposite where inexperienced auditors bring poor time management skills, poorly thought out evidence requests, and negative, accusatory attitudes to audits, putting everyone on guard.

Tips to prepare employees for how to deal with auditors

- "I don't know" is a better answer than guessing. This is especially true if you are not the best subject matter expert for a particular topic. Guessing doesn't get you into trouble, but it does waste time and money.

- Time is money. Audits using third-party assessors are bound by contractual terms with consequences for cost overruns. Wasting the auditor's time also wastes the organization's money.

- Don't try to sound like a lawyer. The best way to be understood is to use language and style you are comfortable with. Don't try to match "auditor jargon" or use labels you aren't familiar with. The surest way to get management's attention, and not in a good way, is to call a minor testing deviation a "material weakness."

- The auditor is not a whistleblower hotline. Gently remind your employees that they should bring internal issues to you or a neutral member of the management team, the legal organization, Human Resources, or another appropriate.

This obstruction causes distrust and adds stress. The distrust comes from the understandable belief that team members are trying to hide something they are uncomfortable exposing or that minor failures will be misinterpreted or used to justify punitive remedies. The stress arises because the audits are scoped for certain resources (on both sides) within a certain timeframe and competing deadlines loom as less progress is made than was expected.

As you can imagine, this distrust and stress often creates a dysfunctional working relationship. Requests for documentation start getting escalated. Escalated or not, documentation is hurriedly assembled and is often incorrect or incomplete. As operational requirements take more time from participants, "just get it done" replaces "do it right." At some point in this dysfunctional downward spiral, "do whatever the auditor says to get this over" becomes the unspoken (and sometimes spoken) strategy to end the pain. The result is that auditors are put in the position of forsaking their independence and process owners are forced to abandon their duty to perform the process in the way they believe yields the best results. Under these circumstances, management receives much less value from the audit and the Board rarely gets an accurate understanding of the state of the business.

So how do we fix this? Building the required trust starts well before the audit fieldwork begins. Management and the auditors need to invest the time to agree on scope, objectives, roles and responsibilities. It's important at this stage to surface issues that otherwise will cause problems later. For instance, does the auditor have past experience with the organization that suggests the likelihood that timeliness will be a problem? Has management had experience with the auditor in the past that suggests that numerous poorly targeted requests will be made due to a lack of understanding about the organization's environment? Both of these problems are quite common and both can be addressed.

How you ask? Well, I'll start by referring to a study (Need Speed? Slow Down) by the Harvard Business Review in 2010 (Atkinson 2010) that looked at the results of driving operational versus strategic speed. The article states in part:

> "Firms sometimes confuse operational speed (moving quickly) with strategic speed (reducing the time it takes to deliver value)—and the two concepts are quite different. Simply increasing the pace of production, for example, may be one way to try to close the speed gap. But that often leads to decreased value over time, in the form of lower-quality products and services. Likewise, new initiatives that move fast may not deliver any value if time isn't taken to identify and adjust the true value proposition.

While certainly a good read, an overview of the FTC's judgment actions is beyond the scope of this chapter. However, there are a couple of actions that warrant specific review. There were two key actions in 2002 that created the precedent for established and audited security practices within an organization. The first is the consent order with Eli Lilly. The impact of this order cannot be overstated. A security breach on the Prozac site resulted in the disclosure of personally-identifiable information for a number of consumers. In response, the FTC ordered Eli Lilly to:

> ... **establish and maintain an information security** *program for the protection of personally identifiable information collected from or about consumers in connection with the advertising, marketing, offering for sale, or sale of any pharmaceutical, medical, or other health-related product or service, in or affecting commerce, by respondent's Lilly USA division, directly or through any corporation, subsidiary, division, or other entity. Such program shall consist of:*
>
> A. **designating appropriate personnel** *to coordinate and oversee the program;*
>
> B. **identifying reasonably foreseeable internal and external risks to the security,** *confidentiality, and integrity of personal information, including any such risks posed by lack of training, and addressing these risks in each relevant area of its operations, whether performed by employees or agents, including: (i) management and training of personnel; (ii) information systems for the processing, storage, transmission, or disposal of personal information; and (iii) prevention and response to attacks, intrusions, unauthorized access, or other information systems failures;*
>
> C. **conducting an annual written review by qualified persons,** *within ninety (90) days after the date of service of this order and yearly thereafter, which review shall monitor and document compliance with the program, evaluate the program's effectiveness, and recommend changes to it; and*
>
> D. **adjusting the program** *in light of any findings and recommendations resulting from reviews or ongoing monitoring, and in light of*

*any material changes to its operations that affect
the program.*[2]

Effectively, the FTC mandated, as part of overall corporate responsibility, the establishment of the following: a security program, the designation of a security officer, a program to evaluate and assess security risks, qualified review of practices, and a program to adjust practices according to material changes in the operating environment.

The December 2002 consent order with Microsoft furthered the FTC's oversight of security to require an independent, qualified, third-party audit of Microsoft's security practices. The FTC order actually required that this third-party report be prepared by a Certified Information System Security Professional (CISSP). This consent order, similar to the case with Eli Lilly, has a 20-year term.[3]

Beyond the operational impact of these orders, the FTC can also impose significant fines for failing to comply with consent orders. The January 2016 amended order with LifeLock includes fines totaling $100,000,000. Clearly, the FTC's impact on cybersecurity practices cannot be underestimated. The impact of these three consent decrees has not been lost on the executives running our organizations. Let's switch gears to bribery.

Interestingly enough, the 1977 Foreign Corrupt Practices Act (FCPA), enforced by the Department of Justice (DOJ) and the Securities and Exchange Commission (SEC) for public companies, indirectly lays the groundwork for the current focus on security controls. Compliance with the FCPA requires the establishment of an appropriate *internal controls* framework to prevent or detect the bribery of foreign officials or other fraudulent activities. While the FCPA does not reference information technology, the Act's provisions require internal controls to be in place to ensure that accounting transactions are accurate, complete, and valid. Effectively these transaction attributes create a level of assurance that accounting procedures and practices reflect managerial authorization and preclude inappropriate financial activity, in this case bribery. The FCPA's emphasis on a program of internal control laid the groundwork for Sarbanes-Oxley's impact on IT, where accounting practices are underpinned and supported by pervasive IT general controls.

---

[2]. https://www.ftc.gov/news-events/press-releases/2002/01/eli-lilly-settles-ftc-charges-concerning-security-breach
[3]. https://www.ftc.gov/enforcement/cases-proceedings/012-3240/microsoft-corporation-matter

Before turning to SOX, let's take a look at the Gramm-Leach-Bliley Act (GLBA) of 1999. GLBA, which is enforced by the FTC and other government agencies, is focused on the privacy and protection of non-public information maintained by financial institutions. While the FTC's consent decrees create an expectation of security practices as noted in the cases of Eli Lilly and Microsoft, the effect of GLBA is to legally mandate specific security requirements for the financial services industry. GLBA requires that financial services organizations – broadly defined as "significantly engaged" in financial services – comply with the security guidelines delineated in Section 501(b) of the Act.[4] The guidelines formally establish the compliance requirements for financial services organizations to include the following:

GLBA Security Compliance Requirements

- The establishment of a response program to address unauthorized access or use of customer information that could result in "substantial harm" or "inconvenience" to a customer. The responses may include the use of Suspicious Activity Reports (SARs) that should be filed with the appropriate regulatory body (e.g. the SEC, Treasury Department, etc.)
- Identity "reasonably" foreseeable threats (both internal and external)
- Assess the "likelihood" and "potential" of these threats
- Implement administrative, physical, and technical security controls to protect customer information
- Assess the efficacy of the overall security program
- Establish procedures to evaluate the security programs and contractual obligations of service provides
- Designate security responsibility within the organization

GLBA is significantly more prescriptive with respect to IT and security practices than Sarbanes-Oxley. The Sarbanes-Oxley Act of 2002 (SOX) barely touches upon IT in the actual language of the law. The role of IT with SOX is largely by inference. It never ceases to amaze me how much is attributed to SOX, especially by vendors, that is actually not part of the law. The Sarbanes-Oxley Act was the direct result of the Enron and Arthur Andersen collapses coupled with other accounting scandals. At the time, investor confidence in the public market and the agencies regulating and auditing these

---

[4]. http://ithandbook.ffiec.gov/it-booklets/information-security/introduction/coordination-with-glba-section-501(b).aspx

firms was low. The Sarbanes-Oxley Act was designed to restore investor confidence in the market.

The focus of SOX, accordingly, is on the internal controls over financial reporting (ICFR) and having mechanisms in place for executive accountability, board oversight, and the independence of external auditors. I've heard numerous vendors proclaim that Sarbanes-Oxley compliance requires e-mail retention. This is actually not part of the law, but it's attributed to SOX based on the requirement in Section 103 for auditors to maintain their records for a period of five years. Caveat emptor to any security professional procuring new products or services based solely on SOX requirements.

While SOX does not overtly prescribe practices such as those required by GLBA, SOX did have an important contribution to cybersecurity in that the law effectively created linkages between accounting and business processes and the underlying IT infrastructure and IT practices. Auditors expanded their review of internal controls to encompass not only enterprise resource planning and general ledger systems but also line-of-business applications that ultimately inform or feed financial data to these accounting systems. The audit community quickly expanded the scope of ICFR to include IT general controls – security being a domain in this assessment. Effectively, publicly-traded firms and certain real estate investment trusts (REITs) meeting a defined threshold of qualified investor are required, similar to FCPA, to establish, test, and report on the effectiveness of ICFR where IT and IT security are lower-level considerations in this assessment.

California's SB 1386 (passed in 2002 and placed into effect in 2003) was the first state law requiring breach notification in the event that non-public information of California citizens was compromised. SB 1386 did provide an exclusion for encrypted data. The law was complemented the next year with AB 1950. AB 1950 added two important extensions to SB 1386's requirements. Specifically, AB 1950 requires "entities...to implement and maintain reasonable security procedures to protect personal information from unauthorized access, destruction, use, modification, or disclosure."[5] AB 1950 further requires that third parties processing NPI on behalf of the entity be protected by similar security procedures, and requires that the service contract contain these provisions. Third-party contractual obligations – effectively requiring supplier due diligence – began with GLBA. As we will see, supplier security standards continue with HIPAA-HITECH in the form of business associate agreements (BAAs).

---

[5]. http://www.leginfo.ca.gov/pub/03-04/bill/asm/ab_1901-1950/ab_1950_bill_20040929_chaptered.html

Breach disclosure laws are present at the federal and international level as well as in 47 of the 50 states in the U. S. In addition to breach notification, organizations are potentially subject to civil legal action and regulatory sanction. In many cases, the "clock starts ticking" for notifying consumers and regulators, and in some cases, public disclosure of the breach. Due to the potential impact on consumers, expect that the regulators will continue to be aggressive.

You should make sure your organization has incident management and breach notification processes, clearly documented with crisp escalation points, that have been reviewed by legal counsel.

Collectively, the culmination of HIPAA-HITECH requirements is driving important security reforms in IT. The impact of HIPAA-HITECH on IT practices, and security and privacy specifically, is similar to the impact of SOX on IT, despite SOX's relatively limited legal requirements for IT and security. While the impacts of both laws on IT and security practices are profound, HIPAA-HITECH shares more common prescriptive elements with GLBA. HIPAA-HITECH requires organizations that store, process, or otherwise use protected health information (PHI), including electronic forms of PHI (ePHI), to implement prescriptive practices spanning administrative, technical, and physical controls. HIPAA-HITECH requirements incorporate both "required" and "addressable" controls that have some nuance related to the size, risk, and complexity of the environment at hand.

Here are some of the fundamental requirements of HIPAA-HITECH:

Administrative Safeguards: Security Management Processes (risk analyses, risk management, system review, and sanction policies) are all considered required activities. There is also a requirement to assign security responsibility. Incident management and contingency planning are also required. Critically, business associate agreements that legally codify security and privacy controls are required of service providers that store, process, or otherwise use PHI or ePHI on behalf of a covered entity or another business associate. CFR 164.308 highlights the required and addressable administrative safeguards mandated by HIPAA-HITECH. These boil down to security and privacy governance. There's a requirement for a designated individual within the organization to establish and be accountable for mandated security programs.

Physical Safeguards: The required and addressable controls related to physical safeguards encompass workstation security, controls over physical media (including disposal), and facility access. These are covered in CFR 164.310.

Technical Safeguards: The required controls related to technical safeguards can be quite challenging where there are "emergency access" procedures that potentially trump other requirements. This strikes at the inherent conflict between the three critical security attributes: confidentiality, integrity, and availability. Availability of systems in healthcare, for example, is truly a life-and-death matter and outweighs the important confidentiality and integrity objectives with security. The necessary balancing act between these three attributes clearly highlights the inherent conflict between confidentiality and integrity (which require potentially performance-impacting controls) and availability. The technical safeguards of HIPAA-HITECH incorporate audit controls, access controls (including unique user identification – required for non-repudiation), and authentication procedures. Unfortunately, perhaps reflecting the challenge of "emergency access," the requirement to encrypt ePHI is noted as addressable. CFR 164.312 outlines the technical safeguards within HIPAA-HITECH. The Department of Health and Human Services' HIPAA Security Information Series are well worth a read for those working in the healthcare industry.[6]

Common Threads of a Cybersecurity Program

As we have seen in this chapter, a combination of federal and state legislation is changing the cybersecurity landscape. Clearly, with so many overlapping standards, frameworks, and legal obligations facing organizations today it can be confusing for the board and executive management (let alone us CISOs) to determine where to begin. I think there are some important common threads that we can derive from the review above that will provide clear guidance on where to start. Specifically, every organization should at a minimum have the following:

- A designated security officer – It's critical that someone within the organization assume responsibility and advocate good security practices. This is required by GLBA, multiple state breach notification laws, as well as HIPAA-HITECH.

- A program to evaluate and assess risk – Ultimately, cyber risk is a subset of overall enterprise risk management (ERM). Organizations need to foment ERM practices and look at risk beyond traditional financial perspectives. Assessing cyber

---

[6]. http://www.hhs.gov/hipaa/for-professionals/security/guidance/index.html

risk is an important organizational competency.

- Data classification – Organizations need to know what type of information they collect, maintain, and share with customers, vendors, service providers, and affiliates. Data flow diagrams (discussed later in this book) are an important tool for gaining this understanding.

- Vendor due diligence – No organization operates in isolation. Organizations rely on service providers that complement and extend the organization's capabilities. Assessing third-party cyber risk, security capabilities, and mandated security practices should be part of standard vendor due diligence. As we will discuss in the next chapter on information controls, it's imperative to know where and how third parties impact cybersecurity for the organization. This third-party evaluation is mandated by GLBA, HIPAA-HITECH, and California's breach notification laws, among other regulations.

- Executive responsibility for internal controls (including security controls) – What is clear from SOX and the FCPA is that executive management is responsible for establishing the *tone at the top* and, more concretely, documenting and testing internal controls.

- The board of directors is responsible for providing oversight of cyber risk management. Boards have a fiduciary responsibility to evaluate the overall risk appetites of the organizations they oversee. Boards need to understand the cyber risk profiles of their organizations and the impact of risk to strategic business operations.

State and federal regulations, coupled with industry and sector frameworks, are removing the ambiguity or mystery associated with security functions. The end result is greater clarity regarding the minimum cybersecurity practices that every organization should employ.

Regulatory and Compliance – Hayslip

> "…compliance does not equate to being fully secure, it is just recommended controls and best practices to reduce risk."

In today's global business climate, we are witnessing technology, business, and compliance regimes converge into new and demanding environments. These dynamic circumstances are being driven by changing global mandates which are shaping business practices in areas such as financial accounting, business process/operations, information security, and data privacy. Organizations' risk, compliance and IT leaders are faced with the recurring heavy responsibility for risk management, corporate compliance, data and records management, and continuous monitoring of compliance-related policies and controls. Within this team of professionals, one of the leaders who is tasked with managing the organization's program for meeting compliance is the Chief Information Security Officer (CISO).

The CISO will work with the CIO and IT compliance staff to address new compliance challenges facing their businesses. One of the constant challenges faced by this team is conflicting compliance requirements that can span across multiple business units. Another challenge is the difficulty in tracking changes to regulations, interpreting how these changes affect the organization, and then putting policies and controls in place to meet the additional audit requirements. Creating and managing an effective compliance program to meet these shifting requirements is one of the greatest challenges for a CISO.

To effectively manage these issues, the CISO and his/her security teams should address compliance using a holistic approach. They must view compliance as it relates to their organization across all of its business channels, data types, and application and technology portfolios. So with that as a backdrop, let's address the three questions we will discuss together and how they relate to helping you, as CISO, manage compliance.

1. As a CISO, do I have any regulatory requirements?
2. As a CISO, how do I position my security program and organization for success with regard to compliance?
3. What policies, processes, or procedures should we leverage to successfully engages our auditors and/or regulators?

What Compliance Requirements?

Compliance is defined as the process of adhering to policies and decisions. These policies can be internally focused and pertain to the organization's directives, procedures, and requirements. These policies can also be outward facing, which means they will be focused on external entities and revolve around laws, regulations, standards, or industry agreements. Whether internal or external, both will put pressure on an organization to meet specific mandated needs and as a CISO you will be an integral part of the team that will manage meeting these needs for your business. This now leads us to our first question to consider, *"As a CISO, do I have regulatory requirements?"*

I would like to say that, based on my 30 years of working in IT, there will be times when you will not have to be concerned with regulatory requirements. However, that is not the case because I have never worked in an industry where there was not some type of internal or external regulation that required my organization to prove it was meeting compliance requirements. So from the beginning, it is safe to say you will have some type of regulation that as a CISO you must help manage. Of course, the fun part is finding out what regulations/compliance mandates apply to your organization. One of the quickest ways I have found to start this process is to do a "walk-about."

As CISO, you will need to build a network of stakeholders, both internal and external, to assist you in protecting your company and its assets. To understand what compliance regulations are applicable to your company and whether or not there is a compliance program in place, you need to talk with stakeholders. Your stakeholders, across the organization, will help you as CISO understand what types of data, applications, business processes, etc. are essentially critical for the company to operate and be successful. This knowledge, especially the knowledge about data, will give you your first glimpse into what regulations and compliance requirements will need to be addressed. I would also recommend that you speak with the Chief Risk Officer and Chief Legal Officer to get their perspective on what they believe applies to the organization.

Once you have this information and have identified any compliance or federal regulations that may pertain to your business, there are some essential questions you still need to get answered:

- How is the company interpreting compliance regulations, internal policies, or contractual agreements with partners and third-party vendors?
  - Corporate counsel will have a say in how they interpret wording on requirements.
- Based on their interpretation, is the company meeting these requirements?
- Is there a documented plan or compliance program in place for meeting requirements?
- If there is a compliance program in place, do you have access to prior reports, audit notes, findings, etc.?
- Are there processes and controls in place to prove that the compliance plan was implemented and being maintained?
  - Is there documentation? How old is it? Is it complete? Is it updated on a recurring basis?
- Is the company continuously monitoring that they meet the level of "compliance attestation" with both internal and external auditors?
  - As CISO, do you have access to these monitoring tools?
  - As CISO, are these tools part of your cybersecurity suite?

The answers to these questions will help you understand the organization's level of maturity with respect to how it is meeting any mandated compliance requirements. It will help you understand whether the current compliance program, if there is one, is a valuable tool for the organization, or if you have work to do in helping get one established. Either way, you need to understand what business practices are essential for your business to operate and you need to know which ones fall under regulatory guidelines.

As CISO, I would recommend approaching compliance with a "business-centric" viewpoint. This will help you understand which departments within your organization have data, applications, or processes that must be managed to meet compliance audits and it will give you a list of stakeholders you need to partner with to protect your organization. It will also help you plan the controls and policies you put in place to meet these regulations. With a business-centric view, you will want to select policies and controls that can span multiple departments and audit regimes, providing economy of scale to the organization. We will speak more on this later.

As we conclude this question, remember that compliance is just another name for risk. As CISO, risk is central to your role and there are four priorities you should focus on when working to meet compliance requirements and reduce the risk exposure to the enterprise:

1. Protect the organization's data
   - As CISO this is essential to your role in an organization
     o Know hot it is used, processes, stored, and backed up –it is the currently that keeps your company in business

2. Know the compliance and regulatory requirements that pertain to your company
   o You need to read them and truly understand them

3. Keep up to date on compliance and regulatory requirements that pertain to your company
   o Not understanding changes and their impact can have devastating consequences for your company

4. Incidents will happen, get used to it
   o If you have an incident that affects compliance:
     o Understand what happened, spend time to figure out the cause
     o Develop remediation to prevent it from recurring, then document it

These four priorities will keep you focused as you grow your cybersecurity program to meet the regulatory mandates required for your organization and its industry.

Build Compliance into Your Program

You are now working for a company and have been informed that there are regulatory requirements that apply to you and your teams. As CISO, you can expect that you will be required to assist in leading the effort to create or manage a compliance program and your teams will maintain the tools that monitor the resultant security controls.

For the sake of our discussion, I am going to approach our next question as if you are evaluating your company's current compliance program and will provide recommendations to help you as CISO. Don't forget, compliance is just another name for risk. Each compliance regime is basically a list of mandatory controls that an organization is expected to put in place to meet the "basics" for security. The compliance type will dictate the level of security. That's right, compliance does not equate to being fully secure, it is just recommended controls and best practices to reduce risk. There is always room for improvement. So let's discuss our next question, *"As a CISO, how do I position my security program and organization for success with regard to compliance?"*

To approach this question, I always go back to the basics. Most recommended controls for compliance requirements are based on cyber hygiene (Confidentiality, Integrity, and Availability) and basic cybersecurity common sense. So to start, I recommend reviewing the business' current security framework or selecting a new one. The right framework is critical. It is used as a baseline for evaluating the effectiveness of the organization's cybersecurity risk management program. A framework such as ISO 27001:2013 (ISO 2015) or NIST Cybersecurity Framework (NIST 2015) is a good start. Either framework would provide structure that your organization, its regulators, and its partners can use to create, assess, or improve their current risk management programs.

I personally would recommend the NIST Cybersecurity Framework. It is designed based on how information and data flows are processed within an organization. This framework has five key core functions: *Identify, Protect, Detect, Respond, and Recover*. This framework provides you with the option of implementing it in tiers, from Tier 1, "Partial," to Tier 4, "Adaptive." Implementation depends on the organization's risk appetite and how rigorously the business wants to incorporate cybersecurity risk management practices. This picture demonstrates the flow of information and decisions required to implement the NIST Cybersecurity Framework. (NIST, 2014)

This framework also contains an annex which lists all of its applicable security controls. This annex lists the individual controls under each of the five core functions and also provides cross references between its individual controls and other risk management frameworks, which may be required depending on the industry of the organization.

Chapter 2 Key Point and Action Item 4

We discussed at length the baseline requirements you need to have in place. Fortunately, there are several frameworks that we have listed that are available to aid you in implementing programs that comply with relevant regulations.

You should evaluate the needs of your organization and select a framework that will allow you to meet your requirements across your organization.

Once you have found that the organization is using a framework to evaluate its compliance program, you will need to verify that it meets your requirements or select a new one. As the CISO, you will also need to review what current security policies your organization has approved with respect to meeting its compliance requirements. You will want to ensure that your security policies are based on some type of standard format. This will provide uniformity in how all policies are created, changed, approved, and decommissioned.

This uniformity is especially critical. Ensuring that your policies meet a standard format will reduce the complexity of your installed corporate information systems. Remember, your policies will be based on the security controls listed in your selected risk management framework, and these same policies will be instrumental in which technologies are selected to enforce your framework's security controls. Keeping your security policies streamlined will help prevent overlapping security controls and the deployment of redundant technologies.

An outstanding white paper on recommended security policies is "Taking Control of Cybersecurity," (Foley & Lardner LLP. 2015). This document lists nine core security policies that an organization must have for its cybersecurity risk management program, with checklists for each policy. I would recommend you read this document and verify that these policies exist for your company. If they do not, you will need to use the supplied checklists and create your own.

By now, as CISO, you will have verified your selected security framework and noted any security controls that are outstanding. You will also have reviewed all current security policies and documented corrections that need to be made. The next step to increase the effectiveness of your cybersecurity risk management program so that it exceeds your regulatory requirements is to set up a security committee. Most organizations will have one. If yours does not, then as CISO you need to put one in place. To meet the requirements of a compliance mandate, it is essential that you understand how compliance applies across all business channels in your organization. To get this visibility, the organization should have an active Executive Security Committee with members from the various business units of the organization.

One recommended model, the "Governance Model," has business leaders from the organization as its members and the CISO as a valued advisor. The CISO presents recommendations regarding non-standard or contentious issues to the committee and its members make decisions for the organization. This places the burden of risk for compliance on the business leaders and allows the CISO to be a partner, making recommendations for remediating security and risk issues.

This model can also be used to provide clarity to the CISO for understanding the organization's risk tolerance as the business leaders on this committee can help articulate the levels of risk that are acceptable to the organization. This knowledge will enable you as CISO to understand what security controls are essential to the business to operate. This knowledge will also provide insight into what compliance requirements can be consolidated to reduce "security control" redundancy. One of the hardest parts of your job is dealing with security controls that overlap each other. If you are able to streamline them and provide a more efficient security control index, then as CISO it's imperative that you make this happen.

At this stage, for you to be effective as the CISO, you have verified that there is a cybersecurity risk management program in place to meet regulatory requirements. You have also verified that the organization is using an assessment framework, has corporate security policies, and that the organization has an executive security committee. You now need only technology to make it all work. This final step in answering the question for our discussion will be centered on how technology is used to provide the organization with visibility into its compliance risks. The technology an organization uses to meet its compliance requirements is driven by three components:

Regulations
- o Can be state, federal, international or industry specific
- o Typically based on the organization's use of "specific" data

Policies
- o Organizations' business rules put in place to meet regulations

Controls
- o Can be security controls, operational controls, financial controls, etc.
- o Used to verify meeting the requirements of a policy

Of these three components, "controls" will be the primary driver for the technology selected by your organization to meet compliance. As the CISO, you will continually review, manage, and monitor any installed technologies currently in place to meet your organization's specific mandates. You will need to continuously monitor your enterprise networks and their underlying security controls in real time. You will also need to document any controls that are non-compliant, as these will need to be investigated and possibly remediated. These "non-compliant" controls will need to be reviewed by your committee of stakeholders to verify whether or not they apply to the organization. If they are required, you will need to review the organization's application and hardware portfolios to validate that the non-compliant controls are not being fulfilled by another installed technology.

After review, if the controls are still non-compliant it will be up to you as CISO to assess the impact to the organization and make recommendations for how this issue can be resolved. It is here where you will see security controls dictate a specific technology to meet their requirements. It is incumbent upon you to not just recommend a new piece of hardware or software, but to remember that a security control can be a new workflow process or a new form used to document that process. Leverage your stakeholders, team members, and security committee to resolve non-compliant security controls, be innovative, and you will likely surprise yourself. With that said, keep in mind that the drive to resolve this issue and maintain compliance can quickly become a project with high visibility in your organization. Be cognizant of the fact that your decisions can impact your organization's ability to operate. Your decisions, if not implemented correctly, can result in fines and substantial liability exposure for your company.

In answering our second question, we touched on several topics that the CISO will require to fulfill compliance requirements. We discussed the fact that the CISO will need to select and implement a solid cybersecurity risk management framework to position his/her teams and organization for success. We also noted that along with the selected framework, the CISO will need to have current security policies in place and will require a security committee. This committee's members should include business leaders and stakeholders from across the organization. This committee will be instrumental in providing the CISO with insight into what level of risk is acceptable to the organization and aide in the prioritization of non-compliant controls and their resultant security projects. Each of these pieces of the compliance life-cycle is connected and feeds one another. It is essential that the CISO and compliance team members recognize that this process is a balanced life-cycle and leverage it to protect the company.

Methods to Make Your Audits Effective

By now in this compliance process you know what regulations apply to your organization and you have started to put the compliance life-cycle and its components in place. You are working with your stakeholders, your leadership teams, and your security committee to meet compliance guidelines. This hard work from you and your teams is going to pay off, and you know you're on the right track for your organization to be certified within its industry standards. Now I have to ask, what have you forgotten? What key group have we not discussed that you must prepare for? If you are starting to stress, you figured it out and that leads into our last question, *"What policies, processes or procedures should we leverage to successfully engage our auditors and/or regulators?"* For the last question in our discourse on compliance, we will discuss some ideas that you as a CISO can implement to better prepare yourself and your organization when you need to speak with your auditors/regulators.

The compliance life-cycle is an ongoing activity. One of the challenging aspects of being a CISO is educating your stakeholders and leadership teams that compliance is not a "one-n-done" project. To help make this case, I believe it will be imperative that you have a "regulatory" change management process and a repository of all regulations that pertain to your company. This collection of documents should be continuously reviewed and any changes to the regulations or security controls need to be immediately noted and reviewed for their impact to the organization's compliance program. Having this repository of data will ensure that you have a true picture of what forms of compliance apply to your business.

You'll want to ensure that you have a true understanding of not only the external compliance regimes that apply to the organization, but also internal contractual (third party vendors, partners) and/or organizational compliance requirements. All three types have requirement mandates that influence the organization, and each has its own level of risk. The CISO must partner with his/her leadership teams and security committee to understand the importance and priority of each. The CISO must know which ones apply to the organization, secure funding to address the risks, implement policies and controls to reduce the risks, and then monitor and report any residual risk to ensure that it's at an acceptable level for the business.

Chapter 2 Key Point and Action Item 5

Regulatory requirements and audit support are recurring obligations. It is this constant diligence that creates both an extra operational burden and an ongoing opportunity to assess and improve. Having a governance program that you keep current and communicate routinely gives you the best chance at success.

You should create a repository of regulatory and contractual obligations and the necessary compliance activities and communicate requirements and status regularly.

You now have an understanding of how to implement a regulatory change management program and create an archive of associated compliance documents for continuous review. It's now time that we look at the major component of our discussion. Which processes should we put in place to fully utilize our compliance management program? The selected processes, if implemented, should be instrumental in positioning the organization to be effective partners with its auditors/regulators. The processes I would recommend are as follows:

1. Employ a clearly defined governance structure
    a. This provides auditors with a view of who has rights for inputs, changes and making final decisions

2. Assess all compliance activities
    a. If we have previous audit reports, do we have non-compliant issues? Have they been resolved?
        i. If not, are there reports tracking the completion rate of these issues with projected completion dates?
    b. Are we collecting metrics on deployed controls to prove we have "effective security measures in place?"
        i. Center for Internet Security – Security Metrics (CIS 2010)
        ii. Center for Internet Security – Top 20 Security Control Metrics (CIS 2015)

3. Architect cross-functional controls
    a. Employ controls designed to support multiple regulatory compliance regimes
        i. Reduce costs
        ii. Automate where possible

4. Architect a data classification program
    a. Know what data is important to your organization
    b. Know the "how," "what," and "where" of all sensitive data
    c. Know how the data is governed
        i. Accessed, processed, stored, backed-up, deleted, etc.

5. Know your compliance regulations
    a. This is where a compliance repository is required.
        i. Organizations have multiple business verticals
            1. Will probably operate with several compliance regimes
        ii. Organizations operate globally
            1. Will often have conflicting compliance regimes that overlap
        iii. Remember that almost all requirements center around cyber-hygiene

6. Manage compliance at the highest level

    a. Use a cybersecurity risk management framework (as discussed)
        i. Establish the organization's risk baseline. Select a framework or standard for use across multiple compliance regimes.
           1. ISO 27001:2013
           2. ISACA – COBIT
           3. NIST – Cybersecurity Framework
           4. NIST SP 800-53
           5. PCI DSS ver3.1
           6. HIPAA/HITECH
    b. Use Policy templates to reduce complexity (as discussed)
        i. Uniform policies can span multiple business verticals in an organization

The key point you should understand is that the more "complexity" you introduce into implementing policies, projects, or processes, the more security gaps you create in your organization. In my decades of working in cybersecurity, I have seen some outrageously complex processes implemented to resolve a known security issue and over time these processes were ignored. Employees would develop work-arounds, which they justified were needed to get work done. In the end, the business is paying for a complex solution that is not being followed and the compliance program has not substantially reduced the organization's risk exposure.

In closing, the CISO will want the organization to have mature processes in place. This will provide him/her a compliance program that spans all business units and can be leveraged for multiple compliance mandates. The CISO and his/her teams will engage leadership and organizational stakeholders, and together they will continuously monitor all policies and deployed security controls.

With an organization's mature compliance program, the CISO and leadership can generate reports from the selected technology suite. These reports will provide real-time scorecard data on the business' compliance risk baseline and document areas that need improvement. These report cards can be used by IT and compliance leadership staff to report to the company's board and present a realistic view of the organization's preparedness for its next regulatory review. As CISO, don't forget that compliance is a life cycle and it starts with you understanding what regulations apply and then using a framework to build your selected policies, security controls, and work processes. As I have stated before, security doesn't work in a vacuum. Leverage your stakeholders and security committee members to develop your program and provide effective value to the enterprise.

Summary

For Chapter 2, we began our discussion by asking these three questions:

- Which regulations apply to my organization?
- What is the status of our current regulatory compliance?
- How efficient is my team in working with auditors and regulators?

Several consistent themes emerged, including the ever-increasing regulatory burden and the difficulty in merely keeping up with the volumes of edicts and orders, the impact of regulations, frameworks and standards on the practice of Information Security, and how central your understanding of where your data resides, how it is protected and who has access to it is in the fulfillment of your duties.

In closing, we would like to leave you with these five key points and next steps:

1. It is extremely important that you understand your regulatory and contractual obligations for data handling, breach disclosure, and policy stewardship and enforcement. Key resources include your organization's legal department, the executive team, especially in finance and procurement, and both internal and external auditors. A common theme in the regulatory requirements for cybersecurity is the designation of responsible roles within the organization to establish and be accountable for mandated security programs. In hiring a CISO, your organization is designating you as that accountable individual. **You should schedule time to review with legal, procurement and finance the set of regulatory requirements as well as contractual obligations which apply to your organization.**

2. Audit functions, whether commissioned by the board or as a result of partners exercising their right to audit are a valuable tool for maintaining confidence in your organization's ability to discharge its duties pertaining to the safeguarding of the data with which you have been entrusted. **You should review your most recent audit reports across all your regulatory and contractual obligations and schedule time with audit leadership and**

the leadership of audited functions to review remedial activities.

3. Breach disclosure laws are present at the federal and international level as well as in 47 of the 50 states in the U. S. In addition to breach notification, organizations are potentially subject to civil legal action and regulatory sanction. In many cases, the "clock starts ticking" for notifying consumers and regulators, and in some cases, public disclosure of the breach. Due to the potential impact on consumers, expect that the regulators will continue to be aggressive. **You should make sure your organization has incident management and breach notification processes, clearly documented with crisp escalation points, that have been reviewed by legal counsel.**

4. We discussed at length the baseline requirements you need to have in place. Fortunately, there are several frameworks that we have listed that are available to aid you in implementing programs that comply with relevant regulations. **You should evaluate the needs of your organization and select a framework that will allow you to meet your requirements across your organization.**

5. Regulatory requirements and audit support are recurring obligations. It is this constant diligence that creates both an extra operational burden and an ongoing opportunity to assess and improve. Having a governance program that you keep current and communicate routinely gives you the best chance at success. **You should create a repository of regulatory and contractual obligations and the necessary compliance activities and communicate requirements and status regularly.**

Your role as the CISO, along with legal counsel and your designated privacy officer, is to ensure that your organization understands your cybersecurity regulatory environment and is prepared to respond in the manner required within the mandated timeframe. The key word is prepared. Without the proper preparation, an embarrassing mea culpa can turn into a regulatory nightmare.

Chapter 3 – How Data and Information Classification Influence the Role of the CISO

<hr>

Introduction

There are few topics more important in cybersecurity than the establishment of good data classification – and by extension protection – programs within an organization. For many organizations, their data and information is every bit as valuable as other assets. Indeed, many economists have observed that data and information are the new currency in the digital economy. As our authors noted in the last chapter, specific types of information are subject to mandated security and privacy practices. In this chapter, we learn how aligning data and information protection with business objectives is a core element of good data governance. The authors note that not all data is created equal.

Bill Bonney begins the chapter by bringing clarity to what is the central role of the CISO, namely protecting information. We are, after all, *Information Security* Officers. Bill provides an important perspective on how data classification influences the three central tenants of security: confidentiality, integrity, and availability (CIA). While each of these three attributes are important, and indeed you cannot have a secure environment without all three being present, their respective values vary notably from industry to industry. As a simple case in point, availability of information in healthcare will trump confidentiality. Bill also offers practical guidance to CISOs in noting that not all data can be protected equally and that a critical part of the CISO's role is to understand which data is most important to the organization and ensure that this data is adequately protected.

Matt Stamper emphasizes the importance of conducting formal data-flow analysis within the organization and notes that the resulting data flow diagrams (DFDs) are a valuable tool in conveying the importance of data and information security and governance to other colleagues and the board of directors. Matt's analysis also enters the world of economics, highlighting the linkages between transactional costs and how much data and information is shared with third parties (be they vendors, clients, independent contractors, or affiliated parties). As part of Matt's guidance, he shares approaches to documenting information flows within an organization that range from non-technical meet-n-greets to more technical packet analysis.

Gary Hayslip brings home the shared perspective of our authors that data is a strategic asset. Gary strongly suggests that data classification activities be made as pragmatic as possible (and aligned with the needs of the organization) and warns that data classification efforts that are too exhaustive become "shelf ware." Overly complex and burdensome classification efforts are doomed to fail and undermine organizational effectiveness. Gary notes how critical it is to have the data classification and governance activities aligned with the organization's risk management practices and ultimately the organization's risk appetite. This risk management perspective on data classification will resonate with other executives in the organization.

Some of the questions the authors used to frame their thoughts for this chapter include:

- What type of information and data does my organization create, use, and share as part of our operations?
- Do we have data that is subject to specific regulatory or contractual controls and practices?
- Do I know the lifecycle of this data and the systems, processes, applications, individuals, and third parties that have access to this data?
- Are our organization's data governance practices consistent with the value of this data and our regulatory or contractual obligations?

Identifying Sensitive Data – Bonney

> "Truth be told, many organizations have done minimal data mapping work, usually driven by needs to estimate storage capacity, develop a retention policy, or because of regulatory requirements."

Information Security is concerned with one thing: protecting certain types of data. Organizations that fail at this, with the exception of the occasional, inevitable breach, do so for two primary reasons. They either don't take their mission to protect certain types of data seriously and fail for lack of diligence, or they try to protect all data equally and fail under the cumulative burden. The key question for you as the CISO then is what is the subset of data that you should be concerned with protecting? This is critical to having a focused and thereby hopefully a successful information security program.

When we strip it down to the essential elements, we are concerned with maintaining privacy, securing financial transactions, protecting intellectual property and safeguarding operational data. Regardless of the specific data elements involved, what we are responsible for is the confidentiality, integrity and availability (CIA) of the data and this is outlined very well in the various information security control frameworks such as NIST 800-53, ISO 27K, and PCI-DSS. Just so the concepts are top of mind, confidentiality pertains to maintaining the proper rights to access, integrity pertains to maintaining the data in an unaltered and accurate state, and availability pertains to ensuring that the data is accessible when needed, i.e., systems are up, data is online, etc.

Start with Privacy

We can easily define privacy and we have a number of helpful guides, also called regulations, along with lots of very helpful docents, also called regulators, prosecutors, and attorneys general, which aid us in that endeavor. While all three elements of CIA are important, systems primarily concerned with organizing and protecting personal information can tolerate a certain level of unavailability, but confidentiality and integrity are both critical. Note that while identifying the data involved is relatively straightforward, ensuring privacy, especially when including choice (a key concept for privacy, allowing the subject to determine what data they want to share and when), is not a trivial task.

Like privacy data, financial transactions fall within the realm of heavy regulation, especially for banks and certain other financial institutions. Many non-financial institutions take on contractual obligations voluntarily when they handle credit and debit cards. As with maintaining privacy, securing financial transactions has regulatory regimes that set an obligatory level of due care. The specific data elements that must be protected are widely available via the references to regulation and data handling standards in the previous chapter. Unlike maintaining privacy, securing financial transactions can have an element of systemic availability as the financial system is considered "critical infrastructure" (to use a U.S. term), and the ability to clear transactions in a timely manner is deemed critical for trust in developed economies. Thus, all three elements of CIA are critical for financial data.

For privacy data, you will be concerned with how personal data, such as personally identifiable information (PII) and Protected Health Information (PHI) is stored, protected, accessed and monitored. Within the legislative frameworks that I mentioned in the last chapter, you will find definitions for the data elements that qualify, the minimum protections you must undertake and the consequences if a failure occurs (i.e., breach notification requirements and regulatory sanctions, to name two). Your compliance team or current auditors should have at least a baseline list of those data elements and systems. You would apply the same technique for financial data, also starting with the regulatory frameworks mentioned in the previous chapter.

Intellectual Property

Intellectual property comes in many varieties, under many names, including "Intellectual Capital," "Proprietary Information," and "Trade Secrets," to list just a few. Some are quite obvious, such as design plans for the organization's next generation product or customer and prospect lists along with the related sales forecast. Some are not so obvious, such as production methodologies and salary structures.

All data is not created equal. Knowing what types of data you have and the sensitivity of that data is critical to your ability to focus your attention and your limited resources in the right way. While some sensitive data types (such as PII and PHI) are obvious and well documented, some (such as intellectual property) are less visible and not always well understood.

You should conduct a data mapping exercise so that you understand what types of data you are responsible for and their relative importance to the organization.

I mentioned our helpful docents and their privacy guidelines above, but proprietary information comes with some legislative heft as well. The Economic Espionage Act of 1996 (EEA), which was in itself modeled on the Uniform Trade Secrets Act (UTSA) (Economic Espionage Act, 18 U.S.C. Ch. 90 § 1839 1996)defines what an organization can or should classify as trade secrets and establishes the behavioral criteria to extend the cloak of legislative protection over what has been designated as proprietary information or trade secrets. Essentially, organizations must take reasonable measures to keep the information secret and its existence as a secret or as something not generally known must give the organization an economic or competitive benefit. Again, all three elements, CIA, are important, but confidentiality clearly trumps both integrity and availability in this case.

For intellectual property and trade secrets, I'm going to list quite a few sample data elements. My point is to show how broadly you should consider what data your organization might wish to protect. You can consider these fields a good start: secret formulas, processes, and methods used in production, a company's business and marketing plans, salary structure, customer lists, contracts, and details of its computer systems (yes, it should go without saying that you should guard your network diagrams jealously). In some cases, the special knowledge and skills that an employee has learned on the job are considered to be a company's proprietary information.

The term "trade secret" means all forms and types of financial, business, scientific, technical, economic, or engineering information, including patterns, plans, compilations, program devices, formulas, designs, prototypes, methods, techniques, processes, procedures, programs, or codes, whether tangible or intangible, and whether or

how stored, compiled, or memorialized p
graphically, photographically, or in writing
yes, it goes much beyond Coca-Cola's secret

Operational Data

Operational integrity is straightforward
with operations teams to understand the
elements that are critical to the business p
includes production output figure
environmental data for physical systems, and pro
capacity, memory utilization, and others for virtual systems. Goals
for handling most operational data have traditionally and will
probably continue in the near term to feature integrity and
availability. A word of caution is in order. Given the advent of
ubiquitous data analytics and the rapid adoption of IoT (and the vast
array of sensors that makes IoT work), the competitive intelligence
that can be gained by intercepting and analyzing what once were
considered low-sensitivity operational data has increased
exponentially. Some industries have already matured to a state
where the confidentiality of all operational data is as important as
the integrity and availability of that data.

Sometimes the same information fits into more than one category.
Salary information about an individual, for instance, may be
considered private information and protecting it may be a matter of
privacy. Salary ranges across a division may be proprietary
information the company wishes to keep confidential to protect
trade advantages they gain from labor arbitrage. Protecting credit
card information might be considered a matter of privacy, also has
an obvious role in financial transactions, and some data elements
from the transaction play an operational role in demand
management and fulfillment.

What is important about all of this is to establish a foundation for
identifying the data over which an organization has control that the
organization should assume responsibility for protecting from
inappropriate use or disclosure. Inappropriate meaning without the
authorization of a data custodian charged with protecting that data
and, when applicable, the explicit permission of the data subject.

Data Classification, Often Neglected

Within these broad categories of data, it is often helpful to do two
things. The first is to classify all the data an organization produces,
collects, processes, and stores into categories that assign levels of
sensitivity. The second is to assign individuals (data custodians)
responsible for each data pool of a certain level of sensitivity. If your

Data Mapping – Stamper

> "It's probably easier than most businesses think to expand internationally. More than likely, their data is already there."

In this chapter, we will be discussing the critical requirement to classify and map data. As I discussed in the previous chapter, laws, regulations, and industry standards are placing greater emphasis on knowing the types of data and its governance within organizations. Before focusing on data governance, let's take a quick detour to the world of economics.

Transaction costs, according to economists, influence which functions are handled internally within the organization or outsourced to an external provider. When transaction costs are high, there is a tendency to maintain these activities internally. When transaction costs are low, these functions will likely be transferred to more cost-effective, external providers. What we have seen over the last twenty-plus years is the widespread reduction of transaction costs for many core enterprise functions and across many industries including healthcare, financial services, manufacturing, and professional services. Outsourcing of wide-scale functions has recently been complemented by outsourcing of niche activities at the margin (think shadow IT). As an economist will note, most everything happens at the margin. So what does this have to do with cybersecurity? Everything.

For the CISO today, it has never been more important to understand the types of information moving in and out of the organization. The effect of reduced transaction costs, coupled with new technologies such as mobile telephony and cloud services, has introduced significant challenges for CISOs charged with protecting organizational assets, including information and data. Let's take a few moments to understand how pervasive outsourcing of certain functions is in today's economy, and its impact on knowing where our data resides.

Most organizations have a number of basic departments including human resources, finance and accounting, sales and marketing, information technology (IT), operations (including manufacturing), and legal. The reduction of transaction costs related to core activities within these departments has effectively made the organizational boundary semi-permeable. What is outside the organization is now inside, and what's inside is now outside. Those of us in security feel this viscerally when we think of our own organization's perimeter. It's hard to find and nearly impossible to secure.

Where's Our Data?

Let's look at some concrete examples of how fluid information is within, and more importantly, outside an organization. It's not uncommon for organizations to outsource their payroll services to third-party processing organizations. Payroll data includes important uniquely-identifiable information, including employees' social security numbers (SSNs), salaries, dates of birth, and addresses. That same organization may also outsource its accounting function. The accounting firm would have access to sensitive financial information including profit and loss detail, the value of assets, and the particulars about significant transactions. External auditors will validate the financial information prepared by the firm and may request samples of specific transactions to support their assertions regarding the quality of the financial reporting.

The organization may leverage external legal counsel to file patent applications, handle merger and acquisition (M&A) activities, and other highly-sensitive projects. A third-party marketing application sends e-mails to clients and prospective clients containing personally-identifiable information (the name and e-mail address of the recipients). Independent contractors may be providing support on key projects with access to material non-public information. Manufacturing may be outsourced to a contract manufacturer in another country. The manufacturer could be using patented processes or other intellectual property of the organization. Application development could be handled by an external DevOps team given real production data to test functionality.

The organization's applications reside in multiple locations across multiple states and in several countries. Some applications and data are "in the cloud" and many lines of business, given the response challenges with *traditional* IT, use SaaS services to meet their requirements. Employees have personal mobile phones that they use to receive e-mail outside of the office. This e-mail includes attachments containing any number of data elements. Employees also bring their devices to work and take these devices with them when they leave the office each day or are terminated from the firm. Employees use third-party file-sharing tools, personal e-mail accounts, and external media to store information. Suffice it to say that the average organization simply does not know where its critical data and information are and, equally important, how they are being protected, if at all, outside the organization.

Outsourcing of business processes has become common place and because of advances in cloud computing, the types of processes that are eligible for outsourcing have expanded significantly. When an organization outsources their business processes they also expose the data upon which those processes depend to a different set of individuals, often allow it to flow outside of the organization's direct control, and extend the data custodianship to third-party organizations. While you can outsource business process activities, you cannot outsource responsibility, which means you are still responsible for how your data and your customers' data are safeguarded.

You should inventory the data you entrust to third parties and validate that appropriate access controls and data safeguards are in place.

All of these challenges are fundamentally the same for third parties providing outsourced services. They too have third parties helping with their core functions. Payroll processing companies may outsource application development and use third-party data centers. Staff turnover, background checks, and other controls are likely to differ from firm to firm. The number of variables impacting the location and controls over information has grown beyond the capacity of most organizations to handle them securely.

To drive the point home, think about how much of our own personal information is shared. How many times have you input your phone number, e-mail address, physical address, or other personally-identifiable information into forms on websites? Using a credit card throughout the day furthers this data footprint. As CISOs, we know that good security practices are rare, so we are left to wonder – just how effective are the security controls of the organizations that have our personal information? Given the number of breach notifications we receive, the answer is obvious. Clearly, knowing where data resides and how it is governed presents unique logistical and technical challenges. Later in this chapter, I'll offer some practical approaches to improve this dynamic.

A Data-Driven Perspective of Cybersecurity

Data governance should fundamentally inform security practices. Few of us work in organizations that have unlimited cybersecurity budgets. As a consequence, it's imperative that we focus cybersecurity efforts on those assets that have the most value to the organization. For the majority of organizations, the asset that has the most value is information – effectively, data with context. This information could include intellectual property, proprietary information, client and vendor lists, health records, employee records, financial records, non-public information (NPI), and personally identifiable information (PII), among other data sets. Information drives and powers today's economy. We rely on accurate, complete, timely, and valid information to make business and personal decisions. Not all data or information is created equal, and devoting resources to protecting information with little intrinsic value does not make sense. This is why it is so important that organizations classify their data and information.

Classification exercises are well-served by using the definitions of the regulatory or standards bodies responsible for oversight. There are exceptions in the cases of intellectual property – which tends to be organization-specific – and government classifications (e.g. Top Secret). Some of the more important data elements within an organization to map and understand include those that move into the domain of privacy. Several examples include Non-Public Information (NPI), Personally Identifiable Information (PII), Protected-Health Information (PHI), electronic Protected-Health Information (ePHI), and credit card data. As we discussed in the last chapter, each of these types of information are subject to mandated controls, either by statute or by standard, as is the case with cardholder data. Definitions for these general classes of information are noted below:

- **Non-Public Information (NPI):** This is specifically addressed in the Gramm-Leach-Bliley Act (GLBA) and defined as name, address, social security number (SSN) or other information provided on an application (typically with a financial services firm). This information is governed by the Act's Privacy Rule, which limits activity related to NPI without notification. With respect to GLBA, if the information is reasonably available in the public domain, the information is no longer classified as NPI. There is also a concept of the combination of unique data elements (e.g. name + address) creating NPI in certain contexts.

- **Personally Identifiable Information (PII):** The National Institute of Standards and Technology (NIST) Special Publication 800-122, "Guide to Protecting the Confidentiality of Personally Identifiable Information (PII)," leverages the 2008 Government Accounting Office's (GAO's) definition of PII as follows: "any information about an individual maintained by an agency, including (1) any information that can be used to distinguish or trace an individual's identity, such as name, social security number, date and place of birth, mother's maiden name, or biometric records; and (2) any other information that is linked or linkable to an individual, such as medical, educational, financial, and employment information."[7] The definitions of both PII and NPI have been widely used by states for their breach notification laws.

- **Protected Health Information (PHI):** PHI is defined in Title 45 C.F.R. § 160.103 as individually-identifiable health information. PHI is effectively any information in the health record of an individual that makes that individual uniquely identifiable. This could include billing information (e.g. name and address) as well as procedural information (e.g. tests, scans, or results from other medical procedures that create information uniquely attributable to the individual). Both PHI and ePHI are subject to the HIPAA Security and Privacy Rules.

- **Electronic Protected Health Information (ePHI):** ePHI is effectively the electronic equivalent of PHI. ePHI's prominence in healthcare was cemented with the Health Information Technology for Economic and Clinical Health Act (HITECH), which provided government incentives to convert medical records into electronic health records (EHRs). HIPAA-HITECH governs how covered entities (typically hospitals and insurance companies) share PHI and ePHI with business associates (third parties) that provide services required to provision health care.

- **Credit Card Data:** The Payment Card Industry (PCI) defines a number of different data elements related to the ubiquitous credit card. Cardholder data is the PII related to the end-user, including data elements such as the name, address, phone number, and the primary account number (PAN). Additionally, PCI provides guidance and definitions related to card validation codes. The Payment Card Industry Data Security Standard (PCI-DSS), now version 3.1, provides required security measures related to protecting this information.

Determining the value of this information, and the associated and commensurate security and governance practices, is a process that requires the CISO to be fully-engaged with colleagues across the organization … certainly beyond traditional IT counterparts. Valued participants in this assessment include other C-level executives,

---

7. NIST Special Publication 800-122 found at:
http://csrc.nist.gov/publications/nistpubs/800-122/sp800-122.pdf.

corporate counsel, line-of-business executives, the board, as well as business partners, vendors, and, potentially, regulatory authorities who may have legally-mandated expectations regarding how certain types of information such as electronic Protected Health Information (ePHI) should be managed within the organization.

While it is almost self-evident that information is the lifeblood of our modern economy, how information – data – is actually handled within companies suggests that this valuable asset is often mistreated and neglected. Regulatory authorities such as the Federal Trade Commission (FTC) and contractual obligations mandated by laws such as HIPAA-HITECH's Business Associates Agreements, require organizations to know what types of information they have, who has access to this information, and how it governed and protected. How do we explain this fundamental disconnect between the value of information, its required governance – often mandated by federal and state laws – and the seemingly negligent treatment of information within organizations?

This disconnect is the result of a confluence of historical issues that are now witness to important changes. First among these issues was the structural distance between IT security and the rest of the organization. As I discussed in the first chapter, CISOs who report into IT structures (e.g. to the CIO or CTO) may lack the business context of the information they are charged with protecting. CISOs who are buried deep in the proverbial org chart may be rendered ineffective in communicating their concerns to the C-suite and the board because their insights are intermediated by their management. This is clearly a separation of duties issue and one of the main reasons why I believe CISOs should report outside of traditional IT. There are also historical perspectives of IT security being largely the domain of Layer 2 and Layer 3. Controls at these layers are important and cannot be neglected, but they are not sufficient to adequately ensure information security. Today's CISO, however, brings an enterprise risk management (ERM) view to cybersecurity operations. This higher-level and business-oriented view of information is changing security practices and how information is understood and valued within an organization.

A Practical Approach to Mapping Your Data

Knowing the types of information, their location, and how they are controlled and governed is a must. There are a number of viable approaches to discover this detail, ranging from highly-informal walkthroughs of processes to more technical packet analyses. Let's review five of these approaches, beginning with the least technical.

- **Meet and Greet:** This is the simplest way to get an understanding of the types of information and data within an organization. Meeting with colleagues and asking questions about the types of data and information that departments use is a great way to learn about the organization, its processes, applications, and, most critically, the information and data processed by these applications. Observation and inquiry will also produce insights that can rarely be obtained via technical means in that they provide direct, meaningful context for the activities and processes within an organization. This is also a great way to assess the staffing levels and competencies required outside of traditional IT to support data governance. If the organization has a privacy officer, they will provide a wealth of insight into privacy practices (and hence data classification) within the firm.

- **Industry Context:** Another simple approach is to understand industry context. Clearly, organizations in regulated industries are likely to create and use data that requires appropriate care. Working in fields such as healthcare, legal, financial, accounting, and government agencies provides indicators for the types of information that are likely to be within the organization. Industry and trade associations can also provide guidance on standards and practices.

- **Legal and Contractual:** I know most CISOs don't welcome the idea of reviewing contracts, but they offer a wealth of important detail on the types of information the organization maintains or is responsible for. This approach clearly requires a strong working relationship with legal counsel. Contracts will often define specific controls, procedures, and activities related to intellectual property or other data sets. Service provider contracts, typically in the form of a master services agreement (MSA), may provide detail on governance practices, service-level objectives (SLOs), and service level agreements (SLAs). Lastly, the CISO should be aware of any breach or incident notification requirements found in the organization's current contracts.

- **Data Flow Diagrams (DFDs):** DFDs are a must for highly-regulated workloads. The beauty of a DFD is in its structured approach to looking at data flowing across an organization. Context diagrams define organizational or operational boundaries that are complemented by decomposed diagrams that go into further detail on a given process or transaction. DFDs effectively map data elements moving into and out of a given process. They clearly show how data is captured, processed, stored, or transferred. The value of DFDs is that they complement the information gathered in the meet and greet activities described above. Linking business processes to applications, data stores, staff, and inputs and outputs at each step informs the types of controls required to protect information at each phase of its lifecycle. Well-crafted DFDs highlight where validation controls are required, where encryption should be employed, and spotlight contractual requirements for governance when information is moved outside of the organizational boundary.

- **Technical Discovery:** Perhaps the most complicated but accurate way to look at data flows within the organization is to literally look at the packets across the network. Network diagrams, complemented by DFDs, can be readily used to determine important access and egress points – and egress is always critical. This analysis requires a combination of technical and protocol knowledge, coupled with the higher-level process detail captured in the meet and greet sessions. In many ways, packet and protocol analysis is a great way to determine if DFDs and other sources of data detail are accurate.

We've seen in this chapter the importance of inventorying and classifying information within the organization. The techniques above offer some initial guidance on the best way to determine what types of information the organization possesses, who has access to this information, and where it resides, including actors outside of the organization such as vendors, independent contractors, and service providers. For today's CISO, security controls and practices are no longer limited to network security within the organization, but now extend more pervasively to all areas within and, equally important, outside the organization.

Securing and Classifying Data – Hayslip

> "Smart companies seeking competitive advantage will look to leverage data governance programs to add to their revenue streams."

As a CISO you will be required to fill multiple roles within your company. Don't be surprised that these roles will traverse the operational landscape. You will be the technical subject matter expert (SME) who provides context on cybersecurity issues and the strategic business partner who provides visibility into your organization's risks. To effectively perform these diverse functions, you will need a thorough understanding of how your organization uses data and what data is important for business operations.

This establishes the framework for our discussion. Today organizations are storing an ever increasing amount of data in numerous categories and database formats. This data comes in categories such as *operational data* (sales, inventory, financial, etc.), *nonoperational data* (sales forecasts, analytics, HR data, etc.) and *metadata* (data about itself, data dictionary, data warehouse design). With this in mind, let's look at the questions for our discussion:

1. As a CISO, do I know what data is important to my organization?
2. As a CISO, what programs or policies should I implement to protect my organization's sensitive data and turn it into a strategic asset?

Not All Data Is Created Equal

When a new CISO starts their job they go through a transition process. Part of that process is to meet stakeholders from the various business channels of their company. As a CISO, I have done these types of meet-and-greets and have found them to be invaluable. In these meetings you have the opportunity to learn what is important to your stakeholders, what problems they currently have, and what services they believe are critical for their respective departments.

During this period of acclimating to a new organization, as CISO you will begin to inventory the enterprise networks and data assets of your new company. You will review previous audit and assessment reports and begin to review standing cybersecurity policies. As you learn more about the organization, its compliance requirements, and its strategic goals, the data you collected from your initial meetings with stakeholders will provide critical insight into projects and policies that are necessary to protect your company. This information should have also highlighted the types of data and information that is critical for their success and provided a more in-depth understanding of its lifecycle as it is created, accessed, processed, archived, and later decommissioned. So with data in mind, let's focus on our first question, *"As a CISO, do I understand what data is important to my organization?"*

Organizations typically believe they understand what data and information they have within their enterprise boundaries. Many corporations will have standard policies in place for data to be archived, with backup schemes and disaster recovery plans. They believe this will ensure that "critical" data is always available for ongoing business operations. But is that enough? I believe for an organization to use its data as a strategic asset it must understand data classification and have gone through the process of organizing and classifying all of its critical data. This is where you, the CISO, become a valuable partner to your business because any data classification project will involve you and your security program.

To start a data classification program, you first need to know the types of data your company uses. You will need to collaborate with your stakeholders, they will need to help you identify some "buckets" that your data can be easily divided into, and this will usually match how the business units use corporate data. Typically, I would look at collected records of data and classify this information into groups, then prioritize the classes of collected records based on requirements such those that are in line with confidentiality or compliance agreements. Starting with these ideas as a reference point, think about what records are critical to the organization and then build out your data map based on organizational priority. Examples of data categories that I have seen used in the past are:

Public – data that is publicly releasable

Internal – internal business information

Confidential/Private – legal, intellectual property, R&D

Restricted/Controlled – compliance related (PII, PCI, HIPAA)

Protecting a Critical Asset

So now you have created two standing policies on how the business classifies its data and how this data should be managed by personnel. Unfortunately, this whole process is still probably viewed by business units within your company as one that IT Department owns and it is only grudgingly followed, if at all. What we need to look at now is you, as the CISO, can lead the effort to mature your Data Classification Policies into a full-fledged organizational Data Governance Program. This leads us to our second question, "*As CISO, what programs or policies should I implement to protect my organization's sensitive data and turn it into a strategic asset*?"

In today's dynamic business environment data is the new currency. Data is the engine that drives today's interconnected economy and data governance is the strategic process of managing this essential engine for your organization. To protect this critical asset, we must create a formal organizational program where data is valued and protected not just by the CISO, but by all employees. This program is called "Data Governance." So what is the official definition of data governance? In an exceptional book called "Non-Invasive Data Governance" (Seiner, 2014) it is described as several processes:

1. Data Governance is the formal execution and enforcement of authority over the management of data and data-related assets.
2. Data Governance is formalizing the behavior around the definition, production, and usage of data to manage risk and improve quality and usability of selected data.
3. Data Governance is formalizing the behavior over the definition, production, and use of information and information-related assets

As you can see from these multiple definitions, data governance involves formalizing organizational behavior. As a CISO, this is a red flag. It means that we will need to get executive buy-in if we expect to move our data classification policies to a mature data governance program. Only through executive leadership can we ensure that our program has the authority to grow and become a strategic asset for our organization.

I personally view governing data as an organizational responsibility. Smart companies seeking competitive advantage will look to leverage data governance programs to add value to their revenue streams. Companies want to know what is happening across their organizations, with their vendors, their partners, and their customers. With a mature data governance program, companies can gain real-time access to their data. They will know where it is located and how it is used, they will understand its strategic worth, and they will know the risks and costs to the organization if it is unavailable.

To transition the data classification policies to an organizational data governance program, it is recommended that we follow these six steps (Adler, 2007):

1. Identify an Executive Sponsor with CEO-delegated authority
   a. Sponsor will champion the program
   b. Sponsor can assist in building consensus among stakeholders

2. Review your organization's use of data (conduct survey)
   a. Inventory the work practices of business units
      i. Document how data is used (should have information from data classification project)
      ii. Document what data is critical for business operations (should have information from data classification policy project)

4. Develop a Data Governance Strategy (stakeholders and partners are essential for this step)
   a. Create strategic vision of where the organization wants to go
      i. Create realistic view of what practices need to be put in place
      ii. Establish milestones and KPIs to verify progress
         ▪ Use Metrics (measure progress)
         ▪ Provide reports to CEO and board of directors

5. Calculate the value of your data
   a. If you don't know the value of your data
      i. Hard to estimate its value to the bottom line
      ii. Hard to protect it if you don't know its value
         ▪ Underestimate value, select wrong security controls to protect information
         ▪ Incorrect security controls can have large liability consequences when dealing with compliance

6. Calculate the probability of risk
   a. Review workflows to understand how data is used by employees, how it has been misused in the past

   i. This information will provide insight into how it could be compromised in the future
  b. Help business transform risk management program
   i. Use this information for "fact-based" decisions
   ii. Use business intelligence and to analyze events

 7. Monitor the efficiency of controls
  a. Data governance is largely about organizational behavior
   iii. Use a risk management framework to assess your security controls
   iv. Assessment timelines may be compliance driven

So now you have assisted in creating a data governance program to ensure the whole organization understands the importance of data, how it is used, the controls in place to protect it, and how it can be analyzed to provide actionable business information. However, as a CISO, once this program becomes an executive-sponsored organizational asset it typically will be out of your hands and managed by other units within the organization such as Operations or Data Analytics. With that said, you will still have an active role in contributing to the program. As the CISO, you will now move into the compliance and data privacy mode as you monitor and police the data flowing in this program.

Part of managing this data will be ensuring that critical data such as PCI-DSS, PHI, and PII is encrypted at the level required to meet its compliance and regulatory regimes. You will also provide guidance on data masking, ensuring it is enabled to obscure sensitive elements of all critical data sets. This is to meet compliance requirements for protecting identified sensitive data so it is not exposed to unauthorized personnel. As data encryption and masking is implemented, controls will need to be installed and monitored to verify that the encryption and masking is active when sensitive data is in a test environment, in the production environment, and finally at rest in archived storage.

Most data handling regulations are concerned with the exposure of the data itself, not necessarily with the custodianship or the availability of the data. Encryption is a key technique for maintaining confidentiality and is referenced as a mitigating control to eliminate or reduce some sanctions in the case of breach or accidental disclosure.

You should ensure that data classified as sensitive is encrypted both in transit (at least outside of your network) and especially at rest, whether in your data center or in the cloud.

One last component of the Data Governance Program that CISOs help manage is data retention and eDiscovery. It is here where you will verify that the program's data retention policies align with organizational record retention policies. Keep in mind that many companies want to reduce storage costs by keeping as little data as possible. However, there will be legal requirements for specific types of data so speak with the Legal Department to make sure you are in compliance.

In closing, when data governance is done correctly it moves the management of data from a primarily IT department-driven process to a business-focused executive program. This program is fueled by specific business drivers that will energize an organization to leverage data governance and turn it into a critical asset. Some of these drivers are as follows:

1. _Growth_ – company wants to increase market share, revenue, product portfolio

2. _Compliance and Risk Reduction_ – reduce compliance and contractual risks, meet information security and data privacy regulations

3. _Efficiency and Cost Reduction_ – improve decision support processes, reduce storage costs, improve efficiencies

4. _Strategic Differentiation_ – optimize customer experience with data, giving better insight into customers' needs; optimize supply chain with data, reducing redundancy and risks

As CISO, you are a valuable partner in first establishing a data classification and handling processes and then helping your organization mature it into a data governance program. As I have stated before, one of the main responsibilities of a CISO is to protect an organization's data and information assets. With these programs in place you will have documented procedures, security controls, and measurable metrics to guide you in providing value to your organization.

Summary

For Chapter 3, we began our discussion by asking these four questions:

- What type of information and data does my organization create, use, and share as part of our operations?
- Do we have data that is subject to specific regulatory or contractual controls and practices?
- Do I know the lifecycle of this data and the systems, processes, applications, individuals, and third parties that have access to this data?
- Are our organization's data governance practices consistent with the value of this data and our regulatory or contractual obligations?

As Bill Bonney states in Chapter 3: "When we strip it down to the essential elements, we are concerned with maintaining privacy, securing financial transactions, protecting intellectual property, and safeguarding operational data."

In closing, we would like to leave you with these five key points and next steps:

1. All data is not created equal. Knowing what types of data you have and the sensitivity of that data is critical to your ability to focus your attention and your limited resources in the right way. While some sensitive data types (such as PII and PHI) are obvious and well documented, some (such as intellectual property) are less visible and not always well understood. **You should conduct a data mapping exercise so that you understand what types of data you are responsible for and their relative importance to the organization.**

2. With the advent of low cost storage, poor or missing data governance programs have amplified the problems many organizations have with managing and, when appropriate, destroying data. However, while a copy of the source of truth is of less operational value than the real thing, the inappropriate disclosure of the data copy is just as damaging and the copy is a legitimate target for legal discovery. **You should establish a data governance program that**

establishes foundational data protection safeguards, oversight within the business units, and policies on data retention and destruction.

3. Outsourcing of business processes has become commonplace and because of advances in cloud computing, the types of processes that are eligible for outsourcing have expanded significantly. When an organization outsources their business processes they also expose the data upon which those processes depend to a different set of individuals, often allow it to flow outside of the organization's direct control, and extend the data custodianship to third-party organizations. While you can outsource business process activities, you cannot outsource responsibility, which means you are still responsible for how your data and your customers' data are safeguarded. **You should inventory the data you entrust to third parties and validate that appropriate access controls and data safeguards are in place.**

4. Specific types of data come with specific legal requirements. For most organizations, this includes, at least, personally identifiable information, protected health information, and credit card or bank information. It is worth repeating that not all data is created equal. **You should evaluate your data asset inventory and segment your network to isolate regulated data from non-regulated data where warranted.**

5. Most data handling regulations are concerned with the exposure of the data itself, not necessarily with the custodianship or the availability of the data. Encryption is a key technique for maintaining confidentiality and is referenced as a mitigating control to eliminate or reduce some sanctions in the case of breach or accidental disclosure. **You should ensure that data classified as sensitive is encrypted both in transit (at least outside of your network) and especially at rest, whether in your data center or in the cloud.**

Chapter 4 – Third Party Risk

Introduction

In Chapter 4 we turn our focus to third party risk. You could say that the first half of this decade was the dawn of a new era of third party risk in cybersecurity. Edward Snowden was an independent contractor when he expropriated and disseminated a trove of sensitive information belonging to the National Security Administration in the spring of 2013. In 2014, Dairy Queen and Taco Bell were breached through third-party Point of Sale (POS) systems. And both Target and Home Depot were breached through inadequately secured vendor logins in 2013 and 2014 respectively. It has never been more evident that how you engage with third parties that have access to your network or your data is a critical component of your risk management program. What you will see from all three authors in this chapter are pragmatic recommendations that will help you understand, explain, and better control the third party risks you encounter as the CISO for your organization.

Bill Bonney starts the discussion by pointing out some red flags that managed to go undetected and the resulting regulatory scrutiny third party risk management now enjoys. Bill touches once again on the importance of knowing how and under whose control data flows into and out of your organization. He provides some practical advice for the new CISO for uncovering and quantifying third party exposure and discusses important legal protections you need to have in place, including a "right to audit" clause for critical third parties. Engagement is the key to Bill's approach, at the individual level for contingent workers and at the center of the relationship for organizations upon which you depend.

Matt Stamper focuses on the vendor management aspect of third parties from a service delivery perspective. He emphasizes how important it is to know the capabilities of the third parties we rely on and helps us use several tools, including the RACI (responsible, accountable, consulted, informed) matrix, third party inventories and assessments, vendor management lifecycle, and independent attestations and audits, to validate the assertions made by prospective vendors. Matt makes it clear that managing vendors is an ongoing activity best approached as a team sport.

Gary Hayslip looks at the five categories of risk, including Financial Risk, Strategic Risk, Operational Risk, Regulatory/Compliance Risk, and Geographic Risk (Ambrose 2014). He reminds us that we can't contract away our responsibility to manage our own risk. We can outsource activity, but we can't outsource responsibility. Gary provides an in-depth discussion of how to set up and run a vendor management program (VMP) and helps us understand how each third-party vendor aligns with the organization's strategic goals. Another key take-away is to be transparent with your vendors about how they are being measured. That helps them stay focused on performance as well.

Some of the questions the authors used to frame their thoughts for this chapter include:

- How do vendors and other third parties impact our cybersecurity program?
- How do I know if my vendors are secure?
- What should I do to protect my organization when using third parties? What controls or processes should I have in place?

Third Parties and Vendors – Bonney

> "Along with privileged access, third-party risk management is the dirty little, poorly kept secret of cybersecurity."

In this chapter, we're discussing third parties and third-party risk management, which includes at a minimum: contractors, consultants, vendors, partners and suppliers. Though similar in some ways, these represent five distinct types of external relationships that come with potentially very different types of risks. I like to think of contractors, consultants and vendors as largely a back-office contribution, partners as largely a go-to-market contribution, and suppliers as largely a production or manufacturing contribution. So in this sense, contractors, consultants and vendors are bottom line contributors, and partners and suppliers are top line contributors. I think it's important to understand how the business depends on your third parties to provide the right context for the risk decisions you will make regarding those relationships.

Along with privileged access, third-party risk management is the dirty little, poorly kept secret of Cybersecurity. The reality is that most organizations do not have a very good understanding of the risks they are assuming with their third-party relationships. This secret was exposed by the now infamous Target and Edward Snowden breaches, both in 2013. For the Target breach, access was originally obtained by the bad actors through the VPN connection maintained for Target's HVAC vendor for direct billing purposes. Edward Snowden was an employee of a sub-contractor of the National Security Administration. He moved from the CIA to Dell to Booz Allen Hamilton under a veil of suspicion after trying to break into classified files while at the CIA.

As a consequence of these breaches, additional attention is now paid to third-party relationships by organizations, regulators and auditors, and as the CISO you will inherit a lot of that responsibility. Even before these breaches, some industries have historically had important controls on third party risk. These include the banking industry, where critical third parties are required to be identified, assessed and tracked, and healthcare, where business associate agreements (BAAs) must be in place and cascade (but do not transfer) responsibilities to apply to each party that handles protected health information (PHI).

With your partners, you are more likely to be sharing data than personnel, so in these cases, concentrate on the data flows. In Chapter 3 I talked about conducting a data mapping exercise and suggested you include third parties in your inventory of data handling activities. That exercise will force you to catalog how data is transmitted, analyzed, retained, and destroyed. It is important to assess both sides of the coin, know where your data goes and know how it is handled. Make sure you know not just how data is stored, but also consider how and when it is destroyed. How you approach the destruction of data is especially important for cloud deployments and should be addressed contractually in those cases.

In addition to your vendors and partners, you'll also want to review relationships with suppliers. The primary difference for suppliers is that they usually contribute directly to the products you are building and therefore may have access to intellectual property such as blueprints and plans, manufacturing processes, customer lists, and release dates. It is essential to have appropriate NDAs in place with all of your critical suppliers.

The Paper Trail

Speaking of NDAs, make sure there are NDAs in place with all third parties. They do more than restrict disclosure, they force the other party to think about obligations and consequences, they usually involve contracts review or legal counsel, and they act as a great starter for formal data handling requirements, beyond non-disclosure. To be effective, make sure an officer or someone with appropriate managerial responsibility to obligate the organization to adhere to the terms of the NDA signs on behalf of the organization. NDAs are useful with all third parties, and should be in place before any discussion takes place.

In addition to the NDA, look for common third-party attestations that are available for your vendors, partners, and suppliers. Include PCI-DSS, SOC 2 and 3 reports, ISO 27K certification and any others common to the industry or the service being provided. While the presence of any of these certifications does not by any means guarantee cyber safety, the lack of common certifications within your third party's domain should be a clear red flag in evaluating that third party. Revalidate annually as a lapsed certification is important to note for changing conditions.

It is also common to include in your agreements with third parties a "right to audit" clause. This is essential to have in place for all third-party organizations, and should be exercised for critical third parties (more on that later), and any third party that has had a significant change in security posture or relationship change with your organization.

Now let's switch to a more practical approach. Any Internet search for "third-party cyber risk" will yield the usual suspects of training options, consultants, frameworks, regulations, white papers, and especially what you should cover in third-party management agreements, or the contracts you use to govern your relationships. You'll be coached to include treatment of information security and privacy, compliance requirements, including service level agreements (SLAs), audit and monitoring terms, enforcement mechanisms, and inheritable, shared, cascaded obligations such as foreign corrupt practices (anti-bribery), and business associates agreements (for HIPAA), and as mentioned above, "right to audit."

Third Party Risk Management Process

Look a little deeper and you'll see results for tools used to conduct and manage third-party risk assessments. These assessments are rightfully identified as essential to help you understand the information security posture of the third parties you are working with. Of course they come in a variety of flavors, including checklists you might include as security attachments on contracts, self-assessments (such as the SIG questionnaire mentioned above), third-party audits or attestations, and on-site audits by you or your team. The tools help you with everything from suggested areas of inquiry through rigorous compliance tracking with applicable regulatory obligations, recording assessment results, and suggested follow-up and remediation.

Whether you choose to use a tool or not will depend on your needs and how you allocate your resources. The mechanics are important but as your search has no doubt demonstrated, you have plenty of help in that department. Before you worry about the tools you might use in your third-party risk management program, the key to success is to understand your objective and the strategy for achieving that objective. The objective is to understand and manage your third-party relationships, including any additional risks associated with using those third parties.

To implement a third-party risk management process, you should include the following activities. (FDIC 2008) Keep in mind that this should be a continuous cycle, not a point-in-time assessment. Also realize that these activities can and should be adjusted based on the type of data being handled as opposed to the size of the financial commitment.

- Develop a plan to manage the relationships

- Conduct due diligence on all potential third parties before signing contracts

- Develop contracts that clearly define the expectations and responsibilities of all third parties

- Perform ongoing monitoring of all third parties

- Develop a contingency plan to ensure that the organization can transition the activities to another third party, bring the activities in-house, or discontinue the activities if necessary

---

Once the relationships are in place, provide for both oversight and accountability, including documentation of performance. Where appropriate, conduct independent reviews of contract performance by your third parties and of your own third-party oversight function.

Be Close to Your Contractors

Coming back to contractors and consultants, there are a number of best practices for managing the non-employee workplace, but in my experience the single most important tactic is to be as close, or closer, to those individuals as you are to your employees. Engage them regularly and ensure that they are part of team activities as much as possible. You want to accomplish two things as a result of a closer relationship: reduce their motivation and opportunity to take inappropriate actions and connect them to fellow workers so that anomalous behavior is more easily detected.

And of course to make this type of approach most effective, start with a known good quantity. Ensure that background checks are conducted for all contractors and consultants, along with all vendor, partner, and supplier personnel that will be granted access to your physical or virtual environment. No exceptions. Make sure the background checks are conducted by an organization you trust and ensure that they are updated every two to three years.

I have used the term "critical" above as a way to describe some of your third parties. When I use the term "critical," I am referring to those third parties that contribute substantially to the strategic goals of your organization or provide services essential for your on-going operations. It is important for your business partners to provide the input on which third parties are critical and it is essential for the CISO to engage with his/her peers at these critical partners. In addition to data handling and NDAs, you'll also want to assess how the third party intends to prevent and recover from any cyber events or physical disasters.

A good indicator for how seriously they take their disaster recovery responsibilities is whether or not they invite you to participate in disaster recovery and business continuity planning. It is also completely acceptable to require disclosure of disaster recovery and business continuity planning during initial due diligence.

Chapter 4 Key Point and Action Item 2

Most organizations do not have a very good understanding of the risks they are assuming with their third-party relationships. As the CISO, it is essential for you to understand the state of your organization's vendor management program. Specifically, you'll want to know who has been entrusted with your sensitive data (as well as whose data you have been entrusted with), who has access to your environment (physical and virtual), and how reliable the information security controls are at the organizations you contract with. This information will provide you visibility into the data flows between the organization and its vendors and provide context for what security controls you may recommend to reduce the risk to essential business operations.

You should meet with colleagues within the organization to create a list of all third party vendors, partners, and external entities; and document what their purpose is and what they have access to.

Why Inventories Are So Important

The order of the first two controls in the often-cited SANS 20 was not an accident.[8] Having an accurate inventory of both systems and software is foundational. As the adage goes, you cannot control and secure something you do not know you have. The same holds true with vendors. It's imperative that an organization accurately inventories and manages its third-party relationships, be they with service providers, vendors, or independent contractors. Knowing the risk profile of these third parties is not just good security, it is good business. Earlier in this book, we noted how important it is to have a CISO report outside of traditional IT. CISOs who sit organizationally within the IT department may lack visibility on and insight into the overall vendor landscape of the firm. This proverbial blind spot exposes the organization to significant risk. CISOs who are engaged with their line-of-business colleagues and who have mapped sensitive data flows within and outside the organization can provide real value in assisting these departments with the security and cyber risk profiles of vendors. In the scenario where the CISO is effectively type-cast in a traditional IT security role, these insights will likely be lost.

Chapter 4 Key Point and Action Item 3

There is significant value in conducting a data mapping exercise for all third parties to inventory what types of data they have access to and their data handling activities. It is important to assess where corporate data goes and know how it is handled. Make sure you know not just how data is stored, but also consider how and when it is destroyed.

You should catalog how data is transmitted, analyzed, retained, and destroyed by all third parties.

I strongly advocate that one of the first actions a CISO should take is to meet with colleagues to inventory third-party providers. Taking a line-of-business or departmental view will make this process easier and offer a fantastic opportunity to really understand the organization from a non-IT perspective. I recommend that CISOs put together a basic list of departments and functions within their organization. As a case in point, almost every organization will have the following departments:

---

[8]. The Center for Internet Security (CIS) has assumed responsibility for the SANS 20 which are now known as Critical Security Controls.

- Finance and Accounting
- Human Resources
- Sales and Marketing
- Operations
- Legal
- General and Administrative

For each of these departments, I strongly recommend establishing a basic narrative of the core procedures within the department as well as a streamlined data flow diagram. Knowing what type of information (especially sensitive information) is used within the department as well as how that information moves into and out of the procedures, processes, and applications related to those processes will inform a number of required controls. This street-level assessment will also highlight where third parties are engaged, what type of information (data) they have access to, and their overall role in the process. The insights gained from this basic discovery will prove invaluable to other security activities and help develop strong working relationships across the organization. The value of this meet and greet cannot be overstated.

The table below offers a quick way to capture this information. The goal is not to have an exhaustive list of attributes and variables by department, but rather to capture the most critical functions, data types, and vendors while determining whether there has been any analysis or assessment of that third party.

Department	Function	Data Type(s)	Third-Party & Application	Status
Finance and Accounting	External Audit	Financial Data	External Auditor	Pending Assessment
Finance and Accounting	General Ledger / ERP	Financial Data Vendor Data Customer Data	Hosted ERP	SSAE 16 SOC 1 & SOC 2 Audits
Human Resources	Payroll Services	Payroll and Taxes	Hosted Payroll System	SSAE 16 SOC 1 & SOC 2 Audits
Sales & Marketing	Client Relationship Management	Client Data Non-Public Information Pricing Contracts	Hosted CRM	SSAE 16 SOC 1 & SOC 2 Audits

While gathering detail on the vendors that are part of the organization's third-party ecosystem, it's important to accomplish two things. First, ask what applications are used by that third party.

These applications may not necessarily be under the direct control of the third party, which will require further diligence. Second, capture detail related to this vendor in the context of a RACI matrix. Who is *responsible* for interacting with this vendor? Who is ultimately *accountable* for the services that are provided by the vendor? And who should be *consulted* and *informed* regarding the activities, controls, and risks associated with the vendor? The RACI matrix effectively widens the proverbial circle of concern with each service provider or vendor and will offer CISOs enhanced context related to the services in question.

Governance and Risk Management Are Vendor Management

Vendor management is now a seminal part of governance, risk, and compliance (GRC) and enterprise risk management (ERM) functions in all but the smallest of organizations. Good vendor management practices require the insights and domain expertise of multiple parties. As a case in point, vendor management could include the engagement of individuals within the legal department, IT, finance and accounting, the GRC team, departmental and business analyst teams, as well as the executive team and potentially the board of directors if the service under review is considered strategic.

There is value in having multiple disciplines engaged with vendor management and assessment. Participants bring their own insights and domain knowledge to the process, which should ideally drive better decision-making with respect to vendor selection. There is, however, a potential efficiency downside to so many participants being engaged with the process. As the saying goes, "Too many cooks in the kitchen…" As a general rule, the individuals requesting the service will likely have a higher risk tolerance than those charged with oversight and governance. This will create an inherent tension between teams. The team that requires the service may see the vendor management and assessment process as too bureaucratic and too slow. Failing to address requirements in a timely manner often results in the use of non-authorized services – shadow IT or non-governed third parties. It's important for all parties to know the business context (including issues related to internal capabilities and competencies, timing, budget, risk tolerance, and executive sponsorship) as well as the potential risks associated with the requested service. This should inform the nature and extent of the diligence required for the provider.

Eight Risk Factors to Assess with Vendors

I strongly recommend looking at vendors across a minimum of eight inherent risk factors, including the following:

1. Operational risk – this is an assessment of the vendor's potential impact to the organization's operations and should be used to measure how dependent your organization is on the vendor's or service provider's underlying services. As a simple case in point, if your organization has developed software that is deployed in a large public cloud, that cloud provider's potential impact to your operations is inherently high risk.

2. Privacy risk – this is an assessment, based on the type of data that is shared with the vendor, including PII and ePHI, that measures the potential exposure to privacy risk associated with the vendor. As a case in point, a hospital (a covered entity in the context of HIPAA-HITECH) may outsource its billing services to a third party (a business associate). Given the type of data that is shared with the vendor, the inherent privacy risk associated with this business associate is high.

3. Reputation risk – this assessment measures the potential impact to your organization's reputation should the vendor not provide services in a secure and available manner.

4. Security risk – this assessment measures the potential security impacts to your organization based on the vendor's own security practices. Security assessments should capture how data is shared between entities and how these communications are protected. Many organizations are now conducting vendor-specific security assessments as part of their vendor due diligence efforts. These activities are beyond the typical SSAE 16 SOC 1 and SOC 2 audit reviews.

5. Regulatory risk – this assessment measures the regulatory exposure associated with a vendor that does not provide adequate protections over its services, notably those related to the security and privacy of data that has been shared. Certain regulations, including HIPAA-HITECH and GLBA, require that organizations assess their vendors and that these assessments thoroughly review the risk considerations associated with these relationships.

6. Revenue risk – this assessment measures the organization's ability to continue to generate revenue should there be an impact on the vendor's services. As a case in point, if your organization derives all of its revenues from an online application or service and the underlying service provider's infrastructure is not available, revenue would be lost.

7. Financial risk – this assessment measures the potential financial exposure related to a vendor's services. This risk

captures items such as exposure to penalties, fees, and other financial costs associated with an incident, including crisis management costs. The assessment should also capture the costs to migrate services to another vendor should it be required.

8. Service risk – similar to operational risk, service risk is a measurement of the competencies and capabilities associated with a vendor's services. In many cases, these are addressed via SSAE 16 SOC 1 and SOC 2 audits, independent assessments, and other alternative means to evaluate the effectiveness of the provider's services. Understanding the depth of the provider's bench, especially for operations that are 7x24 in nature, is an area that's prudent to assess. If a provider delivers services that are designed to be 7x24, it's a good practice to do spot inspections after hours, on major holidays, or at other times where a gap in coverage could present a real risk.

Good vendor management also has its own lifecycle that, when followed correctly, should improve service delivery, security, and operational outcomes for the organization while mitigating risk and improving vendor governance. For too many CISOs, their engagement in the vendor management process is after-the-fact. Vendors have already been selected, contracts executed, and sensitive and proprietary data shared. This places the CISO in a largely reactive role.

Let's take a look at what a proactive vendor management process would look like and then offer some suggestions to handle scenarios where the CISO's input and support is effectively post-selection.

Vendor Management Lifecycle

The vendor-management lifecycle consists of the following basic phases:

- *Requirements* – Requirements are typically captured and documented in requests for information (RFIs) or requests for proposal (RFPs). It's important that the organization's requirements be as detailed as possible and address items beyond the basic function or activity requested by a given department or line of business. This is where the multi-disciplinary approach is so important. Depending upon the requirements, stipulations should be made regarding how non-public information (NPI), electronic protected health information (ePHI), and intellectual property (IP) must be governed and secured. While beyond the scope of this discussion, the requirements should outline specific detail related to invoicing, metrics for invoicing, and service delivery response times. Well-drafted RFIs or RFPs should also inform the subsequent phases of the vendor-management lifecycle and include the following:

- o Evaluation criteria and weighting – Not all selection criteria are of equal importance, so they should be force ranked and weighted. CISOs will want to ensure that governance and security controls are incorporated into the criteria, especially for scenarios where sensitive data is being conveyed, stored, or processed by the third party. The CISO may request special procedures related to data governance. Specifically, including controls related to the information life cycle of the data, notably its validated destruction at the end of the contract, as well as controls related to data in motion and data at rest that generally require encryption of information moving into and out of a service provider's environment are a must.

- o Service-level expectations – Response times, breach notification requirements, demarcation of roles and responsibilities, incident response, and escalation procedures are ideally incorporated into the requirements.

- o Contract expectations – We live in a highly litigious business community so it's important to ensure that contracts are as unambiguous as possible regarding specific requirements. If an item is part of the evaluation criteria or service level expectations, it should be formally captured in the service agreements, e.g. explicitly addressed in the contract.

- *Diligence and Assessment* – Ideally security requirements have been captured in the RFI or RFP documentation. During the vendor diligence and assessment phase, the CISO is a key player in evaluating the security and privacy controls of the potential provider. As part of this diligence, the CISO should review the audit reports of the provider including the provider's statement of standards for attestation agreements (SSAE 16) SOC 1 and SOC 2 audits. These reports address Type I (design) and Type II (operational) effectiveness. A report that only addresses Type I testing is not sufficient and its ability to inform the due diligence effort is questionable at best.

The SOC 1 report focuses on the controls related to financial reporting and the controls are largely defined by the service provider organization. The SOC 2 report focuses on five core principles: security, availability, processing integrity, confidentiality, and privacy. The controls related to each principle are prescriptive and not subject to the service provider's discretion. Depending upon the services that are contemplated, not all SOC 2 reports cover all five of the principles. In the absence of or to complement these audit reports, security assessments should also be considered. Larger organizations are now routinely conducting these assessments – including penetration testing exercises – for applications and services.

- The existence of an audit report suggests that the service provider recognizes the importance of third-party assurance over their services. These audits are also not inexpensive. They can easily cost upwards of six figures depending upon the number of locations and controls that are evaluated. Many organizations simply check the proverbial box when looking at SOC 1 and SOC 2 audit reports. *The audit reports are meant to be read.* There is an important section in each report that describes complementary user controls – those controls that are required to provide reasonable assurance that the service provider's controls can be used correctly. Typically, these controls relate to procedures to designate or authorize users of the services including the revocation of access rights should the user organization dismiss an individual.

  The reports may also provide detail related to exceptions found by the auditors. These exceptions should be reviewed carefully and questioned as part of the overall diligence effort. Are the exceptions indicative of broader issues with the provider? Do they suggest that controls are not functioning correctly in operation?

- While the SOC 1 and SOC 2 audit reports are important, they are no substitute for additional diligence. Simply stated, don't put too much stock in the audit reports. Despite the efforts of the American Institute of Certified Public Accountants (AICPA) – the governing body that oversees the CPA firms that conduct these audits – there are significant quality differences within the audit community. The competencies of the field staff conducting the audit, the nature and extent of their control assessment and testing (including sample selection criteria), as well as their domain knowledge of more complex security reviews does vary notably despite the "standard." If the SOC 1 and SOC 2 reports were issued by a CPA firm that is not widely known, this should be explored.

o   Other diligence is always in order depending upon the nature and scope of services being contracted. One approach to determine the materiality of a vendor and the associated oversight and due diligence required is to determine if sensitive data is shared with the vendor (e.g. PII, ePHI, IP, pricing data, etc.) or if the vendor's services support mission critical operations (e.g. an e-commerce site or other applications supporting the organization's operations).

Site visits are highly recommended. It's important to meet the team that will be providing the services that will be delivered to the organization. Ideally, conduct site visits during non-standard business hours if the service that is going to be provided is 7/24. What do staffing levels and competencies look like at 2:00 AM or on a major holiday? Equally important, learn about the third party's hiring practices. How are applicants screened and assessed? How are certifications and skills evaluated? Look to expand your contacts within the provider's organization beyond those that have a vested interest in the transaction. Stated differently, the sales team offering the services has incentives that may not be aligned with the interests of your organization.

Try to meet your counterpart managing security and governance at the service provider's organization. Meet the team that will be delivering the required services when this is applicable. As part of the site visit, inquire if the service provider has dependencies on other providers or key staff.

o   From an operational perspective, it's important to know about the third party's business continuity and disaster recovery planning. The provider should have client-facing versions of these documents ready for review as part of the due diligence process. How often are the BC/DR plans tested? Are the exercises table top or functional cut-overs of processes? What is the scope of BC/DR procedures? For many service providers, the procedures may only address internal operations and not necessarily those of the clients. How does the service provider assess risk? How frequently are risk assessments conducted? More importantly, what steps are being conducted to remediate known risk?

o   Financial due diligence is also in order. Is the service provider financially viable? Is the service provider profitable? If not, why not? What is their source of funding? Do they have audited financials that can be reviewed? As discussed in the chapter on data mapping, your vendors have vendors and these secondary and tertiary relationships should be incorporated into your vendor assessment efforts.

o   Depending upon the services that are required, the provider's policies and procedures should also be assessed. In many cases, these are reviewed in the context of the SOC 1 and SOC 2 analyses but there may be additional detail warranting further review. Critical policies include those related to security, change, and incident management disciplines. How are the policies enforced within the provider's organization? Are the procedures noted in the policies consistent with the organization's training practices? Are there blind spots in the policies – issues and circumstances that impact service delivery but may not necessarily be captured in existing policies?

A simple case in point would be the service provider's policies (or lack thereof) regarding employee-owned devices. Will your data be accessible on the personal device of some employee of the service provider? Hopefully this is not the case, but if it is, how is this controlled and managed?

o   Due diligence should also include some of the basics, including a thorough reference check. Recognize that the provider is effectively cherry-picking their references. Nevertheless, ask the tough questions related to the services. One way to get the reference to open up on potential issues is to ask the following question: "What would be the one thing you would change in the relationship with this provider?" Additional questions related to response times, after-hours support, incidents, outages, breaches, change-over in personnel, etc. will help get to a closer version of ground truth regarding the provider.

- o As noted above, the nature and extent of the diligence required should reflect the inherent risk and importance of the services being requested, including the type of data and information that will be shared with the service provider or third party. Vendor due diligence practices must be risk-based. Criteria should be documented, force ranked, and evaluated by a group of qualified individuals to help inform the selection process.

- *Selection* – The selection phase should be as transparent as possible to all parties, including prospective suppliers. Unfortunately, this transparency tends to be the exception and not the norm. The reason I advocate transparency is the simple belief that making the wrong vendor decision could place an organization in jeopardy and expose it to a level of risk that would not otherwise be acceptable. Transparency can help mitigate this selection risk. To achieve this transparency, there are some simple things that can done. First and foremost, document decision criteria and weighting. Share these criteria with internal stakeholders as well as prospective suppliers and explain how they will be evaluated. These criteria should be formally captured in the RFI and RFP. Beginning with the end in mind is so important in the vendor selection process. The objective is to make the best possible selection for the organization based on mutually agreed-upon criteria. The goal should be to mitigate the risks of selecting the wrong provider for the wrong reasons.

It may be necessary during the selection process to coach certain providers on the process itself. The "right" provider may be inadvertently disqualified because a response or diligence process did not fully capture the provider's input correctly. The selection process is obviously well-served by having multiple, qualified providers at the table in order to increase negotiating power and improve the terms and conditions the organization ultimately receives from the service provider.

- o Once the selection has been made and where legally acceptable, I strongly believe in communicating the choice and the overall ranking to the participants.

the client to notify the service provider. Proactive SLAs require the service provider to notify the customer when issues occur and to provide for SLA or SLO remedies regardless of whether the client has requested a remedy. This is clearly more than a subtle difference.

o   Documents incorporated by reference are also important. In the managed services industry, services are typically defined in a SOW. The SOW should clearly delineate roles and responsibilities across service layers, define performance metrics, define configuration parameters, and ideally discuss how certain IT service management functions are handled, including change and incident management. These documents should be incorporated by reference into the overall contracts package and should be formally executed by both parties.

o   There is one thing that every CISO should request as part of the contracting phase, which is the inclusion of a right to audit clause. The existence or occurrence of an SSAE audit and the materials provided by the service provider during the RFP process provide a point-in-time snapshot of the provider's viability. Things change. Things change materially. A right to audit clause with provisions to adjust the terms and conditions of the contract – including cancelation – based on findings is now an essential component of good risk management and contracting procedures.

o   While certainly not the last word on the contracting process, I think the CISO's insights on data lifecycle management are especially valuable. Contracts expire. How will the data and information provided to the service provider be handled? What happens if there are retention periods that are federally mandated that extend beyond the service term? How will these scenarios be addressed contractually? The CISO must be a strong advocate for security controls to address these contingencies and work collaboratively with legal counsel to protect the organization's interests at the end of the contract term with as much rigor as when preparing for services to be transferred at the beginning of the process.

- *Provisioning and Implementation* – Inspect what you expect. During the provisioning and implementation phase it's absolutely critical to start the relationship with the service provider correctly. If there's a right to audit clause, audit their services. Ask tough questions and triangulate on the answers by asking more than one contact at the service provider the same question. Assurances are most important in this phase. Validate as many elements associated with the contract as is practicable. I personally view the provisioning and implementation phase as a high-risk period given the number of extenuating circumstances that could impact service delivery.

  Business pressures may rush the implementation phase, resulting in certain procedures not being followed as they would normally be during standard operations. The teams that provision may not be the same teams that operate the service and the provider's handoff from one department to another may not be adequate to ensure knowledge transfer. Equally important and challenging is that many of the key provisions that have been negotiated in the contracting phase may be lost or ignored by the staff conducting the implementation. Verifying key security controls becomes especially critical. If there is a requirement to have sensitive data encrypted, it should be verified to your satisfaction before moving to operational acceptance. Similarly, if there is an expectation that configuration documentation, response times, and other service delivery metrics are to be handled in a specific manner, verify that this is indeed the case.

  Checklists work wonders. Have a checklist that ties to contractual obligations and verify that the requested services or conditions are present. If these conditions are not present, widen the proverbial circle of concern.

    o Outsourcing is like a marriage. The honeymoon occurs during provisioning and implementation. If conditions are not being met or issues arise now, this should be a red flag. Act accordingly. Establish firm expectations on service delivery, response times, and other criteria in a manner that is consistent with the contact.

- *Operational Acceptance and On-going Maintenance* – The foundation of operational acceptance is the conditions precedent noted above. To the extent that requirements are documented and well-understood, the diligence and selection processes were thorough, contracts adequately captured service requirements and obligations, and the provisioning and implementation phases had a strong bias toward validation and verification, the actual service delivery should be routine. Here the critical element is on-going stewardship. The CISO should be actively engaged with key vendors to provide ongoing assessment of their security controls and practices.

If the vendor has committed to performing penetration testing, table-top incident response training, and other activities, these should be reviewed. The transition from provisioning and implementation to operational acceptance should involve a degree of intra-organizational validation. If the IT department liaised with the service provider during the implementation phase, the CISO should validate their findings before moving to operational acceptance.

Certain procedures should also be assessed for their operational impact, notably change and configuration management. Procedures should be established such that no changes can be made to the organization's services without the prior, written authorization of the organization. Change management practices – be they to the specific services being procured or more broadly to the service provider's core infrastructure – should be reviewed thoroughly.

- *Decommissioning* – While we all know that we should have a will or living trust to address our final affairs, many of us simply do not plan for the "end." On a professional level, we should also anticipate the end of a service-provider relationship and have contractually agreed-upon procedures to handle a number of potential scenarios. These include the migration to another service provider (effectively moving to a competitor of the service provider) and the transfer of data and information back to the organization or the destruction of data to agreed-upon standards. None of these activities are particularly easy but planning for their occurrence, despite the challenges, is required for good governance.

Let's take a quick look at the issues of data transference or destruction. In the case of transferring your organization's data back from the service provider, there are a number of technical requirements that need to be understood. Cases in point include the type of media or network to be used, dependencies upon specific platforms or applications, as well as the volume of data to be transferred. Given how large data sets are today, bringing data back home may not be technically feasible or require months to accomplish over traditional network lines. Data destruction may also present challenges when the service provider's infrastructure is effectively multi-tenant. "Destroying" the disks where the data is stored may not be tenable on shared storage arrays. For these scenarios, understanding how the service provider sanitizes its storage is a must.

As noted above, it may also be necessary to plan for longer-term retention periods where the underlying contract has expired. The decommissioning of services should be anticipated and handled contractually during the contract phase of the vendor management lifecycle. These required activities should be documented, have SLAs, and be time-bound.

We've seen throughout this process how CISOs can improve the governance, the nature and extent of required security controls, and the overall assessment of services delivered by third-party providers. This requires that the CISO is aware of these relationships early in the process and fully engaged in the evaluation and assessment of the provider's capabilities.

How to Assess and Work with Vendors Post Selection

What happens when the CISO is engaged after the fact? This is, indeed, the more likely scenario. When a CISO is engaged after contracts are executed and services are being delivered, there is still ample room for him or her to improve the process. Specifically, the CISO should seek to validate operational metrics and controls that impact the security of the services being delivered. If the contracts that were executed incorporated a right to audit clause, the CISO should be part of the auditing team that evaluates the service provider's activities. This is a great opportunity for the CISO to liaise with the CISO at the service provider.

Equally important, if there are on-going stewardship meetings with the provider, the CISO should participate and ask some of the tough questions related to existing practices. Should there be gaps in the provider's governance and security practices, the CISO can provide recommendations for improvement and work with legal counsel if necessary to formalize requests to remediate the issues (effectively to cure). The CISO should also be actively engaged with the incident response and breach notification procedures associated with the provider. Ideally, this engagement will foster better connections with the service provider's own security team and result in the sharing of best practices.

Good vendor management practices are a must. Organizations today depend upon a diverse and growing ecosystem of vendors, service providers, and independent contractors. The security controls and information governance practices of this ecosystem are effectively "in scope" for the CISO. Assessing third-party security practices, ensuring compliance, validating security metrics, creating data-flow diagrams, and reviewing audit reports are as much a part of the CISO's core responsibilities as are internal security practices and policies.[9]

---

[9] In 2014, ISACA issued a great guide - Vendor Management Using COBIT 5 – that offers a solid framework for establishing a vendor-management practice.

Vendor Management Program – Hayslip

> "It's imperative that all parties remember that no matter what services have been contracted, all responsibility and accountability still rests with the organization. We can't contract away our responsibility to manage our own risks."

In your role as CISO, you will deal with many third-party vendors who provide services for your security program and your business. However, be advised that each one of these vendors can bring unique issues and open doors to unknown risks. As CISO, some questions you should ask yourself are: What do I know about my new vendor? They provide a service or an application I require, but are they a good partner for my company? In the long run, do I see them as being financially viable and able to deliver services as promised? These are just a few of the questions that you will have to vet as a CISO. Luckily, there are risk-management frameworks and vendor-management programs that can be implemented to assist companies in understanding the risks of their third-party vendors. This leads us to the two questions we will discuss in this chapter, the answers to which explain why the CISO must understand third-party risk and assist in reducing his/her organization's exposure to it.

1. As the CISO, what are the risks to my organization from our third-party vendors and why is it important that I understand the impact?
2. As the CISO, what is my part in implementing and managing a mature vendor-management program (VMP)?

How Much Risk Do My Third Parties Have?

Today we are witnessing an increasing number of data breaches in both government and private industry. The immense volume of data being stolen and the risks these security threats impose on organizations is impacting their ability to operate as effective business entities. This combination of threats and risks is also increasing the pressure on corporate information technology departments, cybersecurity programs, executive committees, and boards of directors to devise and implement a plan to manage these issues and protect corporate "data." It's this visibility into the executive board's interest in risk that I want you to think about as we proceed to discuss our first question, *"As the CISO, what are the risks to my organization from our third-party vendors and why is it important that I understand their impact?"*

Organizations will typically put controls in place to secure their business assets. The level of these controls will be based on several factors such as:

- The likelihood of an attack on that asset
- The impact to the business if the assets were lost or damaged
- The sensitivity of the data these assets use, process or store

One tool to help measure the maturity of these controls will usually be some type of compliance regime. However, employing these controls still leaves the organization open to an enormous amount of risk—risk that involves third-party vendors, contractors, and partners. This risk is due in part to the fact that we lack visibility into the third party's enterprise networks, business operations, workflows, and financial processes. Remember, your directors and senior management are ultimately responsible for managing activities conducted through third parties. Part of management's due diligence is to identify and control risk. It's imperative that all parties remember that no matter what services have been contracted, "all responsibility and accountability still rests with the organization." We can't contract away our responsibility to manage our own risk.

So as a CISO, you may wonder "why do I want to use third-party vendors, who needs that headache?" Well, that is a good question and it is best viewed in the context of your company's strategic business plan. I'll bet that if you review this plan and its goals, you will find your organization is using third-party contractors to attain some type of strategic objective. They may have an objective to use third-party contractors to quickly increase resources to resolve an issue and ultimately increase revenue. Perhaps they have an objective to use third-party contractors to reduce costs or to gain access to a specific expertise, such as software development, that the company currently lacks. As a CISO, I have employed contractors over the years as staff augmentation for my teams or because we lacked critical skillsets for upcoming organizational projects. What's important to remember here is that there are business reasons why your organization requires the services of third party vendors. However, as security professionals we must thoroughly understand the risks associated with using third-party organizations.

To start this process of understanding third party risk, you will need to know what types of risk "categories" apply to your company. To assist you in understanding these risks, I would first suggest that your organization conduct a risk assessment. This risk assessment will enable you as CISO to better understand the different types of third-party vendor risk exposures, whether or not these risks apply to your organization, and their impact on your company's strategic operations. The first phase of conducting this risk assessment is about establishing a risk framework, a lens through which the organization can proceed to identify risk, understand risk, and mitigate risk. To focus your lens, you need to ask the following questions:

- What activities within the organization are regulated?
- Do you know the data types and data classifications used by these activities?
- Do you know how much data is used by these activities?
- Do you know what vendors have access to these data types and data classifications?
- Do you understand each vendor's responsibility with respect to the organization's sensitive data?
- How does each vendor fit into the organization's overall strategic plan?
- What is the potential impact if this data is breached, manipulated, or lost?

These questions begin to create a picture of how third-party vendors become intertwined in business operations. Once you embark on this assessment, what I expect you will discover is that there are many vendor relationships deemed not only critical to the organization, but vital to its strategic plan. This means that these vendors are viewed as strategic partners and their operations and strategic viewpoints are considered to be consistent with the company's. However, please keep in mind that this doesn't make them less risky. In fact, in my mind, they often bring greater risk exposure to the business because they are deemed critical to the organization's strategic plans and would have a significant impact on those plans if not available.

Management analyzes the benefits, costs, legal aspects, and potential risks of these strategic partnerships. They also conduct risk and reward analyses on relationships deemed to be operationally strategic. However, they can make mistakes as their analysis may be based on data that can be false, manipulated, or out of date. So now you understand some of the concerns and questions that you will need to investigate in conducting a proper risk assessment. Next we will cover the categories of third-party vendor risk and how they impact the organization.

Chapter 4 Key Point and Action Item 4

In Chapter 4 Gary Hayslip provides a list of questions that you as a CISO should ask about each of the vendors on your list. This risk assessment questionnaire will enable you to better understand the different types of third-party vendor risk exposures, whether or not these risks apply to the company, and their impact on the company's strategic operations. The answers to these questions will influence the security controls used to mitigate any documented security gaps and this information will provide a greater strategic view into how the company's data is used by external parties.

You should conduct a risk assessment on the identified third-party vendors that you have documented from the prior two questions.

As I previously stated, many of the risks involved with employing third-party vendors center around the "unknown:" – the lack of visibility into their operations, network environments, corporate culture, etc. These risks fall into categories. There are five categories that I would recommend we use as our grading criteria to view the level of risk that is present with all third-party vendors. These five categories are *"Financial Risk, Strategic Risk, Operational Risk, Regulatory/Compliance Risk, and Geographic Risk."* (Ambrose, 2014)

1. *Financial Risk* – the financial viability of a vendor, the chance the vendor will experience some type of negative financial event
   a. The vendor could develop financial problems that would impair their ability to fulfill contract obligations
   b. They may limit or remove required resources needed to keep their solution or service current to reduce expenses
   c. Factors that affect the financial risk of a vendor:
      i. Financial market volatility
      ii. Vendor's economic climate
      iii. Competition from other third-party vendors
      iv. Vendor's chosen operations and business model

2. *Strategic Risk* – risk imposed on the organization from the vendor's adverse business decisions or failure to implement appropriate decisions. As a strategic partner, changes within

their operations structure can have significant impact on your organization.

    a. Vendor abruptly changes its business strategy
    b. Vendor decides to make changes to its sales and marketing approach
    c. Vendor alters its product and solution strategy without input from customers
    d. Vendor makes changes in its supply chain
    e. Arrival of new "Blue Ocean" competitors (e.g. Uber, Netflix) and vendor doesn't respond appropriately

3. *Operational Risk* – risks imposed on your company because vendor is experiencing challenges in conducting normal business operations
    a. Vendor has challenges providing resources as specified in its contract due to processes, organizational structure, or organizational change
        i. High management turnover
        ii. High unforced-employee turnover
    b. Vendor has major problems responding to external factors such as market trends and forces
        i. Numerous product failures
        ii. Shortage of spare parts
        iii. Business and IT Service shortages
    c. Vendor not meeting SLAs on response to outages, lacks proper business recovery processes

4. *Regulatory/Compliance Risk* – risk that arises due to the third-party vendor violating laws, rules, regulations, or compliance with the organization's internal policies and/or procedures
    a. Vendor has had data breaches with a possible loss of sensitive data such as PII, PHI, PCI, HIPAA, etc.
    b. Vendor's products and services not consistent with governing laws, rules, regulations, or policies
    c. Vendor has inadequate security controls for their financial assessments
    d. Vendor lacks or has failed audits for industry-defined certifications
    e. Vendor financial disclosures and reports are inadequate and don't meet contractual requirements

5. *Geographic Risk* – risk imposed on the organization when it uses vendors who provide products and services from geographic regions outside of its own country
    a. Geopolitical unrest in vendor's country that could have a negative impact on operations

b. Vendor's factories or supply-chain partners may be in regions that are subject to natural disasters such as earthquakes, hurricanes, floods
c. Vendor may have specific legal requirements they must follow that are different than your organization's requirements
d. Vendor may operate in a region that has issues with currency, bank loans, taxes, or partnerships with entities outside of their country
e. Geographic region may have issues with stable power, water, roads, etc. that have a negative impact on vendor's infrastructure including warehouses, ports, or factories

As you can see from these categories, third-party vendors bring many types of risk that must be investigated and, if found to be applicable, mitigated in order to protect your organization. Understand that you will not be doing this risk assessment on your own. As the CISO for your organization, you will probably be a member of a much larger team. This team will assist in identifying which strategic partners have high levels of risk and submitting a plan of action to reduce the organization's exposure to any identified liability.

Now with this said, be advised that this is not a "one and done" process. This is a continuous lifecycle of checks and balances to protect your company. This vendor-risk management process should mature into a program that is part of the organization's overall enterprise risk-management plan. To properly manage third-party vendor risks, you will need to grow this new process and establish a formal program that has executive support and members from across your organization's business units. In essence, to properly assess these risks and manage their impacts to your organization, I would strongly suggest that as CISO you need to champion the establishment of a formal Vendor-Management Program (VMP).

Risk and More Risk, How Do I Manage It?

In review, to properly manage the issue of third-party vendor risks to an organization it is incumbent upon the executive team to assess, measure, monitor, and control any identified risks. A primary strategic tool that should be established to assist them with these duties is a Vendor-Management Program (VMP). There are several reasons why organizations should establish a vendor-management program:

1. _Legal Obligations_ – laws, regulations, compliance. Require the organization to have some type of program to address risk.

2. _Strategic Plans_ – company is outsourcing to increase the breadth of its capabilities to produce revenue.

3. _Financial Management_ – establishing a risk-management program is fiscally responsible.
   a. The program can be used to assess the level of vendor's risk
   b. The program can be instrumental in evaluating vendors at regular intervals
   c. The program can be used for due diligence, assist with identifying problems before they impact the organization
   d. The program can be used to alert organization of problems with a vendor in the early stages, when there is a better chance of correcting the issue and continuing the strategic partnership

You can see that there are several good reasons why your business should have a vendor-management program. This leads us to our next question, _"As the CISO, what is my part in implementing and managing a mature vendor management program (VMP)?"_

Establishing a VMP to increase your company's oversight of third-party vendors requires the following four main elements: _risk assessment, due diligence, contract management,_ and _risk monitoring_ (KPMG, 2013). These four elements are the components of a VMP and as CISO you will find there will be times where you and your team are active participants in this program and other times where you are just passive observers. With that stated, don't forget that a primary responsibility of a CISO is understanding and managing risk. This risk may not be fully within the cybersecurity realm you typically operate in, but it will definitely impact your ability to provide services so you must understand how all of these components interact with each other to provide the proper risk governance oversight for your organization.

1. _Risk Assessment_ - previously, we discussed doing a risk assessment to understand what risk categories applied to your respective third-party vendors and how this risk could possibly impact the business. In a VMP you will take your risk assessment findings and develop them into a mature tool for the organization. To properly use this asset, you will need to understand how the third-party vendor under review aligns with the organization's strategic goals. To gain insight into this alignment, all third-party vendors need to

be assessed and placed into one of four alignment categories (Caldwell, 2009):

a. *Strategic Vendors* – organization is highly dependent on vendor, there is a high cost to replace vendor over time as their operations become essential to the business
b. *Emerging Vendors* – vendors typically are small to mid-size, have a specific service or solution critical to the organization, and will grow over time into a strategic vendor
c. *Legacy Vendors* – vendor has been in place for a period of time and provides services to the organization, but they are not thought of as being "critical" to business operations. Can be replaced easily with minimal cost or disruption to services.
d. *Operational Vendors* – these vendors are focused on daily business operations, and they are not expensive to replace. They have earned their position by providing quality service at minimal cost to the business.

Once you have placed your vendors into these categories, you will have more insight into their strategic importance to the organization's business units and the impact that would result if they were unavailable. However, there are still some questions that need to be answered:

- "Just how dependent is the business on this specific third-party vendor?"
  o Is there an alternate vendor incase the primary vendor is no longer available?
- "Does the business have any resources invested in the third-party vendor's products, supply chain, business operations, etc. and if so, how much?"
- "Is there a possibility for future investment in the third-party vendor?"
- "Is the third party vendor meeting multiple requirements, i.e. do they have different products and services being used by several business units within the company?"

This information is foundational for a VMP and can be used to create a third-party vendor database as a baseline for the other elements of your vendor-management program.

As CISO, many of these vendor-management program requirements and actions will be outside your realm of coverage. Many of your external vendors will require access to corporate data and systems. The management of this is a primary security control that will link your cybersecurity and enterprise risk management program to the organization's overall vendor-management program. This requirement is the reason why you as CISO need to work with the vendor management team and assist them in providing proper governance over all third party contracts. To do this effectively you need to meet with them and educate yourself on how vendors are managed within the organization so that you can assist in protecting the organization.

You should meet with the team responsible for the management of third party vendors for the company.

All third-party vendors need to be assessed, categorized, and prioritized by the amount of risk they generate. As we have discussed, you will need to include their respective categories of risk, (*Financial Risk, Strategic Risk, Operational Risk, Regulatory/Compliance Risk, and Geographic Risk*) in your overall findings. Once the risk assessment is completed, the VMP team will need to ensure that all tabulated data is accurate, and note any vendor that has been found to have an unacceptable level of risk. An example of risk at an unacceptable level would be a strategic vendor with multiple validated risk occurrences, and if these risk occurrences were active, they could cause significant business disruption or negative impact to the company's strategic plans.

I have found as a CISO that using a standard risk framework (such as the NIST Risk Management Framework) as a template can provide teams with the clarity they need to understand the risk their vendors generate and assist in objectively grading them. This clarity is critical, especially when the VMP must prioritize all third-party vendors for review. Obviously, "strategic" vendors identified with multiple risk category issues will be the first ones that need to be reviewed and placed in a schedule for continuous monitoring. This process of review and monitoring is discussed below as one of the critical elements in the VMP. As a CISO, you will have team members who will be part of the VMP and will be required to assist in vetting data on identified high-value vendors. This vendor risk program is a critical piece of a much larger enterprise risk-management program that you as CISO assist in managing for your organization.

2. *Due Diligence* – this is the process by which management, which includes CISOs, performs inquiries into the background of a potential vendor. These inquiries seek to verify such items as the accuracy of past performance history, financial viability, and ability to perform per contract requirements. The level of due diligence conducted will be based on the perceived risks of the vendor, the classification of data required for the vendor's services, and the level of impact they will have on the organization. Some key questions recommended by KPMG (KPMG, 2013) that should be investigated during the due diligence process are as follows:

    a. "Does the vendor have experience in implementing/supporting the proposed service or product?"
    b. "Are third party audited financial reports of the vendor and significant partners available for review?"
    c. "What is the vendor's business reputation?"
    d. "Do they have a history of complaints and litigation?"
    e. "What are the qualifications, backgrounds, reputations of vendor's corporate officers?"
    f. "What is the vendor's level of maturity with respect to internal controls and audit capabilities?"
    g. "Does the vendor have current business continuity; business recovery plans?"
    h. "What is the cost to develop, implement and support vendor's services?"
    i. "What are the vendor's policies for dealing with subcontractors? Do they have a mature program to prevent/reduce fourth party risk?"
    j. "Does the vendor have adequate business insurance? Cyber Insurance?"

It will be the job of the organization's VMP to get answers to these questions. One of the key factors they should consider is performance monitoring of key performance indicators or metrics that are within the current contract. Another key factor I would want to know as a CISO is whether the vendor has personnel with the required professional training and certifications to provide the contracted services. If the organization's VMP is mature, the due-diligence process should include interviews with vendor personnel and reports on vendor work spaces.

Both of these last two factors are important to the due diligence process. They give the VMP program an idea of how vendor personnel provide services to the client organization, what processes the vendor's people use as guidance, what training they currently possess, and what organizational data they require to perform their duties. Be advised that this regular reviewing of prioritized vendors for risk will be a standard workflow item for the company's VMP. It will monitor each third-party vendor for the lifecycle of their contracts. Some strategic vendors will be monitored more often due to their critical relationship with the organization. What is important is that VMP personnel approach this as a professional process. They are protecting the organization and are literally one of the first lines of defense to detect when something goes wrong with a vendor.

3. _Contract Management_ – this is the process of managing vendors through the standing contracts. There will be specific expectations and obligations for both parties outlined in the written contract. All contracts with strategic vendors should have board and/or senior management approval as required. The level of detail in contract provisions will depend on the level of risk and the scope associated with the third-party vendor. For the CISO, contract provisions you should be aware of are as follows:

   a. _Scope_ – this sets forth the rights and responsibilities of each party
      i. The timeframe of the contract
      ii. Specifications of services that will be performed
      iii. Other required services
         • Software support
         • Maintenance and repair
         • Training of organizational personnel
         • Customer service requirements
      iv. Required compliance with applicable laws, regulations, industry rules
      v. Specific authorization to required data classification types
      vi. Required insurance coverage (cyber insurance)
      vii. Assigned deliverables (type, to whom, timeline, etc.)
      viii. Permission/prohibition on the use of fourth-party contractors without organizational approval
      ix. Authorization for organization to monitor and perform periodic review (may have specifications for third-party audit services).

   b. _Cost and Compensation_ – outline of fees, costs, or compensation schemes between organization and third-

c. Review third-party fiscal condition annually
   - Review should be comprehensive
   - Audited financial statements
     - Ability to perform by independent party
d. Review third-party vendor's insurance coverage
   - Is their insurance coverage adequate?
   - Do they have cyber insurance?
e. Review third-party vendor's fiscal obligations to other parties, are they being met?
f. Review adequacy and adherence to internal controls
g. Monitor compliance with required laws, regulations, rules, policies, etc.
h. Review reports for third-party performance
   - Are they meeting contractual requirements?
   - Are they meeting performance standards?
   - Are they meeting service level agreements?

Risk monitoring will require the security teams to assist VMP personnel in maintaining documentation on all aspects of the vendor management program. This paperwork is crucial. It will be required at times to resolve disputes or stand as the performance record on all third-party relationships. Personnel must keep these records current. Third-party vendors perform contracted services more effectively when they know their performance is being regularly monitored and documented.

As CISO, many of these vendor-management program requirements and actions will be outside your realm of coverage. As a security professional, you will normally be tasked with providing enterprise risk management services for all departments across your company. However, because you will be monitoring security controls, Service Level Agreements (SLAs), maturity of services, etc., you still need to understand the full breadth of risks that third-party vendors bring to a business. You must also understand and be situationally aware of all controls and processes that can be implemented through a mature VMP to reduce the company's risk exposure from these vendors.

Vendors, through the execution of their contractual requirements, will require access to enterprise systems, applications, and data; this access will fall under the governance of your cybersecurity programs. It is your responsibility as CISO to provide effective governance of the vendors' authenticated access to organizational enterprise assets and provide a mature security program to efficiently monitor vendors through the lifecycle of their contacts. This management of vendor access to data and systems is the primary control that will couple your cybersecurity and enterprise risk management program with the organization's overall vendor management program. The global awareness of risk that both programs provide you will be instrumental in giving you an expanded view of risk to the organization and its strategic business objectives. This view will also make you a better CISO because you will have a fuller understanding of how risk impacts your business and will be able to provide insight into mitigating this risk from a business perspective.

Summary

For Chapter 4, we began our discussion by asking these three questions:

- What type of information and data does my organization create, use, and share as part of our operations?
- Do we have data that is subject to specific regulatory or contractual controls and practices?
- Do I know the lifecycle of this data and the systems, processes, applications, individuals, and third parties that have access to this data?
- Are our organization's data governance practices consistent with the value of this data and our regulatory or contractual obligations?

Organizations today are fighting battles on many fronts as the threats they face continue to evolve more quickly than they are able to respond. To manage this, a CISO must understand the different avenues of threat/vulnerabilities that can be leveraged to do harm to the organization. As we have discussed in this chapter, an organization's third-party vendors and external partners provide one of the greatest pathways of risk the organization can face. Through proper vendor management, documentation of third party access/controls, and the management of collaborative relationships, the impact of this risk can be minimized. With that said, to establish this type of vendor management and partnership requires a tremendous amount of work and dedication. As CISO, you will be an instrumental team member in addressing this issue due to your insight into technology, risk, and security mitigation.

In closing, we would like to leave you with these five key points and next steps:

1. Having an accurate inventory of both systems and software is foundational. As CISO it is extremely difficult to understand what needs to be protected if you don't know that it exists. This will give you a baseline of what applications are used by the business and what data types are created. **You should conduct an inventory of all hardware and software used by the organization, and work with senior leadership to verify its accuracy and identify which systems and applications are critical to the**

organization.

2. Most organizations do not have a very good understanding of the risks they are assuming with their third-party relationships. As the CISO, it is essential for you to understand the state of your organization's vendor management program. Specifically, you'll want to know who has been entrusted with your sensitive data (as well as whose data you have been entrusted with), who has access to your environment (physical and virtual), and how reliable the information security controls are at the organizations you contract with. This information will provide you visibility into the data flows between the organization and its vendors and provide context for what security controls you may recommend to reduce the risk to essential business operations. **You should meet with colleagues within the organization to create a list of all third party vendors, partners, and external entities; and document what their purpose is and what they have access to.**

3. There is significant value in conducting a data mapping exercise for all third parties to inventory what types of data they have access to and their data handling activities. It is important to assess where corporate data goes and know how it is handled. Make sure you know not just how data is stored, but also consider how and when it is destroyed. **You should catalog how data is transmitted, analyzed, retained, and destroyed by all third parties.**

4. In Chapter 4 we provide a list of questions that you as a CISO should ask about each of the vendors on your list. This risk assessment questionnaire will enable you to better understand the different types of third-party vendor risk exposures, whether or not these risks apply to the company, and their impact on the company's strategic operations. The answers to these questions will influence the security controls used to mitigate any documented security gaps and this information will provide a greater strategic view into how the company's data is used by external parties. **You should conduct a risk assessment on the identified third-party vendors that you have documented from the prior two questions.**

5. As CISO, many of these vendor-management program requirements and actions will be outside your realm of coverage. Many of your external vendors will require access to corporate data and systems. The management of this is a primary security control that will link your cybersecurity and enterprise risk management program to the

organization's overall vendor-management program. This requirement is the reason why you as CISO need to work with the vendor management team and assist them in providing proper governance over all third party contracts. To do this effectively you need to meet with them and educate yourself on how vendors are managed within the organization so that you can assist in protecting the organization. **You should meet with the team responsible for the management of third party vendors for the company.**

Arguably, for a CISO the management of risk from third parties is one of the most challenging roles they will face. However, these third-party relationships are critical to the organization and it's important to develop the relationships between the organization's internal business process owners and selected third parties. These relationships with business stakeholders will allow you as the CISO to have some ability to exert influence on the selection of third parties and the risk level they bring to the organization.

It's also important for the business to develop these relationships with its external partners so that assessments and planning become opportunities for improvement and not merely expressions of risk definition. In fact, good third-party relationships are cooperative, two-way knowledge exchanges that recognize shared risk and shared opportunity for improvement. As CISO you will be one of the key team members providing the governance over managing this risk. Remember, building a resilient cybersecurity program requires you to not only look within the organization with all of its networks, applications and data issues, but also factor in the risk exposure from these critical business relationships with external third parties.

ıı

we look at how to create a metrics program that will ιasure the performance of your entire organization and ιe what to report to your management and your board of ιors. Each of the authors has a bias toward objective ιsurements and sees that as key to fulfilling the role of the trusted authority on your organization's risk posture. They collectively emphasize the value of using widely adopted security frameworks to create a comparable baseline from which to measure improvement and extoll the virtues of being disciplined in the performance of preventive and periodic controls.

Bill Bonney begins with a brief historical review by tying measurement to business objectives and briefly discusses the evolution from control coverage to measuring impact on service delivery. He provides several recommendations for frameworks you can use to establish your baseline. To conclude his section on measuring process effectiveness, he provides a helpful set of principles for deciding what metrics are reported and how to maximize the impact of the reports. Bill then pivots to a discussion on the CISO's role in risk management and how to measure the effectiveness of this strategic function.

Matt Stamper points out that there is no shortage of things to measure and helps the reader understand how detrimental an unchecked onslaught of raw data can be. He skillfully guides the reader through an analysis of key categories of risk and the relevant measurements to capture and report. Some of the categories he covers include legal, financial, human resources, vendor management, software, data, and system hygiene.

Gary Hayslip focuses on how to effectively frame information for management and the board of directors to, in his words, "tell a story." After outlining the criteria for developing the set of metrics the CISO will collect and share, including sample metrics and a formula for creating a good metric, Gary pivots to organizing the information for consumption and action. He brings all of this home for the reader by sharing lessons learned, including the types of reports and dashboards to share (and with whom), establishing relationships with the recipients of the dashboards, and putting the information into context before they even see the report.

Some of the questions the authors used to frame their thoughts for this chapter include:

- What are metrics? Why are metrics important? What steps should the CISO and security team take to create valid metrics for their program?
- What are some examples of dashboards that should be developed as strategic assets?
- What types of reports should a CISO create to educate executive management and sponsor a more resilient, cyber-aware corporate culture?

Measuring and Reporting – Bonney

> "It is important to have a crystal clear understanding of, and communication of, the goals and objectives for both your organization and your metrics and reporting program.

In this chapter I'm going to cover measuring and reporting for the objective of ensuring the successful operation of the CISO function.

It's been said so often that Peter Drucker's famous quote: "If you can't measure it, you can't manage it" is now a cliché. The modern corporation literally has its origin in operationalizing and improving the efficiency and effectiveness of manufacturing goods. Through continual improvement driven by measurement and reporting, we are able to reduce process time, improve quality, and reduce cost.

Manufacturing processes are designed with the need to measure their efficiency and effectiveness in mind. This discipline also appears in the design and creation of computer code, such that quality assurance (QA) test scripts are developed in conjunction with the actual code, rather than as an afterthought once completed applications or modules have been delivered. The advent of agile development methodologies has given rise to DevOps and DevSecOps teams that locate the continual testing of the effectiveness of code and system configurations, along with vulnerability scanning and other security tests, as close as possible to both the development process and the developer community. And of course measuring uptime, throughput, load and the presence of known security vulnerabilities are de rigueur in the modern data center, and remain an area of continued focus as companies migrate their applications to the cloud.

In addition to operational measurements such as those listed above, the CISO has a vast array of functions, processes and outcomes to measure and ways in which to do so. It is important to have a crystal clear understanding of, and communication of, the goals and objectives for both your organization and your metrics and reporting program. This is important because as you communicate progress within your team, to your peers and senior leadership, and to the board of directors, they are each going to need a frame of reference. They need to know your objective, the current behaviors, and change in status over time. They can then participate in a meaningful dialog about the changes in behavior you advocate for the future because you'll be able to tell them what the current and desired states are with confidence grounded in fact.

It is common for CISOs to measure control effectiveness and coverage along with the change in maturity and breadth of coverage over time. We'll start by taking a look at the processes you have responsibility for and discuss assessing and reporting on their maturity. Next, we will examine ways to measure the control effectiveness, or security hygiene, which forms the foundation of your security footing. As we move up the value chain, we'll then discuss the business objectives, specifically in response and recovery, that the CISO is responsible for. Finally, we'll talk about measuring the strategic partnerships that the CISO must nurture to be successful.

A Process Orientation

There are dozens of functions, processes, and outcomes that may apply to your organization. If your organization has used CoBIT (Control Objectives for Information and Related Technology) [10] or a similar framework to establish relevant discrete IT processes, you can start there. Many public companies used CoBIT between 2004 and 2006 to determine which IT processes they needed to assess and/or implement to become compliant with the Sarbanes-Oxley Act and many audit teams, both internal and external, use CoBIT as a reference for their ongoing assessments. A good place to start, then, is with the audit team and IT management to determine which of these control objectives fall within the purview of the CISO and which additional control objectives the CISO should be concerned about. Also refer to Chapters 1-3 for additional relevant processes.

---

[10] Please note that in order to maintain the readability of this chapter, all standards, frameworks and other technical references will be appropriately acknowledged and linked in the bibliography.

Many organizations have been effectively using the ISO 27K framework. This has the advantage of being internationally accepted since it originated in Europe and therefore is appealing to organizations with European operations. To accomplish this, you might use the Information Technology Infrastructure Library (ITIL) to break down IT services into discrete processes, and then apply ITIL Security Management (known as ISMS) and ISO/IEC 27002 to the individual controls applicable to your organization.

Another effective way to start the assessment is to use the tool referenced in the previous chapter, the Capability Maturity Model Integration (CMMI), to look at how mature your processes are on an objective scale. For example, you might assess your vulnerability scanning process to determine if it is "ad hoc," "repeatable," "defined," "managed," or "optimized." The attributes that define these levels of maturity are listed and defined in online publications maintained by the developing organization, Carnegie Mellon· Software Engineering Institute (SEI). Because InfoSec typically provides a service, the CMMI for Services (see link below) is specifically applicable. Once you have completed the process assessment, you can report on the maturity using a well-documented scale of 0 (non-existent) through 5 (fully optimized).

Controls and Hygiene

As you'll see while reviewing CoBIT documentation, processes are described with process steps, and checkpoints, called "key controls" or simply "controls" are identified. By focusing on these key controls, specific measurements can be taken to ensure the proper functioning of the process. To assist with this deconstruction and mapping, the CMMI and its precursor CMM have been mapped to CoBIT by ISACA. ISACA, having developed CoBIT in 1996, in March similar controls in different parts of your environment, such as PCI-DSS for card payment applications and NIST 800-503 for SOX controls. It can also be effective in allowing organizations to quickly understand commonalities and differences in the controls they have implemented in different divisions.

Business Objectives

So far we've discussed IT processes and foundational controls, and while these provide a baseline for implementing and measuring against best practices, the real value is how these foundational controls help you prevent and respond to breaches. As with physical security measures, digital security measures do not prevent breaches. They reduce the likelihood that any particular breach will result in a compromise of critical asset(s) and they help the organization prepare for a quicker recovery in the case that they do. This is accomplished by providing layered protection and enough time for personnel to detect the initial breach and respond with appropriate counter measures.

So how do we measure the ability to detect and respond? We can look at how quickly the security team, and their partners, close vulnerabilities, patch systems, address zero-days, identify and research security events that are identified in the SIEM (security incident and event management) system, and how fast critical technologies (such as end-point protection or web application firewalls) are deployed. Outside of measuring against specific operational goals, this gives us insight into how well our teams know our infrastructure and how easy or hard it is to address problems within that infrastructure.

A simple example would be that if a portion of the infrastructure is so fragile that it cannot be patched or rebooted, then that same portion of the infrastructure is likely to be less resistant to attack and more difficult to recover. Likewise, if the staff has difficulty applying configuration changes due to lack of experience with specific component types, it is less likely they will be able to successfully defend or rapidly recover the same components. On the other hand, while the ability to apply changes to a portion of the infrastructure might not indicate an above-normal ability to defend it from attacks, its stability would likely be an asset in reducing recovery time and allow the team to stay current with patches and upgrades.

Finally, it is also important to track budgetary metrics such as percent of IT budget dedicated to cybersecurity or the number of personnel dedicated to cybersecurity relative to the total number of employees in your organization, or other benchmarks that can provide assurance to leadership that resources are properly aligned or aligned similarly to peer organizations. While these types of metrics lack the granularity to pinpoint what specific changes an organization should make, they can provide a quick shorthand and surface important questions such as:

- Why it is more (or less) expensive to deliver similar services?
- How do we achieve our goals with fewer personnel assigned?
- How do we compare to our peers?

Bring It All Together

We've covered a lot of ground and found a lot to measure: process maturity, control effectiveness, control coverage, speed of remediation, speed of deployment, budget benchmarks, audit results, and several others. Which of these do we actually measure and what do we report on, or are those the same thing?

The answer is, it depends. It depends on your organization's maturity, and on what is currently operating well versus what processes you are struggling with. It depends on how much trust there is in the CISO from the business units and functional groups in your organization. It depends on your industry and the sensitivity of the data you hold. There is no right answer, but there are some principles that can help.

Principles

1. Focus on the data. Stay away from subjective assessments and focus on what you can measure and control.

2. Measure what you need to know but report on what you want to change. You'll likely take dozens of measurements, but other than well-placed pats on the back for good outcomes, only report what you want to focus attention on to change behavior. Remember, everyone is overloaded.

3. Tie your reporting to business goals. "We have 100 servers with the 'Huckleberry' vulnerability" is meaningless to business leaders. "We have 100 servers with the 'Huckleberry' vulnerability, 50 of which potentially expose our 'Goldenrod' product. A breach there would mean $50 million in hard costs and jeopardize $125 million in future revenue," tells the business why they care.

4. Be consistent. Report on the same metrics in the same way over an advertised and dependable frequency.

5. Continually raise the bar. When you achieve success as defined by any particular metric, de-prioritize or deprecate that measurement in favor of another behavior you need to change.

6. Establish your metrics program as the only measurement of the organization's security posture. That way, if you do not have direct control over budget and agenda, you still have the means to change behavior and you can avoid arguments about whether the programs as currently funded and directed are effective or not.

Strategic Measurements

In addition to how you report on the processes, controls and business objectives, it is important to know how prepared you are to help the organization as part of the executive team.

Given the CISO's evolving mandate to help the organization achieve operational resilience, we might now echo within the CISO organization how we traditionally measure successful business continuity plans, namely securing true executive sponsorship. This implies tone at the top, strategic input and responsibility at the board or executive committee level, sufficient funding, and appropriate focus on the most critical business functions. These objectives help in preventing or limiting the scope of breaches and recovering from the significant breaches that still might occur. If the CISO is a key partner to the CIO, the GMs, the functional SVPs, line-of-business colleagues, and the CEO, he or she will have both a voice in setting direction and identifying and articulating the risk that comes with the various strategies the enterprise might adopt, and have a keen sense of the most critical assets to the business. The successful, modern CISO has a seat at the table with executive leadership within the enterprise. The executive team recognizes that the CISO brings a perspective on risk management that is required for organizational governance and that without this insight the organization may face risk that could be existential.

The modern CISO still needs to be a subject matter expert to help the CIO and CTO set technical direction for the enterprise, deal with the ever-expanding compliance and regulatory environment, and rapidly assess the impact of adopting new technologies or delivery platforms such as cloud computing, mobile and BYOD. However, the modern CISO also needs to be able to build a highly effective human network. This human network needs to include the internal security team, cross-functional teams within the organization, and a sufficiently extensive external network of peers, subject matter experts, law enforcement, vendors, and partners. The successful modern CISO will have regular contact with effective leaders internal and external to the organization that will help him or her understand the internal landscape, identify new threat vectors as they become relevant, and rapidly implement contingency plans as needed to overcome outages.

The final measure of success is the strategic focus of the CISO. Recognizing the high percentage of successful attacks that start by compromising the legitimate credentials of employees, the primary focus over the near future for the successful CISO should be on enlisting and empowering the whole organization for better security outcomes. After they have assured themselves that they have the control coverage and technology footprint required, that their business processes are well documented, that operational resiliency and risk management are important value add contributions to the enterprise, successful CISOs will be improving employee education and enhancing their communications and collaboration capabilities so that they can drive systemic change throughout the organization.

indicators could be overlooked. A balanced and thoughtful approach to security metrics is required to ensure that the signal to noise ratio is aligned with your organization's risk tolerance.

I recommend grouping metrics into functional areas. There should be metrics that provide insight on administrative functions such as training, policy review and approval, and non-technical indices. Other metrics should focus on the operational and technical side of security. The development of your organization's metrics dashboard should involve colleagues from the business units and executive management. Their insights and requirements will inform the types of metrics that are ultimately created, implemented, and reviewed. This should be consistent with the core view that the CISO role is transforming into a lead risk management role – evaluating information risk across the entire organization.

Chapter 5 Key Point and Action Item 3

CISOs at times will not have control over budget or agenda to directly influence how cybersecurity will be implemented in their organization's strategic business operations. However, with the correct data a CISO can make an effective case that specific security controls or projects should be implemented to enable the enterprise to be more competitive, securely. Now that you understand what processes and controls are critical, which ones need to be remediated, and new ones that should be implemented, you need to continuously measure their business value.The baseline score will over time provide you with a measurement that reflects how well the organization is addressing its risk and security postures.

You should establish a metrics program as a strategic tool to measure your security program's maturity over time against the established framework you selected above.

Foundational Metrics

Here are some important metrics that I think should be included in every organization's metric assessment. To facilitate collaboration, the metrics are categorized based on function and audience. The CISO's role is to be the steward of the metrics process and ensure that the metrics decided upon meet organizational requirements.

Administrative Metrics (Legal, Financial, HR)

Legal – Metrics related to legal services are frequently overlooked by CISOs. Unfortunately, we live in a highly-litigious business environment and legal risk, including lawsuits, class-action lawsuits, consent decrees and other regulatory actions, should always be assessed and part of the CISO's agenda. Some basic metrics from a legal perspective should include:

- o Percentage of material contracts (defined as contracts that involve transactions or processes with data sets requiring privacy and security controls) that have been evaluated by the security function of the organization.

- o Percentage of all material contracts (defined as contracts that involve services with sensitive information or processes that could impact the core operations of the organization) that require baseline security and privacy controls to be evaluated including specific requirements for breach notification and confidentiality language.

Financial – The financial world is all about baselines, ratios, and comparisons. The worlds of finance and cybersecurity intersect with budgeting, where funding for staffing, tools, and other resources comes into scope. The core financial metric a CISO should be evaluating would be:

- o Percentage of IT budget allocated to cybersecurity (this percentage differs dramatically across sectors and organizations of differing sizes, but a minimum of 5% should be expected).

Human Resources (HR) – Metrics related to HR are also frequently overlooked by CISOs, but human resources and personnel matters are typically a source of notable security risk for an organization. It's quite clear that one of the most significant risk factors and threat vectors we face is our own employees, either through nefarious acts (going rogue) or through inadvertent actions (e.g. responding to phishing e-mail or other ill-advised online behaviors). Some basic metrics from an HR perspective should include:

- o Percentage of employees who have had a thorough background check, including investigation of previous criminal activity.

- o Percentage of job descriptions that highlight each employee's responsibility to protect the organization's assets.

- Percentage of employees who have attended annual security awareness training and passed an assessment that demonstrates retention of core concepts.

- Percentage of employees who have read, acknowledged, and been tested on the organization's security policy.

Vendor Management – Similar to the legal metrics noted above, there are critical security considerations related to the organization's vendor management practices. Most organizations must rely on third parties, vendors, and contractors to support important functions such as payroll, IT infrastructure services (such as hosting and data center services), marketing, and legal. As a consequence, vendor metrics need to be front-and-center for the majority of CISOs. Some important metrics to guide vendor management and assessment practices include:

- Percentage of material vendors (defined as those that have the potential for existential risk for the organization should a service interruption or breach occur) who have been audited either directly by the organization's security function or via a third-party attestation (e.g. a SSAE 16 SOC 1 and SOC 2 audit).

- Percentage of material vendor relationships that are accurately and completely inventoried and documented by the organization.[12]

- Percentage of material vendors that participate in quarterly security reviews with the organization's security function.[13]

Operational Metrics (Security and IT Operations)

Asset (Software) Inventory – Metrics related to asset inventory are among the most fundamental, and typically the most challenging (think shadow IT). These metrics are critical to security operations because as the adage goes, "you cannot secure something you don't know exists." Inventory metrics are also valuable because they tie into an organization's finance and accounting departments – most

---

[12]. This can be a challenging metric given the number of SaaS applications used in many organizations and how pervasive shadow IT can be.

[13]. I strongly recommend, based on the inherent risk profile of the vendor or the services that they provide, structured reviews to assess security incidents, open tickets, or other issues that could impact service delivery and the security of those services. It's very easy to get complacent about a vendor relationship – everything seems to be in good order, so why dig deep – only to discover that critical activities have been overlooked and the services are at risk. As the saying goes, inspect what you expect. This is one of the reasons why it is so important to have a right-to-audit clause in service agreements.

assets should appear in a fixed asset ledger or on an operational budget for items such as software licensing. Two metrics that are simple to state but can be difficult to obtain include:

- o Percentage of Known Assets Accurately Inventoried in an Asset Management System.
- o Percentage of Known Systems Accurately Inventoried in an Asset Management System.

Information (Data) Inventory – As we've discussed elsewhere in this book, for many organizations their greatest asset is their information and data. The compromise of this data is also the largest potential liability for these organizations, especially for organizations that handle ePHI, PII, or cardholder data. Three metrics that should be assessed include:

- o Percentage of Information Assets Accurately Inventoried.
- o Percentage of Information Classified Accurately.[14]
- o Percentage of Systems Documented (e.g. a data flow diagram).

System Upgrades and Patching – We know that systems that are not upgraded or patched on a timely basis are subject to zero-day and other exploits. We also know that most IT departments are understaffed and overworked. Ensuring that adequate attention and resources are assigned to patch management and system upgrade functions should always be on the CISO's agenda. Some of the important operational metrics include:

- o Percentage of systems (defined broadly as both hardware and software, including operating systems) that are still supported by the manufacturer or a validated third party

- o Percentage of systems that are patched within 30 days following notification of critical or security patches. Depending upon the system and its criticality to the organization, this patch interval may offer a level of risk that is unacceptable and tighter patch-response times will be required (e.g. within 24 hours of notification – assuming an assessment of the patch's impact on the system at hand). Conversely, the organization may extend patch management intervals beyond 30 days for

---

[14]. When information is not correctly labeled or classified, there is a high risk of the information not being adequately protected. As a case in point, electronic Protected Health Information (ePHI) that is not adequately inventoried or misclassified could result in regulatory fines or other legal actions.

a disconnect.[17] Key metrics for BC/DR efforts include:

- o Existence of a management-reviewed and approved BC/DR plan.
- o Date since the last BC/DR plan was tested.
- o Percentage of systems, processes, or applications that met RPO/RTO objectives.

The metrics above serve as guide posts for risk management and security operations. There are clearly tens to hundreds of additional metrics that can be used, depending on the size and complexity of the organization. The metrics described above are designed to reduce high-risk blind spots within the organization and to ensure that, at a minimum, certain key planning documents (IR, BIA, BC/DR) exist and certain core security functions are in place (patch management, MFA, inventories, and vulnerability scanning) are in place.

Status on these metrics, even status that suggests real problems are present, should not be guarded within the security function. It is the CISO's role, perhaps the primary function of the CISO's role, to ensure that the fact pattern and consequences associated with these metrics are understood by his or her colleagues in IT, lines-of-business, executive management, and the board. The metrics are strong, clear communication tools that should inform status reporting to the organization's stakeholders.

---

[17]. When I conducted IT general control assessments for publicly-traded firms – required as part of the Sarbanes-Oxley Act – I triangulated my discovery on key applications and processes. I'd speak with line-of-business executives, senior executives, and key members of the IT team. On more occasions than I care to remember, a senior executive would explain how critical a system was to the organization's business, and they assumed that the underlying infrastructure was correctly configured, fault-tolerant, and well managed. When I spoke with IT, I'd discover that the system was on older hardware in a remote server closet and had not recently been patched. This is why it is so important for the CISO to bridge the gap between executive management, line-of-business colleagues, and their counterparts in IT using enterprise risk management (ERM) as the universal language.

> "As the CISO, you must think strategically about the impact of the cybersecurity program on the organization and tailor your metrics and accordingly. Do not be one-dimensional – go 3-D and show how the support your organization's business operations."

As CISO, it will be incumbent upon you to protect your organization and its assets through the creation and management of a mature cybersecurity and risk management program. To effectively provide cybersecurity as a service (CaaS) to your company and its business units, you will need to develop processes that will enable you to measure the maturity of your security services. These processes, which will be instrumental in providing you with the ability to measure your services against a defined standard, are provided through "metrics."

In the discussion that follows, we will examine how CISOs can create metrics, monitor them through dashboards, and then use reports to communicate the maturity of their security program to senior leadership. This leads us to the three questions we will discuss in this chapter on why CISOs must know how to create effective metrics, use them to improve the corporate security program, and report the maturity and risk baseline progress of that program to their senior management teams. The questions under consideration are:

1. What are metrics? Why are metrics important? What steps should the CISO and security team take to create valid metrics for their program?
2. What are some examples of dashboards that should be developed as strategic assets?
3. What types of reports should a CISO create to educate executive management and sponsor a more resilient, cyber aware corporate culture?

Metrics and Data Points Are Essential for The CISO

Today, as we continue to witness an increasing number of cyber incidents across all industry categories, boards of directors and senior management are educating themselves on their organizations' risk exposure to cybersecurity related issues. The field of cybersecurity is relatively new, and many of them do not understand its relevance to their company's strategic operations. They have questions such as, "How secure are we from a particular threat?" and "Can you promise me we won't be the next <hacked company>?" As the CISO, how do you answer them? How do you help them understand that cybersecurity is a lifecycle, a continuous process, and not a simple "one-time" problem to be fixed?

As we begin our discussion, I hope you will gain valuable insight into one of the key components that a CISO needs to protect his/her organization and educate leadership on the value of cybersecurity. So for our first question, let's examine that key component: *What are metrics? Why are metrics important? What steps should the CISO and security team take to create valid metrics for their program?*

Organizations need to understand that cybersecurity and risk management teams do not control the threat landscape facing their company. These teams instead control the company's ability to respond to its risk environment. The ability to respond, to adjust, and to protect the business so it can focus on its strategic goals, is "resiliency." However, even though the security teams are tasked with responding to this risk, a company's board of directors will hold the organization's senior management accountable for the development of a clear strategy to address its threats and vulnerabilities to cybercrime. This strategy, in most organizations, is the domain of the CISO. The CISO is expected to have systems and controls in place that reduce risk to the company, plus processes to monitor program maturity.

To aid the CISO, it is standard best practice to use a cybersecurity/risk management framework such as NIST CSF, ISO 27001, or COBIT 5. These frameworks and their security controls are in effect a platform for the cybersecurity and risk management teams to establish the cybersecurity/risk management baselines for the business. To understand these baselines, the CISO must have established procedures to measure the validity of all installed security controls. To assist the CISO in documenting the maturity of these controls, he/she will use selected metrics as an ongoing measuring device to provide visibility into how well these controls are implemented and any risk exposure from the company's installed technology/application portfolio.

So from the beginning, the CISO must understand that metrics will be used to measure. They will be created and collected to tell a story. That there is no specific template for what should be measured. Every organization's business environment is different. As the CISO, when you report metrics to leadership it will be in the guise of a narrative. You will use them to explain how security services support the organization and its strategic objectives. Some basic considerations for creating metrics are as follows (McMillian, 2015):

1. What is the purpose of the metric?
   a. It should support a business goal, if not why collect it?
   b. Connection to a business goal helps security teams prioritize resources in a more efficient manner

2. It should be controllable
   a. Metrics need to be effective, they must demonstrate that you are meeting specific goals
   b. So metrics should measure processes/outcomes that your team controls
   c. Don't just take an output from a tool and call it a metric, it has to have context – "why are we collecting it, what story does it tell?"

3. Do you understand what "good" is?
   a. We should know the target value we want to achieve.
   b. We should also know who takes action based on the metric and what the action is

4. It should be quantitative
   a. You will want the metric to be a quantitative value so you can compare it and demonstrate trends.
   b. It needs to have a high level of accuracy, precision, reliability and objectivity
   c. Example: "25% of remote users have not logged in within the last 90 days"

5. It should be easy to collect and analyze
   a. You should be able to collect, aggregate, sort, filter and post in a central portal
   b. Collection of data should take no more than 1/3 the length of its reporting frequency. If a report is weekly, it should take two to three days to collect, process and post.
   c. Data should be able to show trends over time, which gives the ability to measure maturity
      i. "Number of critical audit findings over a series of audits"

Management is concerned about the organization's business operations, and as such their dashboards will be designed to provide operational views into the specific business categories (ongoing projects, assessments, compliance level, budgets, operations) they wish to monitor.

To demonstrate how uniquely tailored to their audiences these dashboards are, some examples are shown below.

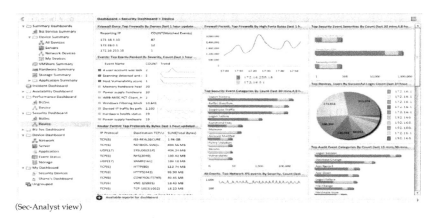

(Sec-Analyst view)

This is an example of a "Security Analyst's dashboard." As you can see, it is very technical. It monitors ports, protocols, and IP addresses. It is designed for the professional whose job is to manage the daily security of an organization's network infrastructure.

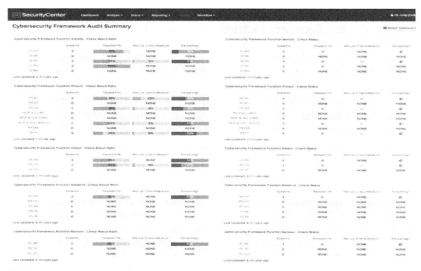

(CISO, Security Executive View)

This is an example of a CISO dashboard. This is one I have personally used to manage the outcome of compliance assessments. As stated above, this is designed for a senior security/risk professional like a CISO who requires a strategic, organization-wide view of risk.

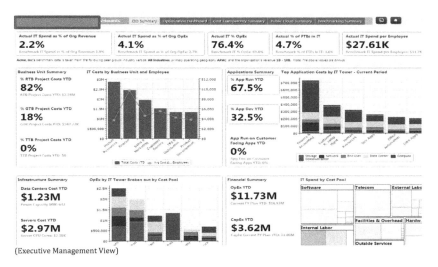

(Executive Management View)

My last example is a dashboard for executive management. This dashboard view is designed for monitoring the IT costs of an organization – definitely from an operational viewpoint.

Now that you have seen examples of several dashboards, let's talk about some guidelines that will help you create your own. As I stated previously about metrics, dashboards tell a story. To be able to tell an engaging story with your dashboards you need to know your audience. You need to spend time with them to understand what information they require – just like with metrics.

Dashboards should answer these questions (BISSON 2015)
1. What risks are important to the business?
2. What is the current accurate security status of the business?
3. What trends are evident in our security data that upper management should know about?
4. How do our assessment results compare with other organizations and industry standards?
5. Are there any predictive qualities in our trends that can assist us with remediating risk?

With this information about your audience, you can proceed to use your metrics and collected data to craft a dashboard display whose data is concise with strong risk visuals. Don't forget, your organizational leaders need to understand the context of the data on display. Vet your dashboards with them to ensure that they communicate business alignment (security risk = business goals). For executive dashboards, remember that executives have limited time. As a CISO, you want to help focus their attention on specific issues. Provide them with a dashboard that allows them to drill down into the data. This will allow you to present trending information quickly and help them focus on critical issues and prioritize where resources can be targeted to resolve a concern.

Chapter 5 Key Point and Action Item 4

CISO's major responsibility to their organization is to ensure that it is kept secure according to the organization's strategic objectives as outlined in the corporate cyber security policy.To do this effectively, the CISO and security team will need to continuously analyze and evaluate large amounts of data.

You should create some technical (team-oriented) and executive - oriented dashboards to monitor the metrics data you are collecting.

As we conclude this discussion, there are a few best practices I want to provide you with so that your dashboards tell the correct story. First, if you use percentages to compare blocks of information, make sure they add up to 100%. Another best practice is if you are providing data on a number of business units within the organization, make sure that you have all of the business units listed in your display. If you don't display all of the business units, the credibility of your data will be called into question. Finally, review your data and make sure it is contextually accurate. Verify that your data points are consistent within timescale, accuracy, and scope. This is one reason you will want to have dashboards and their data viewed and vetted before you release them into production. Make sure they are telling the correct story about your cybersecurity and risk management programs.

To Tell a Story with Metrics, Report It!

With metrics and dashboards, we are collecting information and measuring it against a known quantity. Then we display it in dashboards to monitor and track for trend analysis in order to make effective strategic business decisions. However, there is a third component that these two data elements feed and that is security reports. As CISO, you will create security reports to provide to your executive management. These reports will describe the effectiveness of their cyber security investment, the health of your security program, and any information on specific topics requested by your board of directors. As CISO, you will also be the recipient of reports from your teams and your partners, vendors and compliance professionals. It is this myriad collection of reports that leads us to our last discussion point, *"What types of reports should a CISO create to educate executive management and sponsor a more resilient, cyber aware corporate culture?"*

In July 2015, Gartner reported that by 2017 over 80% of IT risk and cybersecurity organizations will report metrics to non-IT executive decision makers and only 20% of the metrics contained in those reports will be considered useful. As the CISO of an organization, the previous statement should ring some alarm bells in that the information you are collecting to help you manage your security and risk programs may not mean much to your executive management. This doesn't mean that what you are doing is not of value to the organization. Instead, I believe it demonstrates that when you write your reports, you will need to put your information into the context of the audience it is meant to influence and inform.

The reports that you as a CISO will create, manage, contribute to and analyze will typically fall into one of two primary categories. These report categories are technical reports and executive reports. The technical reports that you as a CISO will primarily be focused on will be reports that are created for an IT/technical audience. These reports will predominantly contain daily, weekly, or standard operational data about the work your teams are conducting for the benefit of the organization. Examples of these types of reports are "Daily Maintenance Reports," "Weekly Data/Threat Analysis," and "Server Remediation Updates."

The key here is that these reports will be generated for a technical audience that is within your business unit and they are usually not meant for distribution to executive management. Executive reports, however, are a different breed of information-sharing for a CISO. These reports are written for an audience whose primary driver is to maximize shareholder value and ensure the viability and profitability of the organization. This audience will require you to use a different approach on what subjects you report to them and to present this information in an effective, non-technical way.

So let's discuss some of the reports I have presented, as a CISO, to executive management and boards to educate them on cybersecurity and risk. One of the first reports I created as a CISO and still use to

proud to tell your team's story about how cybersecurity is essential to your company's success.

Photos used for Dashboard examples:
1. *Security Analyst dashboard view* - http://www.accelops.com/products/security-monitoring-siem/
2. *CISO, Security Executive dashboard view* - http://www.tenable.com/sc-dashboards?tid=204
3. *Executive Management dashboard view* - https://www.apptio.com/products/applications/cost-transparency/cost-transparency-foundation

Summary

For Chapter 5, we began our discussion by asking these questions:

- What are metrics? Why are metrics important? What steps should the CISO and security team take to create valid metrics for their program?
- What are some examples of dashboards that should be developed as strategic assets?
- What types of reports should a CISO create to educate executive management and sponsor a more resilient, cyber-aware corporate culture?

In today's global business environment, we are observing exponential growth in the use of technology to achieve strategic business goals. We also see the role of CISO expanding, incorporating more responsibilities within the risk and business operations of an organization. Due to these growing requirements, the CISO has a vast array of functions, processes, and procedures to measure the maturity of their cybersecurity and risk management efforts. It is critical for the CISO to provide a clear understanding of their security goals and risk management objectives for both the organization and its strategic partners.

To effectively communicate the maturity of enterprise security efforts and ongoing risk mitigation issues to the security team, organizational peers, and senior leadership, the CISO will need to have metrics that provide relevant data, reports that provide actionable information, and dashboards where it can be monitored in real time. With this data, all parties within the company can participate in a meaningful dialog about the changes in behavior the CISO will champion to protect enterprise assets and engage stakeholders with the future vision of a more risk tolerant corporate infrastructure.

In closing, we leave you with these five key points and next steps:

1. As CISO, before you can use metrics to measure the maturity of anything you need to understand what critical processes are your responsibility. It's important to work with your audit team, stakeholders, IT management, and executive leadership to determine which business processes fall within the purview of the CISO and which additional security control objectives the CISO should be concerned about. **You should create a list of critical processes and security**

controls that are your responsibility.

2. Once you have created this list of processes and controls, understand that not all of them are created equal. Some will have a greater impact to the organization and are deemed "critical" while others are considered to be the routine "keeping the lights on" processes. You need to understand which processes and security controls are working well and which ones are seriously degraded. **You should select a framework such as ISO/IEC 27002, CoBIT, CIS Critical 20 or NIST CSF to measure the maturity of these processes and conduct an assessment.**

3. CISOs at times will not have control over budget or agenda to directly influence how cybersecurity will be implemented in their organization's strategic business operations. However, with the correct data a CISO can make an effective case that specific security controls or projects should be implemented to enable the enterprise to be more competitive, securely. Now that you understand what processes and controls are critical, which ones need to be remediated, and new ones that should be implemented, you need to continuously measure their business value. The baseline score will over time provide you with a measurement that reflects how well the organization is addressing its risk and security postures. **You should establish a metrics program as a strategic tool to measure your security program's maturity over time against the established framework you selected above.**

4. A CISO's major responsibility to their organization is to ensure that it is kept secure according to the organization's strategic objectives as outlined in the corporate cyber security policy. To do this effectively, the CISO and security team will need to continuously analyze and evaluate large amounts of data. **You should create some technical (team-oriented) and executive-oriented dashboards to monitor the metrics data you are collecting.**

5. The CISO can understand the security controls and processes that are within his/her scope and have a strong metrics program to collect data on their effective management. However, even with all of this in place the CISO will still need to report this information to different audiences. **You should create a set of four to six reports to help you tell the story of what your security program has accomplished and the challenges you face and use them consistently to establish credibility with executive management.**

One of the more challenging aspects of being a CISO is trying to paint a picture of cybersecurity and risk that different audiences with different contextual viewpoints can understand. To be effective in communicating this picture to an organization's executive staff, business stakeholders and external third parties the CISO needs to champion how cybersecurity supports the organization's business goals. To do this effectively will require a metrics program that can be tied into how cybersecurity and all of its controls and processes make the organization more secure and in return enables it to be innovative and compete safely.

As you can imagine, this isn't easy. You need to collect metrics that contain legitimate data. You need dashboards that make the information actionable for the CISO, IT management, business stakeholders, and executive leadership. Finally, in the words of Bill Bonney, you need reports that are tied to the organization's strategic objectives and only "… report on what you want to focus attention on to change behavior." In essence, when you collect metrics and create your dashboards and their associated reports, ensure they have a purpose. Use them to drive change, use them to educate, use them to protect, and finally use them to collaborate with your peers and support the organization.

team and those directly responsible for technical deployments. But do not overlook your duty to teach at the executive level. Keep the message simple. Remember that you are teaching people who are not in your domain. Be mindful about what key messages you want the extended leadership team to be able to communicate to their peers and be open to the follow on questions.

Chapter 6 Key Point and Action Item 1

Boards are elected to represent the true stakeholders in an organization. For publicly-traded companies, this would be the shareholders. The board is expected to exercise its collective duties of oversight and due care. Simply stated, boards are expected to review the strategy, planning, and execution of executive management and to provide guidance on the orga-nization's risk strategies.For executives with little experience communicating with the board, this can be an intimidating prospect and it might be difficult to capture the key points at the right level.

You should ask your management team to designate a business leader within the organization as a sponsor to help you prepare for your first presentation.

Call to Action

Do you want action taken based on the information you are providing? What is the purpose and time frame of that action? What are the consequences for acting and not acting?

Similar to having key takeaways from purely informational interactions, you want the most important actions to rise to the top any time you are calling for action. Don't overwhelm your audience with too many high-priority actions. While your objective for a "full frontal assault" might be to "light a fire," the result is often a feeling of helplessness followed inevitably by paralysis. This is often true even for environments that have been subject to security review for some time, and this creates fatigue as well. People become numb to the inputs and consequences and are paralyzed from taking action. To avoid this overwhelming and numbing effect, consider "grading on a curve." By showing relative performance you can focus management's attention on the largest problems or the lowest hanging fruit, depending on how you want to inspire action within your organization.

A quick story can help illustrate this. Earlier in my career I was sent to help a new business unit formed from a recent acquisition with a rather large backlog of Information Technology General Control (ITGC) deficiencies. We had thirteen weeks to solve a nasty problem. During my obligatory "I'm from corporate and I'm here to help" meet and greet tour I was bluntly told by line management that the problem was unsolvable.

My team set about doing a very quick analysis of the problem set and we built a heat map that showed the full range of ITGCs the business unit was subject to, including the "green" controls, which were functioning just fine. The only controls I recommended the team tackle initially were those marked bright red. The managing director of this group said: "You are the first person from corporate who has told me my team was doing ANYTHING correctly and didn't tell me I had to fix it all at once. You have me and my team's full support." In the ensuring weeks, as they successfully tackled one problem after another, the local team began to own the problem. Nine weeks into the engagement they proudly announced that they'd be done by week eleven. The power of that story isn't what was communicated: 14 of the 16 ITGCs they operated were yellow to red on a heat map. The power was that the call to action was focused. Management understood the relative impact and understood where to direct resources.

To Whom Am I Speaking?

Next, focus on the role of the individual or group you are communicating or interacting with. While the essence of your message is unchanged regardless of who you are interacting with, how you frame that message might be very different. One of the frequent complaints about interacting with CISOs, more so than other highly technical executives that have collectively had longer to assimilate to executive committees, the C-suite and the office of the CEO is that they are often mired in detail or use technical language or jargon that is difficult to decipher. Being aware of your audience's natural filter is essential to being effective in your interactions.

Your peers are more apt to be concerned with the impact to their operations. Do they need to pivot on strategy based on what you are saying? Do they need to take immediate remedial action? Do they need to account for new information in planning? How will this impact their sales or customer service? The CEO or your direct manager might be more interested in the impact across divisions, employee morale, market impact, or public scrutiny. The board, along with the CEO, would be interested in the impact on company strategy, public scrutiny, regulator impact, and any liability you explicitly or implicitly relate.

million in hard costs and jeopardize $125 million in future revenue," tells the business why they care.

The example mentioned here is highly tactical and while it might be something for your peers and management, it is not likely to occupy much time for the board, with a notable exception. We have entered the era of celebrity vulnerabilities and high-profile breaches. It is becoming common for boards to ask how a particular vulnerability affects us or if the most recent high-profile breach can happen to us. It is important to provide succinct answers that quickly and truthfully demonstrate mastery of the issue and relate it to your organization. If this vulnerability or the techniques used to cause that breach pose a real threat, make sure the board knows why, what you are doing about it, and how they can help.

4. Be consistent. Report on the same metrics in the same way over an advertised and dependable frequency.

    As you become more strategic and less tactical, you become more focused on trends and less on point-in-time assessments. While there is a temptation to cherry pick data points to show critical weaknesses or respond to flavor of the month narratives in the press or trade journals, it is extremely important to maintain the consistent data necessary to assess the program and the organization's health over time.

5. Continually raise the bar. When you achieve success as defined by any particular metric, de-prioritize or deprecate that measurement in favor of another behavior you need to change.

    This principle applies at both the tactical and strategic level. Tactically, some of your peers are likely to be very hands on and will want to get quickly to the point of what they need to do to improve. Strategically, everyone in the organization, including management and the board, should know progress against the key initiatives and next steps.

6. Establish your metrics program as the only measurement of the organization's security posture. That way, if you do not have direct control over budget and agenda, you still have the means to change behavior and you can avoid arguments about whether the programs as currently funded and directed are effective or not.

This principle depends very much on the trust you establish in what and how you inform and report. While accuracy is paramount, it is also extremely critical that your messages are consistent, they are targeted to the most important high-level takeaways and they are timely. If management or the board does not get the information they need from you in a way that is immediately consumable and actionable, they will look elsewhere. So a key element in establishing your metrics program as the only measurement of an organization's security posture it to be in constant contact with your peers, management, and to the extent possible, the board and make sure that they are getting the information they need from you.

Finally, "actionable" means different things at different levels. For your peers, and those hands-on managers, actionable means what specific near-term actions can I and my team take to affect a specific metric. For C-level management and the board, actionable means how do we construct training and governance programs, fund initiatives, and enter into relationships that, over the short, medium and long term, would position the organization to achieve its goals.

Chapter 6 Key Point and Action Item 2

For many board members, cybersecurity is a challenging topic, new in its implications to the organization and distinct in its vocabulary and technology. Board members know that they should be concerned and exercise due care and oversight, but they may simply lack the knowledge, context, or even basic cyber vocabulary to address the issue competently.As the lead cybersecurity professional for your organization, your position brings with it an air of competency and professionalism. You can destroy all of that if you don't understand why you are before the board.

You should work with your sponsor and other members of the executive team to determine what the board is expecting from your presentation to ensure you will meet their expectations.

Your Unique Role

A final topic for discussion in this chapter is the unique duties that fall to the CISO and some general guidelines for related communications. The two roles with the most obvious requirements are the CISO's regulatory, audit, and compliance management duties and incident management responsibilities.

In the case of the regulatory and compliance environment, the CFO has traditionally been assigned the task of communicating with regulatory authorities, partners at audit firms, the board, and shareholders. However, several factors have contributed to creating expectations for the CISO in this duty as well.

First, the nature of information security controls that are tested as a part of Sarbanes-Oxley and other government-driven compliance are highly technical and specialized. Also, some compliance activities are almost entirely technical, such as PCI-DSS compliance. Finally, the high profile that non-compliance with these rules creates adds risk for the organization.

Because of this, more CFOs, CEOs, and boards are requiring that the CISO be capable of being the external face of the company in some circumstances to lend credibility to the organization and create confidence in successful outcomes. The communications role in this case is largely with regulators and auditors. The goal of the regulators and auditors is to assess the organization's commitment and management's competence at creating successful programs to ensure compliance. Technical acumen, integrity, and consistency in action are being tested and again, clear, concise communications are key. And while it is at times necessary to demonstrate mastery of the subject or the standards and compliance requirements, it is not expected that you will provide a significant level of detail. Other than remedial plans for addressing deficiencies, you can often leave the technical deep dives for your direct staff.

The final area I'd like to cover also pertains to external communications. As I mentioned above, we've entered the era of the celebrity vulnerability and the high-profile breach. In your role as CISO, one of your first tasks will be to clearly define your role and the roles of your peers and the entire executive leadership team in incident response. Create a response plan early and practice often so you don't have to invent one on the fly.

Because of your role as the CISO, and if the breach was significant enough, your role as the CRO, you'll play an important part in your organization's incident management plan. Key to your success in incident management is to keep your communications timely and consistent and hit on these three themes: "what happened," "what's the impact," and "what are we doing about it." As mentioned above, keep to the facts. It is especially important to keep speculation to an absolute minimum. We've also touched on consistency as a hallmark of good communications; be consistent in format and in timeliness. Remember that nature abhors a vacuum and if you fail to provide a narrative about what transpired, the impact, and your reaction, one will be provided for you.

Board Requirements – Stamper

> "Boards that choose to ignore, or minimize, the importance of cybersecurity oversight responsibility, do so at their own peril."
> Personal Comments of SEC Commissioner
> Luis Aguilar, June 2014

No one likes to be surprised…especially the board of directors. In this chapter, we'll look at the role the CISO plays in informing executive management and the board of directors specifically on the nature and extent of cyber risk for their organization. As Stephen Covey suggests, "seek first to understand and then to be understood." To that end, I would like to use the majority of this chapter to provide a board member's perspective on cybersecurity … effectively seeing this topic not from the CISO's viewpoint, but rather from that of the board. A CISO that appreciates the unique role board members play in overseeing an organization will be well-served in getting their cyber program funded and with the right level of executive attention if he or she first understands why board members think the way they do in their roles.

Chapter 6 Key Point and Action Item 3

To build credibility the CISO has to function on the executive team as a trusted teammate. To that end, a key mantra should be "No Surprises!" If you have information within your presentation that might surprise board members, you will need to work with your sponsor and select key board members to share your information with them before you present to the full board.

You should vet key points being made in any board presentation with select board members and impacted executives before your presentation to the full board.

The Board's Unique Role

Let's take a moment to think about the role of the board. Boards are elected (or in certain organizations appointed) to represent the true stakeholders in an organization. For publicly-traded companies, this would be the shareholders. For other organizations, the fiduciary

- **Tone at the top** – Ultimately, boards represent and function as the voice of the stakeholders of the organization. Proactive and well-informed boards can set the proverbial tone at the top and have a strong influence on the organization's operational effectiveness. CISOs should know the members of their organization's board, their respective roles on the board, and their key interests.

- **Guidance and direction on risk management** – Boards play an integral role in overseeing risk management for the organization. Board members have a fiduciary responsibility to understand the risk environment and to provide guidance on the appropriate risk-treatment strategy for the organization. The board's perspective on risk management will clearly extend beyond cyber to include operational, financial, reputational, and other enterprise risk management considerations. To assist boards in evaluating risk, there are some practical analyses that the CISO can provide to the board, ideally in collaboration with other members of the executive team. Specifically, the CISO should play a leading role in communicating detail and status on the following:

  o *Organizational assets* – The CISO, with support from other colleagues, should provide a list of assets that require due care including the firm's intellectual property (IP), key data sets such as protected health information, cardholder data, and core processes. To keep this information meaningful, a CISO might leverage a data flow diagram to show the board the linkages between organizational assets, information, staff, as well as third parties leveraged by the organization that could impact risk-treatment.

  o *Risk assessment* – The CISO should draft an overall cyber risk assessment for the organization. The risk assessment should take a holistic view of cyber to include third parties, systems, applications, personnel, and data. A summary of the risk factors and their recommended treatment should be provided to the board and executive management at least twice a year, and certainly following any material changes to the organization's operating environment. The use of a trusted third party to facilitate this assessment may also be in order to ensure credibility.

  o *Suppliers and third parties* – As discussed previously in this book, the impact of an organization's supply chain and service providers cannot be overstated. CISOs can play an important role in qualifying the risk of third parties, independent contractors, and service providers. Documenting these dependencies in a board-friendly manner is an exceptionally valuable exercise.

o *Threat landscape* – Boards are concerned about a number of risk factors facing the organization, including changes to the industry, regulations, new competitors, and changes to the executive team. It's important that the board is also aware of the threat landscape facing the organization's systems, applications, and IT infrastructure. A CISO can provide quarterly updates summarizing these changes in the threat landscape.

- **Evaluation of incident response capabilities** – Boards should be aware of their organization's capabilities to respond to a cyber incident or a breach. While the board may not be expected to read the full incident response plan in detail, they will want to know that the incident response plan exists, that it's been tested (and the results of this testing), and the role of executive management in implementing the plan effectively. CISOs should provide an overview of incident response capabilities, requirements for additional resources to support incident response, and an escalation matrix that includes designated members of the board when a breach is discovered or another cyber-related matter puts the organization at material risk.

  o Counsel – The board should know the role of the organization's legal counsel in handling incident response. For many organizations, the first call following the discovery of a breach should be to counsel to invoke attorney-client privilege. CISOs, with the guidance and support of the extended executive team, should have these procedures clearly documented and tested.

  o Regulatory and law enforcement – The board will also need to know how law enforcement and regulators are to be engaged depending upon the nature and extent of the incident. These are procedures that should be routinely practiced through the use of table-top exercises and other methods to ensure the executive team is prepared.

  o Notifications and escalation – A basic RACI matrix should be provided to the board that includes the board itself and details how notifications and escalation should be triaged when an event occurs. The last thing that anyone wants to do during an incident is to determine who should be notified. A breach is an activity that should be anticipated and documented within the incident response plan.

- **Review and authorization of budgets** – Boards have an important role reviewing the overall budget of the organization. Part of their assessment is to ensure that the organization's strategy is commensurately tied to the funding associated with key activities. Unfortunately, cybersecurity is too frequently seen as a cost to the organization versus a business or process enabler. Even under the best of circumstances, cybersecurity is viewed as something analogous to an insurance premium – begrudgingly paid, with an emphasis on paying the least amount possible. The CISO needs to work closely with the board – and clearly with executive management as well – to ensure that the cyber budget is tied to the organization's overall risk appetite. The adequacy of the budget and the funding of key cyber activities should also be seen in the context of contractual and regulatory obligations.

  o CISOs should help the board baseline security spending in the broader context of the organization's industry as well as other risk variables, notably the cost of a breach. Does the organization have the right cybersecurity capabilities to address its specific threat landscape; are the staffing levels and competencies sufficient for the work at hand; and can the organization adequately address third party risk? These are all important topics that translate into budget decision-making. CISOs should help the board understand the context of the cybersecurity budget and to make recommendations that lower overall security costs for the organization while still providing adequate protections. CISOs should also provide a detailed review of their options and preferences if more budget were available.

- **Adequacy of insurance** – Insurance is an important risk treatment vehicle. The advent of cyber liability insurance reflects the importance of cybersecurity to an organization's overall risk management practices. Cyber liability insurance is a key tool for mitigating financial exposure following a breach. Expenses after a breach may include penalties and fines, consumer notifications and credit monitoring, legal expenses, as well as other costs including damage to an organization's reputation. There is also the opportunity cost facing the organization as key staff are focused on incident response and clean up rather than their normal responsibilities. Numerous studies suggest that the cost of a breach is approximately $200.00 per record and averages between $3 million and $6 million in total (the Ponemon Institute's analyses on this topic are well-regarded and should be provided to the board as background). The CISO can assist the board and executive management in evaluating the adequacy of the cyber-liability coverage and facilitate the application process.

- **Validation of current practices against industry norms and baselines (essentially legally-defensible security)** – Boards, especially those of publicly-traded firms, leverage comparison and baselining as a tool to oversee the performance of the organization. Financial ratios help the board determine how well the organization is performing, the effectiveness of its use of capital, and whether the company is heading in the right direction in general. Boards relish an opportunity to compare and contrast. CISOs should provide detail on how the organization compares to such key frameworks and standards as the NIST Cybersecurity Framework, COBIT, ISO, or other recognized approaches to cybersecurity management. Every organization has its challenges so a CISO should be prepared to convey the ground truth to the board. If certain key controls or activities are ineffective, the board should know. Helping the board develop a level of comfort with basic security metrics is an important element in successful board and executive management communication.

- **Ensuring organizational accountability** – The board should know who is ultimately accountable for cybersecurity within the organization. Board members are ill-served if their oversight is limited because they do not have access to – or much worse, knowledge of – the leader who oversees cybersecurity within the organization. Under ideal circumstances, the board should have unfettered access to the CISO and there should be routine, calendared updates on all items cyber. As noted in the incident response section above, a basic RACI matrix is an important first step in this regard.

- **Evaluation and assessment of controls and disclosures** – The SEC's guidance, coupled with other recommendations from board-focused groups, clearly suggests that boards need to develop a level of cyber-acumen to ensure the ability to provide competent oversight. There are analogies to other

Are You Board Ready?

To begin, let's assume you have a mature security program in place and you are collecting metrics that you will use to measure the maturity and growth of its value to the organization. To analyze this data and use it to implement change, you have created dashboards to display this information to support your organization's business units. Now as CISO, you are excited about the trends you are seeing in the information you have collected and you communicate this news to upper management. Then one afternoon you get "the email," that's right the email that comes from your organization's executive assistant for the board of directors. The board is requesting that you present to them the information you have on your cybersecurity program and the current risks the organization faces. At first, if you have never done an executive presentation, you may be apprehensive. However, recognize that this is an incredible opportunity.

You, as the CISO, have the chance to educate the board and executive management on how cybersecurity is providing value to the organization. So let's discuss how you can approach this opportunity and not lose your job with the following questions, *"What are recommended practices for reporting cybersecurity requirements to the board? How should the information be presented? What important aspects of cybersecurity and risk should the CISO ensure are conveyed to the board?"*

Boards of directors are tasked with protecting their organizations from significant risk. Their duties generally fall within six areas (Leech, 2015):

1. Governance
2. Strategy
3. Risk
4. Talent
5. Compliance
6. Culture

To corporate boards, cybersecurity risk is as significant to the business as risks posed by strategic, operational, financial or compliance operations. For the board, providing effective oversight of cybersecurity risk means the difference between learning about cybersecurity after a breach with significant damages and having a mature cybersecurity program in place that can mitigate the damages of a breach with minimal exposure to the company. In today's fast-moving business environment, boards can't claim lack of awareness as a defense against allegations of improper oversight. Boards of directors and executive management must educate themselves about cybersecurity and its risk exposure to their organizations. This knowledge is crucial; it enables board members to make strategic decisions with the full knowledge of how cyber risk impacts their business plans. So with this strategic view in mind, let's discuss how the CISO, the security program, and security teams can assist the board with its mission of providing proper strategic oversight.

At the executive management level, the CEO is ultimately responsible to the board of directors for the business' cybersecurity risk strategy. However, the CEO will typically look to an executive, (CIO, CTO, CRO, etc.) who has governance responsibilities over information technology or risk management to execute this strategy. This executive will be expected to interface with the board and be held accountable to the CEO for this strategy's implementation and overall management.

As I mentioned in Chapter 1, it's my opinion that the CISO should report to another C-level executive who understands the importance of the CISO position and how cybersecurity can be used as a valuable asset to support the organization's strategic objectives. This senior executive is critical to the CISO. Business tends to try to decentralize itself in order to be nimble and competitive while cybersecurity programs tend to try to centralize the business in order to be more effective in managing risk. It's obvious that these conflicting views will be in a constant state of opposition unless there is a senior executive to provide context and mentorship to the CISO. It's this partnership between senior executive and CISO that enables the CISO to see cybersecurity and risk from a more strategic viewpoint and understand its impact on the business.

So back to our quandary. You have been informed that your presence is requested to report to the board of directors on the state of your cybersecurity program and the company's current level of exposure to cybersecurity risk. This is where the senior executive you report to is critical. He/she will be able to assist you in articulating the value of cybersecurity in business terms and demonstrating how the program provides clear business value.

Ideas for painting this picture on business value

- Approach this opportunity as is presenting a financial report on a budget.
- Provide a balanced cost-benefit analysis on cybersecurity projects based on expected results.
- Describe a reduction in risk based on the use of specific cybersecurity controls or work processes (it is good to have metrics here to back up this picture).?
- Demonstrate some quantifiable financial returns.
  - Increase in a specific cyber metrics allows a more specific service or reduces risk to a critical service.
  - A mature cybersecurity risk management program increases productivity or allows for a reduction in cost – automation of controls or processes reduces time requires to touch equipment or rewrite code.
- Discuss how the cybersecurity program enables corporate competitiveness. The company can leverage

Management has the responsibility to develop and implement the cybersecurity strategy; however, the board has an obligation to fully understand the company's risk exposure to cyber related issues. Boards, due to their positions and breadth of governance, tend to look at issues from a broader macro level of operations while management operates at a more tactical level within their specific departments or divisions. Your job when you present to the board is to tell a story, a story that is concise, simple and connects the organization's business goals to your cybersecurity program's risk management objectives. As you can see, this is very similar to the process you implemented when you created security metrics for your program and architected dashboard views to manage them. When you address the board, your story needs to have a beginning, middle, and end. It also needs to be interesting and should have a goal:

1. _Inform and Educate_ – you wish to tell the board that leveraging a new technology provides opportunities, however it also provides new risks that must be addressed.
2. _Influence a Decision_ – make the case for why a specific action should be taken, for example the cybersecurity program should be moved out of the IT department to address "segregation of duties" issues.
3. _Change Behavior_ – show how a current organizational process, behavior, standard, etc. is opening the organization to substantial risk. Demonstrate workable alternatives that

will reduce risk exposure with minimal impact to business operations.

Since you are in effect telling a story, it is crucial to know how you want your audience to feel. To ensure that you are constructing the correct message, test it on one or more business executives to get their opinion on the information you present and whether it seems valid. Ask them to review your terminology and provide suggestions. You want to be sure that your story is demonstrating how cybersecurity is providing value to the business.

To assist in preparing for your board presentation, ask senior management for a board-level sponsor. This sponsor will be your sounding board as you create your presentation and can help you convey your message and answer the dreaded question, "What do you need from us?" There are multiple strategies to assist you in formulating your narrative. One that I would suggest you start with is to increase your business operations knowledge. You need to review the organization's strategic plans and annual reports and interview executives within your company. This will give you more insight into the business drivers that are critical to the board. They are also critical to you – you must ensure that your metrics and presentation are aligned to support them. Another strategy I would suggest is to compare/contrast with your peers if possible or use a framework such as NIST CSF or ISO 27001. Risk posture is difficult to measure.

Chapter 6 Key Point and Action Item 4

As CISO, you will be the center of an ecosystem — creating metrics to measure your program's effectiveness, producing and managing dashboards to execute strategy, and reporting maturity to executive management. There are multiple strategies to assist you in formulating your narrative as you create your slide deck. Make sure you demonstrate alignment with the organization's strategic plans, use industry common industry benchmarks to allow for comparisons with peer companies and use data to create an objectiveassessment.

You should validate that your presentation is at a sufficiently high level by previewing it with your sponsor and other select members of the executive team.

Using a framework to provide visual data on the maturity of a process is a good proxy for risk posture and it provides a picture for

dashboards to execute strategy, and reporting maturity to executive management. This will be a continuous process, one that you will need to fine tune to your organization's business strategy. Understand that you will not be able to do all of this immediately; it will take time to develop. Do not be afraid to reach out and ask for assistance from the business leaders in your organization. In the end, your program, its security controls, metrics, and dashboards provide the business with an intimate view of their risk footprint and the impact to the organization if there is a breach.

Because your program will directly influence your organization, it is critical that you are collecting the correct metrics, you are telling a story that provides value, and you remain flexible as your organization adjusts in its cycle to remain competitive. It is also critical that as the senior cybersecurity professional for your organization, you can effectively present to senior management a true picture of its risk with respect to cybersecurity related issues. This will enable senior management to make informed strategic decisions based on sound knowledge and will provide you with further insight into how your security program can continue to support your organization's business operations.

Summary

In Chapter 6, we began our discussion by asking these questions:

- If the CISO were a board member, what would the data the he/she would most want to see? What would he dashboard look like?
- What does the CISO want from the board in support of their information security responsibilities?
- What are recommended practices for reporting cybersecurity requirements to the board?
- How should the information be presented?
- What important aspects of cybersecurity and risk should the CISO ensure are conveyed to the board?

In recent years there have been numerous cyber related incidents that have adversely impacted organizations and have affected their brand, stock price, executive leadership, and market share. Unfortunately, as trends have shown over the last five years, these adverse cyber oriented events are increasing and their impact on industries is driving new legislation, regulatory requirements, and the growth of risk-mitigating tools such as cyber liability insurance.

Because of this unstable digital landscape, corporate boards of directors and executive management teams are requiring their CISOs to brief them on the cyber risks the organization currently faces, the status of ongoing security projects, and recommendations for improvement. The growing sentiment by corporate boards and management teams that they must understand cybersecurity has moved the role of CISO into a position of executive visibility which is relatively new for many. One of the frequent complaints about interacting with CISOs is that they are often mired in detail or use technical language or jargon that is difficult to decipher.

Be aware that if you speak to your audience in a manner that is too technical you can lose them and thus lose the opportunity to educate them on the value of your security program.

In closing, we leave you with these five key points and next steps:

1. Boards are elected to represent the true stakeholders in an organization. For publicly-traded companies, this would be the shareholders. The board is expected to exercise its

collective duties of oversight and due care. Simply stated, boards are expected to review the strategy, planning, and execution of executive management and to provide guidance on the organization's risk strategies. For executives with little experience communicating with the board, this can be an intimidating prospect and it might be difficult to capture the key points at the right level. **You should ask your management team to designate a business leader within the organization as a sponsor to help you prepare for your first presentation.**

2. For many board members, cybersecurity is a challenging topic, new in its implications to the organization and distinct in its vocabulary and technology. Board members know that they should be concerned and exercise due care and oversight, but they may simply lack the knowledge, context, or even basic cyber vocabulary to address the issue competently. As the lead cybersecurity professional for your organization, your position brings with it an air of competency and professionalism. You can destroy all of that if you don't understand why you are before the board. **You should work with your sponsor and other members of the executive team to determine what the board is expecting from your presentation to ensure you will meet their expectations.**

3. To build credibility the CISO has to function on the executive team as a trusted teammate. To that end, a key mantra should be "No Surprises!" If you have information within your presentation that might surprise board members, you will need to work with your sponsor and select key board members to share your information with them before you present to the full board. **You should vet key points being made in any board presentation with select board members and impacted executives before your presentation to the full board.**

4. As CISO, you will be the center of an ecosystem — creating metrics to measure your program's effectiveness, producing and managing dashboards to execute strategy, and reporting maturity to executive management. There are multiple strategies to assist you in formulating your narrative as you create your slide deck. Make sure you demonstrate alignment with the organization's strategic plans, use industry common industry benchmarks to allow for comparisons with peer companies and use data to create an objective assessment. **You should validate that your presentation is at a sufficiently high level by previewing it with your sponsor and other select members of the**

executive team.

5.   Presenting before the board of an organization can be a unique opportunity for a CISO who is growing their cybersecurity program. It is a chance for you to articulate the value of cybersecurity in business terms and illustrate how the cybersecurity and risk management programs support the organization's business objectives. **You should recognize the opportunity and ensure you ask for any funding, staffing, board sponsorship, or board access you might need to successfully carry out your role.**

Although preparing to present before an organization's board of directors can be an excruciating trial for a new CISO, you don't have to do it alone. You also need to understand that in truth you are telling a story about how your security and risk mitigation operations are providing value to the organization. Now how that story is told by you and how it is received by executive leadership can be quite different. This is why in today's business environment it is incumbent on you as the CISO to not just champion your cybersecurity program to stakeholders, but understand how your company operates and what changes you may need to make to align your cybersecurity strategy to the corporation's overall business goals.

Chapter 7 – Risk Management and Cyber Liability Insurance

Introduction

In this chapter we will talk about the one fundamental issue that drives most CISOs and influences how they create and manage their security programs. That issue is risk. Our authors will note that there are numerous types of risk facing an organization from both an internal and external perspective. They will also discuss the various components of risk and its impact to an organization when it's not properly managed. The discussions that follow will highlight our authors' unique viewpoints on risk in its disparate forms and how it can be managed through security controls and new tools such as a cyber liability insurance policy.

Our authors collectively believe risk is one of the primary drivers that influences an organization and its ability to be successful. It is because of risk's enterprise-wide impact that our authors believe the modern CISO must understand their organization's industry, regulatory requirements, and strategic initiatives. This business context will provide critical insight for CISOs as they use their security program, policies, tools, and cyber insurance to protect their organization and reduce its risk exposure to an acceptable level.

Bill Bonney highlights the four fundamental approaches that organizations will use to manage their risk. He provides a thorough analysis of how the risk function within the organization has changed due to many of the dynamic threats now facing enterprise business environments. He describes the multitude of ways that risk can impact an organization, and from his in-depth experience provides several options that organizations can use to mitigate risk and its impact to their business operations.

Matt Stamper approaches the discussion of risk through the lens of cyber liability insurance. He breaks down how to view the management of risk through tools like an insurance policy and how this new capability should be leveraged for the organization. In his discussion, Matt emphasizes that for the CISO to consider using cyber insurance, they must have an understanding of the current risks facing the business, the present risk management controls that are in place, and the resultant gaps that need to be addressed. He believes that with this knowledge a CISO is in a better position to help their organization reduce their risk exposure by implementing an appropriate cyber insurance policy.

Gary Hayslip begins his discussion on risk with a pragmatic view that for CISOs to be productive in mitigating the risks facing their organization they first must establish a risk baseline. The CISO must understand what is critical to the organization and must have executive management support to ensure that cyber risk is prioritized correctly. Gary delivers a thorough treatment of cyber insurance and its numerous components and provides recommendations on how cyber liability insurance can be used as an effective tool to protect the organization.

Some of the questions the authors used to frame their thoughts for this chapter include:

- How to I assess my organization's current cybersecurity status? What do I need to protect first?
- What mist my executive team do to ensure that cybersecurity is prioritized in the organization? As CISO, what components and policies must be part of my cybersecurity program to effectively manage risk and keep my executive team informed?
- Should my organization consider cyber insurance to reduce its risk exposure? What is actually covered/not covered in a policy? What types of coverage should my organization consider (first party/third party)?

Risk Management Techniques – Bonney

> "The target list for industrial espionage has expanded as more relative economic value is managed via interconnected computer networks."

We are all familiar with the definition of risk in the context of Information Security. The National Institute of Standards and Technology tells us (NIST 800-30 r1 2012) that "risk is a function of the likelihood of a given *threat-source's* exercising a particular potential vulnerability, and the *resulting impact* of that adverse event on the organization." We're also aware of the four fundamental ways of managing risk: avoid the risk by exiting the business, mitigate the risk with various methods to counter the threat, transfer the risk by contracting for insurance or with partners to share the consequence, and accepting the risk as a natural outcome of doing business. Let's unpack these statements.

A *threat source* is an actor, in a cybersecurity context; these are hackers, hacktivists, industrial spies, malicious insiders, careless users, organized crime, terrorists, and nation states. If, as we discussed in Chapter 1, the role of CISO includes the role of chief resilience officer, then we should add nature and environmental factors to the list of threat sources. Floods, earthquakes, pandemics, power outages, terrorist attacks, and acts of war, for example, are all potential sources of risk.

In order to exercise a particular vulnerability several factors need to line up. The organization must be exposed to that vulnerability, without adequate mitigation, and the threat actor must know (or be able to reasonably guess) that the vulnerability is there. How could a threat actor make a reasonable guess? Pack a malicious payload with multiple, frequently successful exploits, as the Angler Kit does. It uses multiple techniques to infest the target computers and then multiple techniques to gain control. As the criminal underground becomes aware of vulnerabilities, exploit kits such as Angler are updated to include these new attacks.

The *resulting impact* to the organization refers to a step beyond the immediate technical result, such as corrupting the compromised computer's hard drive or establishing a link from the compromised computer to a command and control system outside the organization's network and control for later harvesting. We're interested in the impact to the business. The corrupted files, for example, cause a productivity impact on the staff, or in some cases, impede some functions entirely until the files are decrypted (in the case of ransomware), recovered from backup, or recreated. The infested computer controlled by cyber criminals can be used to collect personal information about customers or employees, commit fraud, expropriate intellectual property, or launch other more devastating attacks. These can be aimed at the organization itself or the assets that are now controlled by cyber criminals can be used or rented out to the highest bidder to conduct malicious acts around the world.

The Changing Risk Landscape

There are a few aspects of this risk function that have changed dramatically over the last few years. Threat sources for most organizations in the past were largely limited to cybercriminals and what the industry referred to as "script kiddies." Script kiddies are basically bored teenagers with access to malicious code and a willingness to apply themselves to mayhem, but no true understanding of the capabilities they were deploying. I say most organizations because militaries and governments, along with large multi-nationals and defense contractors, have long had to contend with nation states, industrial spies, and terrorists.

Over the last few years, nation states, industrial spies, and terrorists have moved "down the food chain" to attack many more targets. They have done so for a number of reasons. The target list for industrial espionage has expanded as more relative economic value is managed via interconnected computer networks. We have also seen an increase in what I call "stepping stone" attacks. Stepping stone attacks involve stealing one piece of data, such as one-time password "salt" keys, from one victim in order to be able to steal something else, like the plans for the F-35 fighter jet, from another. A stepping stone attack makes more members of the value chain attractive targets.

Finally, I would be remiss if I didn't mention the rise of cybercrime syndicates and cybercrime eco-systems that have created a black market for specialized products and talents. Cybercriminals can procure lists of credit cards, collections of user names and passwords, virus kits, exploit kits, and zero-day vulnerabilities. All of these can come complete with customer service, consulting, contract labor for customization, call centers, and boiler pits to "work" the leads (victims).

The example I noted above involved RSA and Lockheed Martin. Cyber criminals carry out similar attacks to obtain social security numbers or PHI (protected health information) from one organization so that fraudulent tax refunds or fraudulent Medicare claims can be filed with another. Because there is more economic value embedded in computer networks, there are more cyber criminals attracted to criminal cyber activity.

Another aspect of the risk function that has changed is the likelihood factor. There are an exploding number of vulnerabilities available to exploit, made possible by a larger and larger number of interconnected systems running heterogeneous and sometimes incompatible hardware and software. The amount of work involved to identify and mitigate these vulnerabilities is daunting for many large companies and overwhelming for most small to medium sized companies. And as I mentioned above, the ability to attack multiple vulnerabilities simultaneously has drastically changed the game.

A third and equally important changing factor in the risk function is the impact that the adverse event can have on the organization. While large companies with significant financial resources have demonstrated the ability to withstand devastating cybersecurity breaches over the last few years and continue as going and growing concerns, the impact can be existential for small to medium sized organizations. In some rare cases, a cybersecurity event can lead directly to the ultimate demise of the organization. For example, DigiNotar, a Dutch certificate authority, was taken over by the Dutch government and subsequently went bankrupt, was sold, and eventually ceased activities as a direct outcome of a cyber breach.

However, impacts far short of the organization's demise can be extremely detrimental. The example of ransomware noted above is certainly disruptive to the organization while the infected hard drive is being recovered. But the fallout from adverse effects such as cybersecurity breaches that involve personal data loss also includes lawsuits, settlements, regulatory investigation and sanction, loss of customers, and worst of all, the distraction of management while the organization recovers from the incident. Time and energy is consumed that is not then available for running the organization to the full benefit of its customers and shareholders.

The point of breaking down the risk function is not to paint a picture of gloom, but to show how the situation has changed over the last few years. In the past, cybercrime affected mostly large companies who often had relatively poorly secured systems. The combination of unsophisticated attack tools, relatively few bad actors (as compared to current numbers) and the natural lag for smaller firms in interconnecting operations skewed the risk function toward larger companies and comparatively smaller losses. In the recent past, "it won't happen to us" or "we can handle that level of loss" were common sentiments. "It won't happen to us" is a statement of the likelihood that a threat source would exploit a potential vulnerability. "We can handle that level of loss" designates the resulting impact as acceptable and not worthy of additional mitigation.

Communicating Risk to Senior Leadership

In trying to educate executives and boards, Information Security professionals focused too much on the technical aspects of the "it won't happen to us" side of the equation, discussing system vulnerabilities and programmatic attacks, without properly setting the context of the business reasons why the likelihood was going up (i.e., the changing risk/reward equation for cyber criminals) and the business impact (for example, disruptions in supply chain) of successful attacks. Without this context, it is very difficult to inspire the changes in behavior required to address the growing risks.

In trying to address this, some Information Security professionals have focused on the ROI of security programs versus the impact of cyber incidents. It is certainly a good idea to focus on ROI, but the calculations are often subject to error. Two contributing factors are misunderstanding the changing values for likelihood as the number of actors, the number of vulnerabilities and the economic incentives of cybercrime continue to alter the discussion from "if we get breached" to "when we get breached," and underestimating the cost in time, focus and money of recovering from an actual breach.

Most Information Security professionals have accepted as axiomatic the near certainty of a breach for well over a decade, but the executive team has only recently been starting to agree. Worse, very few organizations can successfully determine the likely cost to the organization if a breach were to occur. Insurance companies are charging a wide range of premiums for policies, and each new breach brings a new collection of publicly-minded and litigation-prone groups with a point to make. Compensating individuals for the loss of their data, paying the regulator's fines, and replacing credit cards are no longer the largest cost factors.

In addition, there are a number of biases that impact our reasoning when we are less than certain of the outcomes. These biases, such as the status quo bias (taking the current state as a baseline), present bias (valuing current certainties over future uncertain outcomes), and the overconfidence effect (rating ourselves better than objectivity would suggest is warranted) operate against us when we are not certain of our facts or the outcome of our actions. Attempting to explain the risk and the changes in behavior we're advocating in response in a non-technical way often leads to over-simplification, which is reinforced by the media's relentless over-dramatization.

impact, etc.), and the cost to implement additional mitigation. This will help you prioritize the challenging systems and at the same time make the case to a skeptical executive that the certain impact of downtime is a worthwhile investment to mitigate a potentially exploited vulnerability.

Other technical mitigation strategies are often available. Understanding the complete environment in which a system operates, along with good working partnerships with the CIO staff and business teams, can lead to designed solutions that any single group might not have been able to devise on its own. The outcome: reducing the probability of exploitation from a vulnerability to an acceptable level given that the likely impact if successfully exploited is more important than the particular method or group responsible. Work together to get to the outcome; don't get caught up in the "right" way to resolve any particular engineering problem.

In addition to the purely technical mitigation activities, the CISO should employ these soft skills as well:

- Provide leadership and obtain buy-in for cybersecurity programs. The largest single risk factor for cybersecurity is the workforce. A visible cybersecurity program is essential for motivating behavior change throughout the day-to-day activities of the organization's workforce.

- Provide training and education to your team, the executive team and the entire organization's workforce. Everyone should understand their role in both the prevention of cybersecurity incidents and in recovery operations in the event of a cybersecurity incident. This includes routine incidents (such as malware infections and ransomware attacks) and disasters caused by cybersecurity incidents, natural disasters, outages and pandemics. Planning for contingencies is a critical part of risk management. Knowing that the overwhelming likelihood is that you will be breached makes planning to be resilient a business imperative.

- Approach talent management as a risk mitigation strategy and not just an HR function. As I mentioned in Chapter 1, the entire Information Security team should be engaged at their peer level throughout the organization. A key assumption is that your team members have the prerequisite skills and learning agility to help the organization stay on top of the threat environment and are prepared to address incidents as they occur. It is the CISO's job to make sure that is the case.

- Advocate for and obtain proper placement and funding for the Information Security program. Again, in Chapter one I made the point that it is incumbent on the CISO to identify and advocate for a reporting structure that will best position the role for success in the organization. This extends to ensuring that important programs are identified and funded so that vital capabilities are in place.

I turn now to the final two options for risk management: whatever risks we cannot avoid or mitigate we must either transfer or accept. Typically, transfer of risk involves a contract of some sort. To transfer the risk of currency fluctuation, for example, you could purchase a currency hedge. To transfer the risk of running afoul of employment law, you could outsource the performance of certain HR functions to a firm that specializes in the performance of these functions, with explicit guarantees of outcomes compliant with applicable laws and regulations.

Where Does Cyber Liability Insurance Fit?

Transfer of risk is also the foundation of insurance transactions. When you enter into an insurance contract, you take a specific risk, or basket of risks, all spelled out precisely in the insurance contract, and transfer that risk from the policyholder to the insurer in exchange for a premium. It's important to recognize that the only portion of the risk that is being transferred via insurance is the cost. You cannot transfer the risk of an adverse event occurring, but you can transfer certain portions of the monetary impact to the insurance company.

Another important realization is that while there are often questions CISOs field pertaining to cybersecurity as part of the application process for the organization's General Liability insurance, this part of the application is being used by the underwriter to determine if you are taking due care with your information assets as they relate to other business processes. Your General Liability policy usually has exclusions for Internet activity, cyber breach, data loss, etc.

I mentioned above that you cannot transfer the risk of an adverse risk occurring with cyber liability insurance. However, if you partner with your insurance company to go beyond the due diligence of the application process and work to improve your security posture, the process of obtaining and maintaining coverage can have an overall positive effect on your organization's resiliency. Work with an insurance company that has a track record of driving down the occurrence of cyber incidences (not necessarily payouts). The point of the insurance is to transfer a portion of the risk. Reducing the likelihood of the event occurring in the first place pays dividends as well, as you learn from the community that is pooling resources to share the risks (the policy customer base).

Chapter 7 Key Point and Action Item 1

Cyber insurance has become an important tool in the organization's risk management toolbox. Cyber insurance policies may cover both first party and third party expenses and should be evaluated and assessed on their respective coverage limits and sub-limits. Given the complexities of cyber liability coverage, we recommend that you use an insurance broker to help determine which type of policy is appropriate based on the organization's workloads, risk appetite, and budget.

You should review your organization's current cyber liability policy, validate that it is adequate given your recent assessment of the organization's risks, and make any needed updates.

When determining whether or not to purchase cyber liability insurance, review the types of data you hold, and the impact of a cyber event, including business interruption, sanctions and fines, customer damages, court costs, and lawyer fees. Price policies that provide coverage that addresses these potential losses. Make the purchase if you are comfortable with the amount of financial risk you can transfer for the cost of the premiums.

The final option for managing risk is to accept the risks we cannot avoid, mitigate or transfer. There are plenty of valid reasons to "self-insure," and as a prudent risk manager, you should address this question with a data-driven approach. As I mentioned above, there are a number of biases that impact our reasoning when we are less than certain of outcomes. Using a data-driven approach can help your organization avoid falling victim to these biases.

First, for each risk that you decide to accept you should do an impact analysis. Even if it's a relatively high-level analysis, be aware of the impact to the organization if the adverse event occurs. Low probability, low impact risks might be easy decisions and are generally good candidates for risk acceptance, except where compliance is legally mandated. Risks that come with potentially high impacts require more thought and discussion. In those cases, you may choose to implement prudent mitigation strategies and accept the residual risk. While you are reviewing the potential impact of an adverse event, assess whether the organization is prepared to respond if the event occurs. Contingency plans and recovery plans should be in place as appropriate, including having contracts in place for backup facilities and backup data centers.

Chapter 7 Key Point and Action Item 2

Risk management requires the CISO to work and collaborate with individuals across the organization and not just with their colleagues in IT. Knowing the business impacts of the organization's cyber risks will help translate cyber risk into enterprise risk terms. This in turn will help ensure that your cyber risk mitigation requirements are understood by your non-cyber colleagues. Spend time with other departments and learn as much as you can about what systems, processes, and activities are important to their areas and help to qualify and quantify that risk exposure.

You should, within the next 90 days, conduct exercises with the C-suite to assess the organization's cyber risk in this context.

Finally, avoid the trap of allowing the organization to put the burden of risk acceptance entirely on you. Your job is to help the leadership team understand the risks and make thoughtful decisions about the risks to which the organization is exposed.

Beyond the basic cost-per-record metric, the C-suite and board will also want to understand other contractual obligations and associated exposure. To help address this context, working with the organization's legal counsel is invaluable. This contractual review could be tied to specific client and vendor relationships or contracts required by regulation such as the business associate agreement (BAA) used between covered entities and their vendors (business associates) that have access to PHI, as is the case in the healthcare sector. Covenants within these contracts should be evaluated in terms of the overall financial exposure should a cyber event occur. There may be other breach notification clauses related to the stewardship of PII in the organization's possession. Contracts between organizations are not commonly requiring certain minimal security practices and controls to be in place (e.g. the adoption of the NIST framework, ISO 27001, or the Center for Internet Security's Critical Security Controls – formerly the SANS Top 20).

There will also be questions relating to current cybersecurity practices and their effectiveness in mitigating or reducing risk. CISOs will need to provide up-to-date status on how well the overall cybersecurity program is functioning. This update should be complemented with data-flow diagrams (DFDs) showing how sensitive information moves into and out of the organization and which applications and individuals have access to this data. These DFDs, coupled with an accurate record count, will help the C-suite and the board estimate the overall financial exposure to the organization.

Also important in this effort is an understanding of the organization's risk appetite as evidenced in its business impact assessment (the result of this assessment is an understanding of the organization's important processes and its tolerance for data and service interruption, as quantified in the recovery point and recovery time objectives of the organization (RPO and RTO respectively)). The business impact assessment should determine the approach to the organization's business continuity and disaster recovery plans. This context will inform what type of cyber liability insurance (if any) is required and the policy limits that should be established to appropriately protect the organization.

---

indicating that "Small and midsize businesses are ideal candidates for cyber insurance, because they may be less prepared for a data breach and less able to absorb the costs associated with a breach." (McGuire Woods, October, 2, 2013 – L.D. Simmons II).

Risk is diverse. It's important for a CISO to understand the different types of risk (including operational, financial, reputational, security, and privacy) and be familiar with risk-management techniques, including avoidance, mitigation, transfer, and acceptance.

You should ensure that cyber risk is incorporated into the enterprise risk management framework and that as the CISO, you are a key member of the risk management apparatus.

Risks Covered by Cyber Insurance

Let's take a look at the types of risks that cyber insurance is designed to cover. As noted above, breaches are not covered by traditional property insurance and the assets that tend to be most valuable to the organization – its intellectual property, customer lists, price lists, client records, and data – are also not covered. Cyber insurance covers two distinct categories of expenses: first-party expenses (the organization's specific expenses) and third-party claims (the exposure to claims against the organization given a breach or other such incident).

First-party expense coverage is designed to cover those expenses that are directly tied to the organization, including cyber extortion coverage, business interruption coverage, and other business-related expenses associated with the breach. The latter includes items such as the costs of digital forensics and the hard costs associated with breach response (customer notifications, credit monitoring services, increased staffing to field client inquiries – crisis management, if you will).

Third-party expense coverage addresses penalties and regulatory actions related to privacy and security violations resulting from the inadequacy of privacy and security protections within the organization. Third-party coverage may also include content-related issues, including copyright infringements, libel, and slander. Policies generally have coverage limits, with sub-limits for specific first-party and third-party damage. It's highly recommended that a qualified insurance broker assist with validating what's covered and to what extent by the various insurance providers. The cyber insurance marketplace is becoming more competitive, so vetting several providers should be the norm – try to get quotes from at least three carriers.

As part of the policy due diligence, it's important to validate explicit exclusions and effective date clauses. Given how nuanced this type of insurance may be, a given exclusion could be the difference between a policy that has value to the organization and one that should have never been purchased. Similarly, we know that it can take months to discover a breach. Sophisticated attacks are extremely difficult to discover and often go unnoticed for half a year or more. Work closely with the broker to ensure that there is some retroactive date available with the policy.

A good practice is to create a simple matrix that outlines the key variables associated with each policy, including aggregate limits, sub-limits, exclusions, and effective (retroactive) dates along with associated costs. Cyber liability insurance varies in cost of coverages more notably from carrier to carrier than other types of insurance, so really work with your selected broker to vet the options carefully. Caveat emptor has never been more critical than for this type of purchase.

Cyber liability insurance applications have also expanded over the years. Early policy applications were relatively straightforward, suggesting that the complexity and technical nuance of cyber risk was not fully understood by the insurance industry.[24] Applications today can routinely reach 15 to 20 pages and they cover a broad range of cybersecurity issues. Underwriters are seeking to reduce their liability by validating the existence or occurrence of certain cybersecurity practices within the organization. At times, this validation crosses the line by being too prescriptive and consequently losing sight of the actual objective versus the means to achieving that objective.

As a case in point, on one recent application there was a section to capture which security technologies are in place. One of the questions on the application asked if there was a "web application firewall" and the response options were simply "yes" or "no." There was no question regarding whether the web application firewall (WAF) was configured correctly (WAFs typically require a significant amount of tuning as they learn the normal behavior of the applications that they protect) or whether the WAF was protecting applications that are material to the policy's coverage (e.g. an application containing PII, cardholder data, or ePHI).

---

[24]. Unlike other types of coverages where there are actuarial tables that provide very accurate detail on the likelihood of a claim (think life insurance), cyber liability insurance does not benefit from this maturity. There is also the challenge that prescribed activities (security policies, controls, and other actions) have not necessarily translated into reduced risk in the same way that "don't smoke and get exercise" translates into longer and healthier lifespans.

There are similar challenges with other questions that are often asked in policy applications. Cases in point include the existence of a security policy or a disaster recovery plan. The anticipated "yes" response (e.g. the organization has a security policy and a disaster recovery plan) does not provide context on the effectiveness of the plan and the completeness of the policy. Further, a simple yes response does not indicate if the security policy has been reviewed and approved by management, conveyed to all employees, or is current. We'll cover the topic of security policies in Chapter 9.

It Takes a Village

Cyber liability applications require the input of not just the CISO or CIO to address current security and IT practices, but also the input of the Chief Privacy Officer to help validate the extent of the organization's PII, cardholder data, or ePHI record counts. There are also sections within most applications that are clearly in the human resources domain, including questions related to hiring practices, background checks, and training. Some particularly challenging questions relate to known past cyber events. If these incidents have been kept from the CEO, CFO, or another designated officer, they will be known now.

Applications typically require the signature of an executive officer of the organization, and there is also a section that discusses insurance fraud should information knowingly be withheld from the application. The bottom line is that the application requires open and honest collaboration between multiple organizational domains – including human resources, security, IT, vendor management, and privacy departments – to be completed adequately. If you are the CISO of an organization that has a cyber liability policy in place and you were not involved with the application process, this is a serious red flag.

Cyber insurance reflects how our economy has changed over the last few decades. Organizations are increasingly interconnected and reliant upon technologies and vendors. More than ever, digital assets drive the economy. The complexity of our business environment continues to increase as organizations adopt new applications and technologies to improve efficiency, profitability, and time to market. As CISOs, we're focused on mitigating as much of this interconnected risk as we can through the careful use of policies, procedures, controls, and security tools. But we cannot reduce this risk completely, which means that this residual risk must be either accepted or insured or both. Cyber insurance is now one of our most important risk management tools.

Cybersecurity, Risk Management and Cyber Insurance – Hayslip

> "I like to think that organizations come together under the umbrella of cybersecurity, with the board of directors leading the effort."

Across our planet, the Internet is making inroads into every society as technology moves forward in exponential fashion. With this increase in connectivity, we see new business platforms being created and these societies reaping the benefits of access to new business opportunities and services.

However, there is a dimmer view of this amazing growth in technology. With every tool that is used for one's benefit there is always the dark side of how it can be used to one's detriment. This drama of how today's technology is being used against organizations highlights the unique position of the CISO.

The CISO within an organization is the subject matter expert on the dilemma of this dark side. It is incumbent upon the CISO to know the organization's risk exposure to cybercrime, compliance and regulatory issues and new evolving threats. To do this effectively, the CISO must establish an executive-sponsored cybersecurity program, create relationships within their organization's internal and external stakeholder communities, and continuously evaluate their organization for risk and take immediate steps to protect it from harm.

This leads us to the questions we will discuss in this chapter on why CISOs must know their security posture, understand their organization's risk exposure, and look at alternative solutions such as cyber insurance to protect their company and its business interests.

The questions under consideration are:

---

1. How do I assess my organization's current cybersecurity status? What do I need to protect first?
2. What must my executive team do to ensure that cybersecurity is prioritized in the company? As CISO, what components and policies much be part of my cybersecurity program to effectively manage risk and keep my executive team informed?
3. Should my organization consider cyber insurance to reduce its risk exposure? What is actually covered/not covered in a policy? What types of coverage should my company consider (first party/third party)?

You Want Me to Protect What?

As we begin our first discussion, it is incumbent on me to remind you that the CISO is the focal point for an organization's effort to deploy cybersecurity as a service (CaaS) and reduce the company's risk exposure to its current technology portfolio. As previously mentioned, one of the first steps a CISO will take is to establish an executive-sponsored cybersecurity program.

This program will be the platform that a CISO can employ to gain a better understanding of the organization's exposure to technological risk and create a mitigation plan for how to address it based on the organization's business requirements. As it matures, this security program will also provide a foundation for the CISO to pivot from and use new workflows, security controls and technologies to enable the business to understand its risks and its partners' risks and reduce them where appropriate.

So to begin our first discussion, we will talk about cybersecurity and the inherent risk it manages for the business. We will also discuss how the CISO gains visibility into the corporate enterprise environment and how this knowledge will be used for the betterment of the cybersecurity program and the company's strategic business plans. So let's discuss how you, as CISO, will approach this first question and how you should proceed to look for viable answers, *"How do I assess my organization's current cybersecurity status? What do I need to protect first?"*

To begin our discussion, let's first understand what type of risk we are concerned about as a CISO. In our position we must understand *"cybersecurity inherent risk,"* which is the risk posed by an organization's business activities and its connections to partners, as well as any risk-mitigating controls that are currently in place. An organization's cybersecurity risk incorporates the type, volume, and complexity of its cyber operational components. These are the types of connections used by the applications and technology required by the organization to conduct its business operations.

To understand this risk, we must approach the business departments within the organization and gain insight into how they do work. We must understand the applications, data, workflows and technologies that are required by their personnel and any projects they wish to initiate to improve their capabilities. To collect this information quickly and effectively, I would suggest you begin with an enterprise risk assessment. I have completed several of these in the past and would recommend using a framework like the NIST Risk Management Framework or the COSO Enterprise Risk Management Framework. These frameworks will provide you with a solid foundation to begin your discussion about risk within your enterprise.

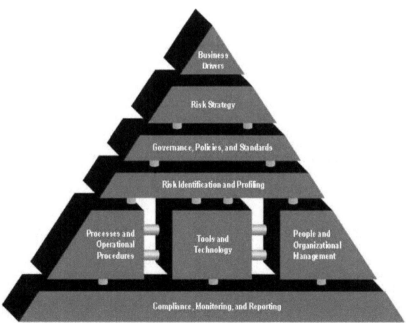

COSO Enterprise Risk Management Framework

As you begin your assessment, there will be components that will require you to directly interact with your various business departments. Use this assessment as an opportunity to begin building the relationships you will need as a CISO. Your stakeholders have critical knowledge about your organization and you will need them to help your program mature and grow a cyber culture within these departments.

So as you work with these stakeholders, you should seek to gain the insight that you will need as a CISO, which is to understand what assets must be protected for the organization to be successful.

Questions for the CISO to Gain Insight to Critical Assets

- Do I understand which applications and services are critical for my organization?
- Do I know what data these critical applications create and where this data is stored and backed up?
- Does my organization have formal agreements with its critical partners that allow us visibility into how they are managing their technology-based risks??
- Does my executive leadership team understand what threats and/or vulnerabilities are being used by our adversaries the target the products the company presently has it its technology portfolio?

As you begin discussions with your stakeholders, there is one crucial point I want you as CISO to pay attention to and document. This critical point is the tone that you and your teams get from these stakeholders for anything associated with your cybersecurity program. Most boards of directors only speak about cybersecurity when there is a breach. If the board is routinely addressing security and senior executive management is sponsoring your security program, you should see the beginnings of cybersecurity awareness taking root in the organization's culture.

However, if this is not the case, it will be harder for you to get true information when conducting your assessment. I bring this point up because it will give you much-needed insight into how you should address your stakeholders and the responses you might receive from them.

As a CISO, I have found in the past that there will be departments that will want to work with me as a partner and departments that will try to ignore me. Those that were partners I treated as equals in the process, and I championed their projects at tech review. I also included their inputs in new security policies and work processes and requested their assistance with my reluctant departments to eventually grow the trust required to conduct a full cyber risk assessment with all departments.

So back to our cyber risk assessment. As CISO you should also review current practices and overall company preparedness. Several critical processes that should be a focus of the risk assessment are:

1. *"Risk Management and Governance"* – this component is about strong governance with clearly-defined roles and responsibilities. There should be assigned accountability to adequately identify, assess, and manage risks across the organization. How well does management account for cyber risk when implementing new technologies? Is there a formal process to review and mitigate issues as required? It is also in this process that we look at our personnel, who are the company's first line of defense. It is here that we address whether the organization is providing cyber awareness training to employees and whether this training is effective in providing employees with an awareness of ongoing cyber risk.

2. *"Threat Intelligence and Collaboration"* – this component is about the processes the business has in place to collect and analyze information to identify, track and predict the intentions and activities of your adversaries. This information can be used to enhance your decision-making capabilities, providing needed visibility into the risks associated with large strategic projects. Participation in information-sharing forums such as: CERT, NIST, InfraGard, MS-ISAC or FS-ISAC are considered critical to the CISO. A key element of the CISO's job is assisting with organizational risk management and the information from these partners is instrumental in the CISO's ability to identify, respond to, and mitigate cyber threats/incidents.

3. *"Security Controls"* – this component focuses on the employment of security methodologies that can be preventive, detective, and/or corrective. Most organizations will use preventive controls, controls that are focused on preventing unauthorized access to enterprise assets. However, a mature cybersecurity program will employ multiple control types, interwoven to provide more resilient coverage against the changing cyber threat landscape. The types of controls that can be deployed to work together are:

   • Preventive Controls – processes such as patch management, encryption of data in transit or at rest. These controls need to be periodically reviewed and updated as the organization's technology portfolio changes.

- Detective Controls – tools that are used to scan for vulnerabilities or anomalous behavior. Some of these controls are anti-virus/anti-malware solutions or new endpoint solutions.
- Corrective Controls – these are controls designed to fix issues. Examples are organizational policies such as change management, patch management, and third-party vendor management.

4. With the deployment of these controls don't forget to ask yourself "what are the processes for implementing them?" Are these security control processes documented and are they periodically reviewed? What are the procedures to mitigate risk identified by these processes? As you can see, controls are like children. They will need to be fed, monitored, cared for and as they mature updated to ensure they effectively provide value to the organization.

5. "*External Third Party Management*" – this component is about the management of connectivity to the business' third party providers, partners, customers, and others. What processes/policies should the company have in place to manage these relationships? Part of this component will be organizational directives that document company policy for executing contracts with third party entities. Does current contract policy spell out what types of connections will be required to corporate networks? Does current contract policy spell out what data will be required and document who will access it? Does current contract policy include as part of the contract a "verification of risk standard" with respect to the external partner's disaster recovery/incident response plans?

6. "*Incident Management*" – this component is critical for the organization. It is focused on cyber incident detection and response, mitigation of identified risks, incident escalation/reporting procedures, and overall cyber resiliency. In the assessment process you will need to identify whether the business has documented procedures for the notification of customers, regulators, and law enforcement in respect to a breach. You will also need to verify that metrics are being collected on this component and its maturity is being periodically reported to senior management. One last essential process that will need to be verified through this risk assessment is "does the organization have documented Disaster Recovery and Business Continuity plans?" In answering this question be sure to verify that the plans have been tested, there are

communication policies in place, and there is a documented process for how trusted third parties are included for effective communications.

As you can see from our discussion so far, in assessing the organization to develop a more thorough understanding of its cybersecurity inherent risk, you will generate an inordinate amount of data. This data will be focused on the essential technology and business process components required by the organization to execute its strategic business plans. This information will be extensive and can be overwhelming, especially if the organization has numerous business verticals and/or international business channels. However, as CISO you now have a decision to make and that is "what do I protect first?" Not all assets are created equally and now it is time to prioritize with your stakeholders which ones require the most protection and the focus of your cybersecurity risk management program.

As CISO, the level of protection you will dedicate for an asset will be based on a process called "asset classification." You will find that organizations tend to overprotect assets and data. In the world of technology, not all data and assets require the same level of protection. As CISO, you will want to understand what assets make up the category of "most valuable assets" as prioritized by the business stakeholders. This means that your stakeholders will assist you in prioritizing what is important to them. A good rule of thumb to help you in this process is to ask "if these assets are stolen, compromised, used inappropriately, or destroyed, would this result in significant hardship to the organization." If the answer is yes, then they are critical assets and will require added protection. Once you have this list you will also need to understand where they are located and, most crucially, who has access to them.

I am sure by now you are wondering what baseline should be used to assist the organization in grading these assets. You know that you will be working with the business' various departments to identify what assets are critical and you have some good questions to ask yourself as you review the data that is collected. However, there is a methodology for determining what is important and requires extra protection. Some steps I would recommend are as follows:

1. *Identify the critical assets and business processes* - following the steps I listed above, work with your stakeholders to create a prioritized list of important assets. Some examples of asset types that fall into this category are trade secrets, market research, trading algorithms, product designs, and R&D research.

2.   *Determine the assets' value to the organization* - "one size fits all" doesn't apply when you are assessing technology, work processes and data types. I gave you some questions to measure the criticality of the assets under scrutiny, however there is also the topic of compliance. You will have asset types that fall into a regulatory/compliance regime and as such they will have laws and fines associated with them. What this means to a CISO is that once you have your prioritized list, you will still need to review it for any items that are governed by compliance and move them towards the top of the list. You will want to ensure your business has visibility on compliance-related assets when they help you set the priorities for this list.

3.   *Determine the risk tolerance of the organization* – once you have identified and ranked the organizations assets, you need to determine how much risk the business is willing to accept. This idea of risk tolerance will be focused around how much protection the business is willing to employ provided it doesn't interfere with its ability to conduct operations. I have found, as CISO, that there will be times where a critical asset will not receive a specific level of protection for fear of degrading a business process. This becomes a risk the organization is willing to accept, and it is one you will need to document and develop other compensating security controls or methodologies to monitor and manage. The key part of this step is listing those assets that have degraded protection, developing compensating controls to mitigate as much risk as possible, and then documenting the residual risk for monitoring and hopefully eventual mitigation.

4.   *Set appropriate levels of protection for each asset type* – This last step is a recommendation for organizations with large numbers of assets. I have used this step to separate my data into asset groups that have already been prioritized in the previous steps. Now with these identified groups, you can establish a level of controls that apply to the specific asset types and you can identify who has responsibility for the assets. With responsibility identified, you can create a matrix of management to document who is responsible for the assets, who can make decisions about whether to accept or mitigate risk, and who will assist you and your teams in remediating any security issues.

One final aspect of identifying what needs to be protected and establishing an appropriate level of security is developing training scenarios for staff to protect their assigned assets. The CISO is expected to not only understand the complexity of risks facing the organization, but know how to quickly mitigate any cyber related is is why you will want to create training scenarios. k previously completed in assessing the organization's turity level and establishing what assets are critical, the v take these training scenarios and include them as an the organizational incident response manual. These .... should be used to test the organization's response to the ongoing list of threats it faces on a daily basis and assist it in improving its business continuity.

Cybersecurity Must Be a Priority, or Is It?

In December 2015, an international survey was completed by the Information Systems Audit and Control Association (ISACA). This survey, titled *"State of Cybersecurity, Implications for 2016"* (ISACA, 2015), had over 461 cybersecurity managers and security professionals respond and confirmed that the rate of cyber incidents continues to grow at an alarming rate and the sophistication of attack methods is evolving. Two interesting statistics from this report that I found particularly daunting were that 75% of respondents reported that they expect their organizations to fall prey to some type of cyberattack this year, and 60% felt their security staffs were not mature enough to handle anything beyond simple cyber incidents.

So I am sure you are asking, "Why is this important?" Well, the reason is that as CISO it is your job to understand the maturity of your organization with respect to cybersecurity. It is also your responsibility to ensure that your organization is prioritizing the risks your security program is designed to manage and if is not, that you have the policies and procedures in place to educate your organization's officers and directors accordingly. This brings us to our next topic of discussion, *"What must my executive team do to ensure that cybersecurity is prioritized in the company? As CISO, what components and policies must be part of my cybersecurity program to effectively manage risk and keep my executive team informed?"*

Corporate laws in every state of the United States impose fiduciary obligations on all officers and directors of companies. To fulfill these obligations, the senior management and board of directors must assume an active role in the governance, management and corporate culture of their respective organizations. In fulfilling these obligations, they must address issues that would put their business at risk. One of the greatest risks they face today is how the organization responds to the threat of cybercrime.

I like to think that organizations come together under the umbrella of cybersecurity, with the board of directors leading the effort, combined with multiple organizational components, including business units, HR, Compliance, finance, internal audit and procurement. Through collaboration with the CISO and his or her team they can effectively execute the organization's cybersecurity Strategy – cybersecurity does not flourish in a vacuum. For this collaboration to happen, it must start at the top with the executive team. This team must demonstrate, through its actions, that cybersecurity is a priority for the business. Some specific actions that a CISO should observe from their board of directors and executive leadership teams that indicate that cybersecurity is a strategic priority are as follows (Foley & Lardner LLP, 2015):

- Executive staff are educating themselves on the risk to the organization from cybercrime.
- Leadership is reviewing the status of the corporate cybersecurity program and requesting periodic updates of its maturity level and the status of any outstanding issues.
- The executive staff is reviewing current security plans and standing policies.
- Leadership is prioritizing cybersecurity projects.
- The board of directors and executive leadership are requesting briefings on incident response and disaster recovery policies and any testing results.
  - They are especially asking for information on how the organization will manage a breach and if this policy has been tested recently.
- Executive leadership and the organization is aware of the risk from current third party relationships and procedures have been put in place to document and mitigate this risk to the organization.
- Policies are in place for the business to document and manage technology risks associated with all new third party relationship decisions.

As the above steps demonstrate, the CISO and his/her team will be involved in assisting company leadership in addressing and reducing the risk of cybercrime. However, even with these steps we need to remember that every organization that uses technology and employs some type of risk reduction controls is still exposed to cybersecurity threats. Because of this evolving exposure, it is essential that business' cybersecurity and risk management programs be integrated into the strategic operations of the company so they minimize any disruptions with respect to cyber incidents. For this type of well-managed program to exist, executive leadership will need to be actively involved and the CISO will need to work with his/her leadership teams to effectively demonstrate a "standard of reasonableness," or as it is known in the legal profession a "standard of care."

What this means to the CISO and executive team is a legal determination that the organization is conducting a cybersecurity risk reduction program with applicable standards of care and best practices to reduce its risk exposure. This is important, because we know as cybersecurity professionals that breaches will occur; however, with an engaged executive team and a mature cybersecurity program we can demonstrate that the organization is taking all reasonable steps to protect itself and the interests of its stakeholders.

Understand that in the triage of a breach cleanup many of the organization's steps to prioritize cybersecurity will be evaluated to determine if the organization committed appropriate financial, technical, and human resources to the cybersecurity and risk management programs. The answer to these questions are critical. They could either lead to proper payments from the organization's cyber insurance policies or the opposite, lawsuits from partners and/or customers who seek to recover from losses generated by the resultant cyber incident.

Chapter 7 Key Point and Action Item 4

CISOs need to express cyber risk in business-accessible terms. As our authors note, describing threats and vulnerabilities in technical jargon will almost assuredly result in the message being lost on the recipients. Make sure that everyone understands the organization's current risk environment even if there is disagreement on approaches to minimizing that risk. Remember that it's a contact sport.

You should schedule a briefing with senior leadership and ideally the board of directors to review the findings of both the threat modeling and risk assessment exercises.

The scenario above and how it is coupled with executive leadership engagement and a properly prioritized cybersecurity program demonstrates one side of an ecosystem that is required for a CISO to be effective in managing his/her organization's cyber risk. The other side of this evolving ecosystem is directly controlled by the CISO and is focused on the very components that they have deployed to build their security program. Does their program follow standard "cyber hygiene" recommendations from security/risk management frameworks such as NIST, ISO, and COBIT? Have certain standard policies or procedures not been implemented due to the impact on business operations?

Truthfully, the answer to these questions will demonstrate the maturity level of the cybersecurity program and the organization's support of its cyber and risk management programs. Either way, a CISO should know which components are essential for a mature cybersecurity program and which policies they should have in place to manage it. Some components and policies that are recommended are as follows (Foley & Lardner LLP, 2015):

1. *Components* – essential processes or procedures that an effective cybersecurity program will use as a template to reduce risk.

    - Incident Management
    - User Education and Awareness
    - Identity and Access Management
    - Remote and Mobile Working
    - Removable Media Controls
    - Malware Protection
    - Scanning/Monitoring
    - Secure Configuration
    - Network Security
    - Cyber Insurance

2. *Core Policies* – this is the basic set of strategies for how your cybersecurity program will incorporate the components listed above into documented step-by-step guidelines. Your teams and organization will use these policies to measure your program's effectiveness in reducing risk and providing value to the organization.

    - Cybersecurity Policy, also known as Information Security Policy
    - Acceptable Use Policy
    - Back-up/Disaster Recovery/Business Continuity Policy
    - Mobile Computing/Remote Access Policy
    - Bring Your Own Device/Use of Personal Assets Policy
    - Employee Education and Training Policy (focused on Cyber Awareness and Compliance Training)
    - Incident Response Policy
    - Social Media Acceptable Use Policy
    - Vendor Due Diligence and Contracting Policy
    - Data Governance Policy
    - Use of Cloud Technologies Policy

As we close this discussion there are a couple of things I want to touch on to bring everything that we have learned together. Risk management is the coordinated management of information, technology and business operations to productively manage the organization's digital assets and prevent unwanted consequences.

New Solutions to Manage Risk

Cyber risk management, on the other hand, is a very complex issue. It requires executive management's engagement, ongoing governance and risk management, an effective cybersecurity program, and organizational collaboration. The ultimate goal for cyber risk management is for the organization to operate at a high level of "cyber resiliency." When an organization's cyber risk management program operates at this high level, you as a CISO will see cyber incorporated into the organization's culture and business operations.

You will also see that while "cyber resiliency" doesn't completely eliminate risk, it does allow the executive team to make informed decisions that will help avoid concerns such as financial damage, negative publicity or loss of customer/partner trust in the event of a cyber incident. As CISO, you will also understand that for cyber resiliency to be effective, you must have a solid cybersecurity program in place that is based on best practice "cyber hygiene" policies and procedures that provide your team and organization a solid foundation to manage its cyber risk portfolio.

Chapter 7 Key Point and Action Item 5

Threat modeling is a highly valued skill. The organization's business impact assessments help define which business processes, applications, and systems are integral to the organization. Once these have been defined and their organizational value is understood, think imaginatively about how these systems would be compromised and attacked.

You should schedule and conduct a high-level threat modeling exercise with senior leaders to ensure the business perspective is incorporated into the risk management program.

As previously stated, it is incumbent upon the organization's board of directors and executive management to educate themselves on the complexities of risk associated with cybercrime. They must also educate themselves on the approaches risk professionals advocate to reduce the organization's exposure to risk. One relatively new risk reduction methodology for cybercrime is cyber insurance. For our final point of discussion, we will consider cyber insurance and whether it is an effective approach for cyber risk management. The questions under consideration are as follows: *"Should my organization consider cyber insurance to reduce its risk exposure? What is actually covered/not covered in a policy? What types of coverage should my company consider (first party/third party)?"*

Main Costs to the Organization from a Cybercrime Incident

- Loss of business due to critical assets damaged, impact on organization's business operations.
- Customer/partners leave, organization's reputation and brand damaged.
- Cost to restore critical assets that were affected by the incident.
- Cost of resources required to manage the incident and resolve any findings.
- Cost of possible fines, lawsuits, regulatory actions if compliance-related assets were involved.

For today's businesses, it is no longer a matter of whether they will be hacked, rather it is a question of whether they will have cyber insurance in place to assist them in mitigating the damage as they recover from an incident. In 2015, IBM sponsored a research document from the Ponemon Institute titled "2015 Cost of a Data Breach: Global Analysis" (IBM & Ponemon, 2015). This report found that the costs associated with the increasing number of cyber incidents continue to rise. The total costs to an organization for each breach are now averaging $3.79 million, up from $3.52 million in 2014. This report also documented that 79% of the "C-level" respondents to the Ponemon survey believe executive-level involvement is necessary and 70% believe board-level oversight is critical. This report documented that the main costs to the organization from a cybercrime incident.

As malicious cyber activity becomes the norm, companies are looking at alternative methods to reduce their organization's risk exposure. As mentioned previously, one method is transferring some of this risk through a cyber insurance policy. Companies that store data such as PII or PHI face significant losses in the case of a data breach due to "notification laws." Cyber insurance can help an organization mitigate the costs of notifying affected clients/customers, and it can be used for forensics and breach response costs as well.

In September 2014, Home Depot was hacked by cyber criminals who used a third party vendor's account credentials to gain access to the company's network. Over several days, the hackers moved within the corporation's network and in the end information on over 53 million credit cards and debit cards was stolen. The total cost to Home Depot to resolve this breach included the costs of notifying 53 million customers, the forensic costs of investigating how the breach occurred, and the costs to upgrade their networks and cybersecurity program. This total cost was $252 million. Interestingly enough, Home Depot had over $100 million in cyber insurance (Greenwald, 2014) to assist them with reducing these costs.

Some key provisions and terms that will assist you in the following discussion on cyber insurance are as follows:

Trigger – Loss/Claim: cyber policies are triggered by either a loss of data or a claim. The claim comes from an event experienced by the organization and reported to the insurance company.
- o *Claim type policies* are more restrictive in terms of events that could trigger the coverage of the policy.
- o *Loss type policies* are preferable; however, the cost of coverage will be higher.

Trigger – Defense: cyber policy where there is a "defense" obligation triggered by a suit/claim.
- o Requires a lawsuit or written demand against the insured (the organization).
- o May preclude reimbursement for defense of a claim that has not evolved into a lawsuit or written demand.
  - ▪ You would want less restrictive defense language.
  - ▪ In some cyber policies the "suit limitation" doesn't apply to government action/investigations.

Defense – Choice of Counsel: in some cyber policies, defense costs are only covered to a certain extent, and the insured is required to choose from a list of insurers' "panel" of law firms.
- o Substantial costs involved with significant data breach.
  - ▪ Insured would ideally have input in selecting choice of counsel.
  - ▪ Should look for policies with more balanced choice of counsel language.
    - • Insured/insurer will initially agree on counsel, if they cannot, the insured selects who they wish and insurer pays up to a specific amount.

Retroactive Coverage: losses arising from events prior to the retroactive date will not be covered.

- Insurers often fix the retroactive date at the initial date of coverage.
  - May be able to negotiate a date further back in time, but this will be at significant cost due to the risk to the insurer.

Acts and Omissions of Third Parties: acts/omissions of third parties may not be fully covered or may be excluded.
- Some cyber policies provide coverage for breaches of data between the insured and third parties (typically you will have a written services agreement between the insured and the vendor).
- If the organization has sensitive data retained by a third party vendor (e.g., cloud storage)
  - Seek a policy that expressly covers breaches of data maintained by third parties.

Coverage of Unencrypted Devices: many policies exclude coverage for data lost from unencrypted devices. Coverage without this requirement is preferable.

Coverage for Corporations and Other Entities: cyber policies define "covered persons" for liability purposes as a "natural person." However, entities affected by data breaches can be corporate and business entities. Ensure coverage properly defines the scope of entities affected by a data breach.

Policy Territory – Occurrence Outside Country: insured may not have operations outside of their home country. What happens if an employee loses their laptop or device while traveling abroad?
- Policies may restrict applicable coverage territory to home country and its territories.
  - As CISO you should verify that your coverage is not this restrictive.
- Some cyber policies may only cover data loss if it was electronic data, versus paper printouts or reports.
  - Ensure coverage is for a data breach that involves both electronic and non-electronic records.

Location of Security Failure: coverage for some policies is only for theft of data from company premises.
- This could be an issue if you have theft of data from a laptop at an airport.
- Some policies also limit coverage of data breaches from password theft to situations where credentials have been obtained through only non-electronic means.

- This doesn't take into account the theft of credentials online and leveraging them for access.
- Organization should assess these limitations; I would be wary of them because they don't take into account the new threats companies are facing today.

Exclusions for Generalized Acts or Omissions: some policies may exclude coverage for losses arising from:
- Shortcomings of the security program which the insured was aware of before purchasing the policy.
- Insured's failure to take reasonable care.
  - Follow best practices to design, maintain, and upgrade security program and respective architecture.
- Exclusions for this issue can be overly broad and lack adequate definition. They can be potentially subject to how the insurer wants to apply them.
  - Suggest they be limited appropriately through negotiation or removed entirely.

Exclusions for Acts of Terrorism or War: common type of exclusion added to policy.
- Unclear the extent to which insurer will want to leverage this exclusion if cyber incident is due to a foreign nation or hostile foreign organization.
- The breadth of this exclusion should be negotiated. If that's not feasible, it is recommended that the organization consider alternative secondary insurance coverage.

So with these terms in mind, let's talk about why a company may wish to purchase cyber insurance. To begin, it is recommended that organizations first proceed to establish a mature cybersecurity program and then conduct an enterprise-wide security assessment. Once you have this assessment, you then look at cyber insurance to reduce the residual risk left after the employment of security controls. What this means to the CISO is that you will be working with your organization's Chief Risk Officer or Director of Risk Management to identify which residual risks cannot be mitigated through your security program and are thus good candidates for a cyber insurance policy. Understand that cyber insurance is not a substitute for making smart investments in cybersecurity and following best practices. Cyber insurance is just one of many resources a company can employ to reduce its exposure to risk and there are several reasons why an organization should consider cyber insurance, as follows (Lockton Affinity, 2015):

- *Data is the organization's most important asset* – An organizations standard property insurance doesn't cover digital assets like data. Cyber insurance provides comprehensive coverage for data restoration.

- *Critical systems downtime is not covered by standard business interruption policy* – Cyber insurance covers loss of profits due to system outages caused by "non-physical" perils such as a virus or DDOS attack.

- *Cybercrime is not covered by standard property or crime insurance policies* – Businesses are connected to the Internet and as such exposed to digital crimes such as phishing scams, identity theft and social hacking. These types of crimes are not covered under traditional insurance policies; however, cyber insurance provides coverage for a wide range of electronic crimes.

- *Company held liable if they lose third party data* – An organization holds data that belongs to customers, partners, and suppliers. NDAs and contracts with these external parties can contain warranties and indemnities in relation to how the organization secures their data. If the organization experiences a breach, this event could trigger expensive damage claims.

- *Severe penalties if the company loses credit card data* – Credit card crime continues to accelerate; risk is being transferred to the retailers that lose data. Under merchant service agreements, compromised merchants can be held accountable for forensic investigation costs, credit card reissuance costs, and actual fraud conducted on stolen credit cards. Cyber insurance can help mitigate these claims.

- *Complying with breach notification laws costs time/money* – New breach notification laws are being introduced across the globe. They typically require the business that lost the sensitive data to provide written notification to the affected individuals. There is a growing trend amongst organizations that have been hacked to "voluntarily" notify in order to protect their brand/reputation. Customers who have had their data compromised expect openness/transparency from the organization with whom they entrusted their data. Cyber insurance policies can provide coverage for the costs associated with breach notification.

- *The reputation of the business is its #1 asset, why not insure it?* – Businesses survive by their reputation, and there are reputational risks that can't be insured. However, you can insure your reputation in the case of a cyber incident. Cyber insurance can help pay for the cost of hiring a public relations firm to help restore the organization's reputation.

- *Social media usage is quickly increasing as are the claims associated with it* – Social media is the fastest growing entertainment channel in the world, with little control exercised over what is said and how it is presented. This use of social media increases the liability for businesses responsible for their employees and what they say on social media sites. Cyber insurance can provide coverage for claims arising from leaked corporate information, defamatory statements and copyright infringement.

- *Portable devices increase the risk of loss/theft* – With the increasing use of portable devices, it is becoming easier to steal or lose sensitive data. Devices such as USB thumb drives, laptops, and tablets are being targeted with a growing number of malware payloads. Cyber insurance can help cover the cost of a breach caused by the theft of a device.

As you can see, there are multiple reasons why organizations should look at purchasing a cyber insurance policy to mitigate the liability of their exposure to cyber risk. With that said, there are some issues a CISO should keep in mind when discussing the possibility of using a cyber insurance policy as part of his/her cyber risk portfolio. One of the biggest issues is that policies are sold under a number of names such as "cyber risk," "information security," and "privacy or medical liability" coverage.

There is also no set standard for cyber insurance policies. In fact, most policies currently on the market are a combination of traditional liability coverage and protection against claims from third parties. Remember that as CISO you will need to help educate your organization that cyber insurance is not a cure all. Basically, you cannot expect to secure every available security gap with cyber insurance coverage. So now that I have really depressed you, it's actually not that bad.

The market for cyber insurance is maturing and insurance companies are starting to offer policies with coverages that can be adjusted to address unique business situations. We should discuss these coverages next because as the CISO for an organization, you will need to understand the important features of both third party and first party cyber insurance coverage (Raptis, 2015), and you should also understand their limitations.

A quick note on the definitions of third party versus first party for those of you who are new to purchasing insurance. Liability insurance is purchased by the organization (first party) from the insurer (second party) for protection against the claims of another (third party). So organizations can purchase cyber insurance for themselves, internally, and for protection against claims from external third parties.

The coverage and features commonly offered for _third party cyber insurance_ are as follows:

- _Privacy Liability Coverage_ – liability to insured customers, clients and employees if there is a breach and loss/damage of private information.
    - The organization should seek to have the trigger (activation) language of the insurance policy focus on the insured's failure to protect confidential information, regardless of cause, versus language which could state "intentional breach." This is because the definition of intentional breach is vague and breaches can be caused by numerous issues.
    - Insurance Policy should provide coverage for insured's failure to disclose a breach in accordance with applicable breach notification laws.
    - Insurance Policy should provide defense from the earliest stages of investigation, should include requirements for civil investigative demand (request from civil authorities, regulators, government).

- _Regulatory Action_ – there is substantial variation among cyber insurance policies regarding what is covered with respect to regulatory or government action.
    - Some policies require that a formal suit be initiated before a "trigger of coverage."
        - This can be problematic because it would preclude reimbursement for defense of the investigative stage (forensic investigation) of a regulatory/government action.
        - This is typically the most expensive stage for an organization under investigation. It's after this is done that the regulatory/government entity would possibly file a formal complaint, which would then "trigger" coverage.
    - Policies that include defense from the earliest stages of investigation are preferable.

- o Civil fines/penalties are covered under most cyber insurance policies.
    - ▪ Pay attention if the insurer seeks to exclude these specific coverages.

- *Notification Costs* - breach laws are constantly evolving; these are the costs of notifying third parties potentially affected by a data breach.
    - o Coverage is included in most cyber insurance policies.
        - ▪ Many policies limit the number of persons that may be notified and the methods of notification.
        - ▪ Some policies may vest some control over the notification process with the insurer.

- *Crisis Management* – coverage should include the cost of managing the public relations fall out of a data breach.
    - o Most policies have some form of coverage for this.
        - ▪ May require the insured to choose from a list of vendors provided by the insurer.

- *Call Centers* – this portion of a cyber insurance policy may be covered within the notification or crisis management coverages. This coverage can be purchased separately. Be advised that this tends to be one of the highest costs in a data breach investigation.
    - o Is this coverage included? Are there specific limitations?
        - ▪ Limitation on the number of affected people who are eligible to receive call center services.
        - ▪ Hours/locations of call center, specific services the call center will provide.

- *Credit/Identity Monitoring* – included in most cyber insurance policies, will typically state that it is limited to the number of affected people who can receive services and the insured may be required to pick from a prescribed list of vendors provided by the insurer.

- *Transmission of Viruses/Malicious Code* – coverage protects against liability claims alleging damages from transmission of viruses and other malicious code/data. Not all policies will have this coverage, so before requesting it you need to consider how likely it is that your systems could be a source of this type of liability.

- The coverage and features commonly offered for *first party (internal) cyber insurance* are as follows:

  o *Theft and Fraud Coverage* – covers certain costs with respect to the theft/destruction of the organization's data and the theft of the organization's funds.

  o *Forensic Investigation* – covers the cost of determining the cause of the loss of data.

  o *Network Business Operation* – covers the cost of business loss and additional costs due to the interruption of the company's computer systems.
    - Some policies may state the interruption must be caused by an "intentional cyber-attack."
      - This is not recommended because interruptions can be caused by internal staff due to maintenance, mistakes or by the use of legacy equipment.
    - Some policies may have limitations on interruption coverage.
      - Interruption must last a specific time period before trigger of coverage.
      - Total length of coverage calculated after the trigger goes into effect.
    - Be sure that you understand when your trigger goes into effect. If you need to adjust this, it may require negotiation and added expense. Calculate the cost to the organization without it.

  o *Extortion* – covers the cost of "ransom" if third party entities demand payment to refrain from releasing information to the public or causing damage to the organization's critical digital assets.

  o *Data Loss Prevention* – included in some cyber insurance policies, covers the cost of restoring data that is lost and diagnosing/repair of the cause that precipitated the loss.
    - This will have some limits on the size of data to recover.
    - This will also have limits on the cause of data loss that the policy will pay to repair.

In comparing these policy types, you can see that third party coverage has many exceptions that you, as CISO, must be aware of and understand. I would suggest that you have the company's cyber insurance policy reviewed by in-house counsel to ensure you are properly covered for those risks that you are unable to mitigate with your cybersecurity program. Remember that cyber insurance is a good tool to transfer some of the organization's residual risk. However, it will rarely cover the full loss of critical assets like intellectual property or the disruption of critical supply chains required for business operations. Cyber insurance policies will also rarely cover data breaches that are part of a cyber war campaign by state actors/terrorists nor will they cover the full losses due to a compromise caused by an employee-owned device (BYOD coverage may be negotiated).

As we draw our conversation to a close, what I'd like you to recognize is that in order to effectively scope what coverage is required for cyber insurance, you will need to go back to the beginning. At the beginning, as the CISO for the organization, you were required to assess what assets were important to your stakeholders and prioritize them with respect to your stakeholders' business requirements. Next, you did a risk assessment on these identified assets and you evaluated the company's board of directors and executive staff with respect to cybersecurity and their understanding of cyber risk. Finally, you conducted an impact analysis and with input from your stakeholders you gained insight into the risks facing the organization and the potential shock of these risks to business operations.

As CISO, you identified which risks could be mitigated by your cybersecurity program and which residual risks were candidates for transfer via a corporate cyber insurance policy. As CISO, you also learned the differences in policy coverage and which exclusions the organization should remove or negotiate for better terms. This whole process of risk inventory, organizational assessment, asset prioritization, security scanning, monitoring and risk remediation is the cybersecurity lifecycle. As the CISO, you are responsible for implementing it, maintaining it and collaborating with stakeholders to grow it throughout the organization with the end goal of enhancing business operations by reducing risk and providing the visibility the board and executive staff need to make effective strategic decisions.

Summary

In Chapter 7 we began our discussion by asking these three questions:

- If the CISO were a board member, what would the data the he/she would most want to see? What would he dashboard look like?
- What does the CISO want from the board in support of their information security responsibilities?
- What are recommended practices for reporting cybersecurity requirements to the board?
- How should the information be presented?
- What important aspects of cybersecurity and risk should the CISO ensure are conveyed to the board?

Each of our authors looked at cyber risk management as a subset of overall enterprise risk management practices and emphasized the business and regulatory context of the cybersecurity program. Indeed, it's this organizational or business context that should inform cyber risk management practices and their specific policy guidelines.

In closing, we would like to leave you with these five key points and next steps:

1. Cyber insurance has become an important tool in the organization's risk management toolbox. Cyber insurance policies may cover both first party and third party expenses and should be evaluated and assessed on their respective coverage limits and sub-limits. Given the complexities of cyber liability coverage, we recommend that you use an insurance broker to help determine which type of policy is appropriate based on the organization's workloads, risk appetite, and budget. **You should review your organization's current cyber liability policy, validate that it is adequate given your recent assessment of the organization's risks, and make any needed updates.**

2. Risk management requires the CISO to work and collaborate with individuals across the organization and not just with their colleagues in IT. Knowing the business impacts of the organization's cyber risks will help translate cyber risk into enterprise risk terms. This in turn will help ensure that your cyber risk mitigation requirements are understood by your non-

cyber colleagues. Spend time with other departments and learn as much as you can about what systems, processes, and activities are important to their areas and help to qualify and quantify that risk exposure. **You should, within the next 90 days, conduct exercises with the C-suite to assess the organization's cyber risk in this context.**

3. Risk is diverse. It's important for a CISO to understand the different types of risk (including operational, financial, reputational, security, and privacy) and be familiar with risk-management techniques, including avoidance, mitigation, transfer, and acceptance. **You should ensure that cyber risk is incorporated into the enterprise risk management framework and that as the CISO, you are a key member of the risk management apparatus.**

4. CISOs need to express cyber risk in business-accessible terms. As our authors note, describing threats and vulnerabilities in technical jargon will almost assuredly result in the message being lost on the recipients. Make sure that everyone understands the organization's current risk environment even if there is disagreement on approaches to minimizing that risk. Remember that it's a contact sport. **You should schedule a briefing with senior leadership and ideally the board of directors to review the findings of both the threat modeling and risk assessment exercises.**

5. Threat modeling is a highly valued skill. The organization's business impact assessments help define which business processes, applications, and systems are integral to the organization. Once these have been defined and their organizational value is understood, think imaginatively about how these systems would be compromised and attacked. **You should schedule and conduct a high-level threat modeling exercise with senior leaders to ensure the business perspective is incorporated into the risk management program.**

CISOs are quickly becoming an extension of the organization's risk management team and, depending upon the industry in question, the CISO may actually function as the organization's Chief Risk Officer. CISOs should embrace this role. It broadens their perspective on their organization and their industry, and facilitates greater cooperation and collaboration with their peers. Be comfortable with and embrace good risk management.

Chapter 8 – Tools and Techniques

Introduction

In Chapter 8, our authors discuss their views on the use of tools and critical strategies and techniques that the CISO can use to validate an organization's security controls. Each of our authors will provide guidance on how they have used specific tools and techniques and will examine the importance of understanding a tool's role with respect to risk and providing actionable information. All of the authors emphasize the importance of collaborating with stakeholders to select the best approach for deploying new critical processes and the use of tools to measure their maturity.

Through the aggregate of their different approaches, they provide the new CISO a unique opportunity to understand the importance of tools and critical strategies to an organization and their detrimental impact to business operations if not implemented correctly.

Bill Bonney approaches this discussion of tools and techniques for CISOs by focusing on inherent business processes and deployed technology. He advocates that the CISO must conduct an inventory of tools used to support critical business objectives and that the enterprise should focus on building a mature process portfolio. Bill makes the case that with a mature process portfolio and the required tools to measure their impact, the business will be more secure through the use of proper security controls.

Matt Stamper starts his discussion with the statement that common sense is one of the best tools a CISO can use to protect their organization. He states that with common sense and some context on the processes/techniques the tools are used to serve, the CISO can provide better service to the company versus purchasing a new technology. Matt makes the case that through the use of tools such as a Business Impact Assessment (BIA), the CISO can collaborate with his/her fellow stakeholders to understand the organization's risks, resulting in a selection of techniques and tools more finely tuned for its strategic business operations.

Gary Hayslip begins his discussion with a list of best practices he has compiled over the years that an organization and a mature cybersecurity program should use to reduce risk exposure. Gary then provides a list of recommended techniques a CISO and the security program should use to sustain a more business-centric "cybersecurity as a service" to the company. He concludes his discussion by listing and describing the various domains of common tools that are available to organizations and their security programs to protect enterprise assets.

Some of the questions the authors used to frame their thoughts for this chapter include:

- What best practices would I recommend that new CISOs implement to reduce risk and provide value to their business?
- What actions or techniques can the security program proactively take to better protect organizational assets and preempt threats?
- What are some core tools/solutions that I would recommend to a new CISO to support cybersecurity operations?

Tools and Techniques – Bonney

> "The discipline to think in horizons helps you to
> construct layers of protection and the permission
> for your team to experiment and learn will help
> you amplify the impact of your efforts."

In this chapter we're going to cover tools and techniques with an equal emphasis on both process and technology. The temptation among those of us in the technical fields is to think tools first. While tools are often helpful in solving various process problems, especially by using automation, an over-reliance on tools is often expensive and usually decreases the effectiveness of any given program. The outcome of working through this chapter should be a roadmap that will allow you to right level your processes for your current requirements and build a technology roadmap for your future needs.

Build the Process Inventory

We're going to start with an important data-gathering step. Whether inheriting a mature program or building a new program, the key first steps are to document your process inventory, and take an inventory of the tools your organization uses to assist with each process. It's fundamental that you focus first on your process inventory, understanding how these processes map to your organization's business objectives. Make sure you understand specifically what you are protecting, and from what threats. Know how are you reporting effectiveness of these processes to management and communicating expectations to your entire organization. It's important to keep these points in mind as you inventory your tools and map that inventory to your process inventory.

To make sure you get a complete list, use the same information security framework you use for measuring and reporting. In Chapter 5 on measuring and reporting, I listed several options for security frameworks and standards that you can use to determine where you need to have processes and controls in place. PCI-DSS with its 12 high-level requirements and 300+ detailed requirements is a necessary standard for any portions of your network that handle payment card data. Likewise, NIST 800-53 with its 18 security control families and detailed implementation guides provides a wonderful blueprint for a robust collection of processes. Finally, the CISSP 8 Practice Domains and CIS Critical 20 Security Controls would provide any nascent or recovering program with an inventory of critical must-have processes with which to build a solid program. Any of these will help you create a baseline of processes upon which you can build your inventory and perform your assessment.

Chapter 8 Key Point and Action Item 1

Leverage frameworks and standards such as the NIST Cybersecurity Framework and/or the Center for Internet Security's Critical Security Controls to establish a roadmap to baseline your current security practices and controls.

You should formally select an information security framework that reflects your organization's industry and is best suited to baseline your process maturity.

For each process, you should uncover activities, organized into procedures and described as work instructions, along with metrics for measuring effectiveness and the roles that individuals will play in those processes. Mature, well-documented processes will also describe opportunities for improvement. Wherever activities, procedures or work instructions call out an interaction with a tool, which can be commercially purchased (referred to as COTS or Commercial Off the Shelf), licensed as a SaaS (Software as a Service) offering, a personal productivity application such as MS Excel, or a homegrown tool, that should be recorded in your tools inventory.

In many cases you'll have more than one process that relies on the same tool and you'll often have several tools that are used for a single process. Make sure you note these inter-relationships, because they will be important later when you are forced to make decisions about how to allocate your scarce resources. It's also important to note that some tools that play a part in processes that you own, in whole or in part, are not actually owned or possibly even administered by the Information Security team. Finally, remember to include tools you use purely for reporting or governance activities in addition to your prevention and detection tools you use to protect your organization from threats.

Because we technologists so often place so much of our faith in tools, we often miss the importance of people and process in producing any business outcome. For this reason, I recommend that you seek out people within your operations teams who must bridge the gaps between what your tools produce and the outcomes the business requires. Also sit down with your auditors, internal and external, to understand how they audit key IT processes and your organization's contractual performance. Regardless of the tools in place, the work must get done and the operations personnel and audit community know how tools are used, augmented and worked around. Looks for gaps, ask about what is not covered, and determine what is done manually.

Once that you have your process portfolio documented and you know what tools you have, which processes they are used for, and who owns and administers them, you are ready for the next steps. Now you will assess the effectiveness of your processes and assess the suitability of your tools to your processes.

The Capability Maturity Model

In chapter 2 I described two different methods for rating your processes. Using the Capability Maturity Model Integration (CMMI) would allow you to rate your processes on a maturity scale of 0 through 5 (for non-existent through fully optimized). While you can certainly do a more detailed assessment using the ISO 27K framework, NIST 800-53 Standard, CISSP 8 Practice Domains, or CIS Critical 20 Security Controls and conducting performance testing, and should to continue improving your performance over time, I think the CMMI assessment is ideally suited for the process inventory/tools mapping task. The approach I recommend is to do a maturity assessment using the descriptors for CMMI maturity levels.

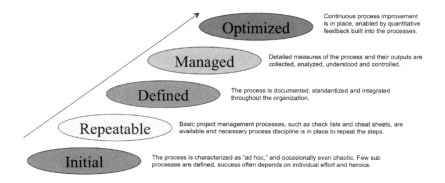

	Level 1 Initial	Level 2 Repeatable	Level 3 Defined	Level 4 Managed	Level 5 Optimized
Process	Ad hoc, informal	Semi-formal process, business unit specific	Defined processes are consistent across business units	Formal and intergrated	Mature and optimized
Metrics	Basic information is collected	Basic metrics, informal reporting	Defined metrics, manual reporting	Advanced metrics and semi-automated reporting	Fully automated reporting
Tools	Some templates or checklists exist	Manual remediation	Remediation automated	Automated prevention	Integrated with threat intelligence

A common mistake at this point, after you have done your inventory and completed your assessment, is to be overly aggressive with respect to desired maturity. Keep in mind that not every process needs to be fully optimized and the "right" level of maturity for any process depends entirely on the organization's risk environment. A small company with low staffing turnover may find a 2.5 rating for onboarding completely adequate, whereas a large company with significant hiring or staff turnover may need onboarding operating at a 4.5 maturity level to avoid unacceptable risk, avoidable idle time, and undue cost.

With that in mind, review the inventory of processes and your CMMI assessments and determine the desired maturity level for each process based on your organization's risk environment. Perform this at the holistic level, i.e., not at the metrics or tools level, but at the process level. Once this is complete, for each process that currently rates below the maturity your organization requires, determine if you need managerial support (perhaps to effectively evangelize the process to additional business units, either by education, mandatory adoption, or awareness using better metric collection and reporting) or if you need to improve the skills sets of the people executing the process or to update the tools your team is using.

Organizational size, complexity, and maturity have significant and material impact on the organization's techniques. As we note throughout, "security doesn't exist in a vacuum." This situational awareness of the organization's capabilities has a profound influence on how cybersecurity programs are implemented within organizations. It is important that your organization clearly understands the maturity and capabilities of the cybersecurity program.

You should create a maturity model to baseline your current practices vis-à-vis your organization's size, complexity, and industry and review this baseline analysis with senior leadership and the board of directors.

Line Up to Your Business Plan

The final step in building your process and technology roadmap is to review your organization's 1-3-5-year business plan and assess how your Information Security processes need to mature to support that plan.

What you have in hand now is a roadmap for improving your process portfolio to achieve the capability you need today as well as what you must plan for in the future. Once again, as technologists, we might be tempted to sit down with a few trusted vendors and start listing requirements for RFPs and pilot projects. And once again I suggest taking a different approach. Look first at each of the processes that don't operate at the desired level and evaluate the skillsets of the people, the documentation and organizational adoption of the processes and the extent to which the current tools are contributing to positive and negative outcomes.

Ask the people executing the processes how they are using the tools they have. It is often easy to blame the tool for process problems, so be alert to that and ask the next level questions: How was this tool selected? How were you trained? Is the tool properly maintained? If the tools in use were selected via a thorough vetting process and properly implemented, it's hard to imagine a better outcome with a different tool.

While you are assessing the under-performing processes, look also at what tools the team relies on the most. What tools can they truly not live without? When there are emergencies, what tools do they count on? Which tools show up as reliable across multiple processes? Now look at the nature of these tools. Are they homegrown? Are they from a single vendor or from single trusted systems integrator? Why? Is it training, fit, functionality, or a combination of these attributes? What makes a tool successful in your organization? Throughout this part of the assessment, make special note of the tools you use versus merely the tools you own.

So to recap, at this point you have an inventory of all your processes, using your default Information Security framework as a baseline. You've captured which tools you use for which processes and you've assessed the maturity of each of these processes. You have recorded which tools in your portfolio are relied on the most, and have noted which tools you use rarely, if at all. You are almost ready to build a roadmap of improvement for your process portfolio, along with a roadmap for the tools in your arsenal. Before we tackle that, let's take a brief philosophical detour and talk about an approach for putting people, process, and technology together to solve problems.

Horizon Planning for Cybersecurity

I'm going to start by drawing an analogy from the business world and talk about horizon planning. For those not familiar with this, briefly you design your product portfolio with products with different time horizons.

H1, or time horizon 1, is categorized by products that are extremely mature, need very little investment, have loyal customers, and earn lots of profits. But, because they are somewhat long in the tooth, there isn't a lot of investment that can be made (perhaps the technology is captive on an old platform or some other barrier exists) and the loyal customer base is loath to change.

Products that are maturing and gaining traction in the market categorize H2, or time horizon 2. They still require significant investment and along with that investment comes a growing customer base, market enthusiasm, and dynamic development and product feature additions.

Finally, H3, or time horizon 3 products are barely MVPs (minimum viable products). They are often experimental and there is a real concern that they will not deliver their promised value to the market or that a significant customer base will not adopt them. Many of these products will fail without generating any profit at all. For a deeper understanding of horizon planning, please see the original work "Alchemy of Growth" by Mehrdad Baghai and others at McKinsey & Company.

The point I am making is purposeful. You need to think of your process inventory as a "business portfolio" and you need to structure your use of technology within that portfolio with an eye toward the tried and true that works today (H1), the emerging technologies (H2) that solve problems that were either left unsolved by the H1 technologies or that have surfaced since the H1 technologies reached their innovation zenith, and the experimental technologies (H3) that hold promise and are worth the investment of your time and your staff's time, even if you aren't spending hard dollars. The discipline to think in horizons helps you to construct layers of protection and the permission for your team to experiment and learn will help you amplify the impact of your efforts.

Here is a simple example of how to apply this approach. In the domain of end-point protection for personal workstations and handheld computers, for example, malware detection capabilities have evolved significantly since Fred Cohen first coined the term "computer virus" in a paper in 1984. First generation anti-virus (also known as anti-malware) software initially used "signatures" to recognize software known to be malicious based on a common string in the program that was unique to that piece of software. Several factors, including the rapid rate at which new strains of malware are released (as many as 250,000 unique pieces of malware are released in a single day as early as 2015) and various counter-measures, such as polymorphic code (programs that change themselves each time they replicate) render that method alone subject to failure.

To improve the ability to recognize malicious code that hadn't been seen before, anti-virus software adopted heuristic algorithms to detect behavior of a program that was indicative of different viruses. This technique has a higher rate of false positives than purely signature based software, which creates friction and impacts productivity. As anti-virus manufacturers were adding heuristic capabilities to their products, some were initially better at it than others. In some cases, new products were built that eschewed signature detection and relied entirely on heuristics. This is a high-level depiction of the early evolution of anti-virus software for illustrative purposed only.

This process took several years to play out. Information Security teams using the layered portfolio approach would run multiple tools, perhaps selecting their favorite H1 mainstream signature-based tool using a range of common procurement factors, such as suitability to their environment, ease of administration, and cost. They might also deploy heuristic tools in select circumstances where new viruses might be more prevalent, such as customer service or marketing where more computer files are exchanged, while avoiding more isolated functions who might be less tolerant of false positives.

As more anti-virus products incorporated both signature detection and heuristics, they replaced signature-only products as the H1 tool. As viruses continue to improve their stealth, for instance disabling the anti-virus program before the heuristic engine can recognize it as malware, new techniques, such as examining the binaries for capabilities as opposed to looking for signature strings might take over as an H2 tool for the organization. Meanwhile, the team might experiment with network anomaly detection, trusted computing (extreme white listing), trustless computing (blockchain-like approaches) and other early-stage end-point protection techniques to try to find the malware that gets through by recognizing activity that is out of place and therefore indicative of malicious behavior.

This approach is different than buying a single product from a single vendor based on the best match to an RFP. The team must understand the outcome they want (protection from computer viruses that exceeds the protection they can get from a single product), they must understand their environment and the behavior of their users, they must understand enough about how the various products work to understand how to build a complementary strategy, have an experimental mindset, and be meticulous in measuring the effectiveness of their processes. This mindset of understanding the environment, the business imperatives, and the technologies is critical for successfully managing a process portfolio.

Is That in the Budget?

The final mindset I want to address in this chapter is the need to be judicious in how you manage the cost of your process portfolio. Certainly, every organization faces budget realities and in the vast majority of cases, the Information Security department has very limited funding. You'll frequently be asked to "self-fund" new projects, which of course if a euphemism for cutting spending somewhere else.

To set yourself up for success, become comfortable with force-ranking your tools, look for tools that assist with more than one process and span multiple data center strategies such as on premise, bare metal, virtual, cloud and hybrid, and routinely "clear the decks." I am not recommending you change direction without good cause; you don't want to acquire a reputation for poor budget stewardship. But to remain agile with your technology budget, try to use a pay-as-you-go model when you can and be very careful with multi-year lock-in contracts. Also keep in mind that support is not always mandatory. Repeat your assessments at least every other year and as you map tools back to outcomes and processes, be prepared to drop what is not helping the cause.

With a budget conscious mindset, focused on process over tools, keenly aware of your outcomes and willing to experiment to construct the right kind of layered approach, you'll be in a position to put together an effective information security portfolio and deliver on your mandate for your organization.

Security Domains and Control Families

CISSP Domains (8)		NIST 800-53 Security Control Families (18)	
• Security and Risk Management		AC	Access Control
• Asset Security		AT	Awareness Training
• Security Engineering		AU	Audit and Accountability
• Communication and Network Security		CA	Security Assessment and Authorization
• Identity and Access Management		CM	Configuration Management
• Security Assessment and Testing		CP	Contingency Planning
• Security Operations		IA	Identification and Authentication
• Software Development Security		IR	Incident Response
PCI DSS Requirements (12)		MA	Maintenance
		MP	Media Protection
• Network Segmentation		PE	Physical and Environment Protection
• Default Configurations		PL	Planning
• Protect the data		PS	Personnel Security
• Encrypt network traffic		RA	Risk Assessment
• End-point protection		SA	System and Service Acquisition
• Application and System Engineering		SC	System and Communications Protection
• Least Privilege		SI	System and Information Integrity
• Non-repudiation		PM	Program Management
• Physical Access			
• Logging and monitoring			
• Security assessment and testing			
• Security policy			

Cyber Tools and Techniques – Stamper

> "A cyber-focused business impact assessment (BIA) is one of the most important tools that a CISO should develop."

I was tempted to begin this chapter with a laundry list of vendors...next-generation firewalls, web application firewalls, intrusion prevention and detection platforms, end-point protection, anti-malware, URL filtering, security analytics (both user and network), penetration tools, monitoring tools, among hundreds of other categories of tools that we would ideally have access to as CISOs. The risk of naming a number of different vendors is that it quickly becomes akin to discussing religion or politics...you never know where the discussion will go and how alienated your friends and colleagues will be when you express your perspective on a given tool or vendor.

I believe it's important to pause and put our tools and the techniques for their usage into a broader context. When we think of the various tools that we can leverage to protect our organization's operations, information, and other assets, let's not lose sight of what a tool is...it's a means to an end. Tools are used for their effectiveness in addressing a given workload. For those of us who work in technology and try to protect it, it can be too easy to fall in love with the next great technique or tool, without necessarily capturing the broader context of how that same desired outcome could be achieved without the latest technology or a huge dent in our budget. In many cases, as we will see, common sense and some basic business context will be some of the best security techniques and tools you'll have.

Addressing Cybersecurity with a Limited Budget

Equally important, not all organizations have the luxury of budgets that allow them to deploy the latest and greatest security tools into their environment. One of my greatest concerns as a CISO is the disparity of security practices, competencies, and access to resources given an organization's size and industry. The small-to-medium enterprise (SME) may simply lack the resources to acquire next-generation firewalls, hire skilled security architects and analysts, and deploy sophisticated end-point protection for their mobile devices and laptops. These same resource-challenged organizations may actually be strategic suppliers to larger enterprises supporting critical infrastructure, healthcare, or national defense. This asymmetry in resources should concern everyone because our economy's job growth and innovation typically comes from the SME space, precisely those organizations that are ill-equipped to address the myriad of security objectives required to protect their intellectual property and business models.

The question then becomes not necessarily what new tools to deploy, but rather, how can I best protect my organization using the assets and capabilities at hand? Effectively, how can I reduce the attack surface my organization presents to cyber adversaries with the organization's current capabilities? Equally important, how can I, as the organization's CISO, advocate for better capabilities and enhanced resources given my organization's inherent risk profile? As we have discussed elsewhere in this book, cybersecurity should be seen in an enterprise risk management (ERM) context. C-suite executives and boards know and think about risk. They may not know or care about things like web application firewalls (WAFs) designed to protect against SQL injection and other layer 7 exploits. But describe these capabilities in terms of enterprise risk management, and you'll likely pique their interest.

An Unconventional Tool Box

This leads me to the first "tool" and "technique" that a CISO should employ. You should describe cybersecurity in the context of risk management and evaluate the organization's cyber exposure in business terms. Here are the impacts to our organization's revenue, to our reputation, and our customers, and here is our potential legal and regulatory exposure should a breach or service interruption occur. Here is how we believe we can mitigate this risk. A cyber-focused business impact assessment (BIA) is one of the most important tools that a CISO should develop. The artifact of this BIA is a basic document or spreadsheet. The value of doing this BIA is that it necessitates knowledge of the organization's business (processes, vendors, customers, etc.). This knowledge requires that the CISO work collaboratively with other departments and executives within the organization. The return on investment for this "tool" cannot be overstated.

As a subset of the BIA, another assessment that is absolutely required is a list of material vendors and their risk profiles. Given a number of high-profile breaches involving large, publically-traded firms, there should be no ambiguity regarding how impactful vendors can be on security. Critical in this effort is an understanding of what type of data is shared with vendors and which processes they support. Chapter 4 provides a number of approaches to evaluating vendor and third party risk. Minimally, evaluating vendors and third parties for operational, privacy, and security risk factors is in order.

Defining the materiality or force ranking the importance of vendors becomes fairly self-evident once these risk factors are documented. As with the criticality of business processes coming from the business impact assessment, reviewing the findings from the vendor assessment analysis with your colleagues shines the light on where an organization's limited resources should be focused. The results of the BIA and vendor assessment should provide a more in-depth understanding of the organization's information sets (data assets if you will) and how this data flows into and out of the organization with vendors, processes, applications, and clients. Knowing how data moves within and outside the organization provides invaluable context for the types of security controls that may be required (e.g. access control lists, rule sets related to ports and processes, encryption, and user access rights). The artifact of this data flow analysis is the data flow diagram (DFD) that was discussed earlier in this book[25]. A basic drawing tool or, in the extreme, a blank piece of paper can suffice to help capture this critical information.

---

[25]. DFDs should capture the starting, transactional, and ending phases of a process or procedure. They should also clearly capture applications, organizational boundaries, people, roles, and departments, data sets, and locations, among other variables.

The results of the BIA, vendor assessment, and DFD documentation should inform the types of controls and procedures that will have the most impact on the security and governance of the organization. These are typically captured and described in security and other policies, which are discussed in our next chapter. This data, business process, and vendor context can also be used to provide insights into threat modeling exercises.[26]

There is a common thread associated with these first four techniques (BIAs, vendor assessments, DFDs, and policies). None of them require specialized tools or significant budget. What they do require is the commitment of the CISO to have a deep working knowledge of the organization, its industry, and its information and data coupled with strong working relationships with colleagues across departments and divisions within the organization.

Chapter 8 Key Point and Action Item 4

Tie tools and techniques to processes and business objectives. A business impact assessment (BIA) can be the CISO's best friend in aligning cybersecurity objectives with those of the rest of the organization. It is critical to know the linkages between processes, applications, their data, and the value to the organization with the security practices at hand.

You should draft a BIA and validate with your colleagues throughout the organization that they agree with the organizational value and recovery point and recovery time objectives.

There are some basic security techniques, beyond the governance practices described above, that should be used in every organization regardless of its size and complexity. First and foremost, the Center for Internet Security's (CIS') Critical Security Controls[27], begins with two foundational controls: inventory of authorized and unauthorized devices (effectively assets) and inventory of authorized and unauthorized software (effectively applications and systems). As the saying goes, you cannot secure what you do not know exists. Here again, collaboration with partners within the organization is key.

---

[26]. There are a number of great resources to support threat-modeling exercises including OWASP (https://www.owasp.org/index.php/Application_Threat_Modeling) and Microsoft's guidance (https://msdn.microsoft.com/en-us/library/ff648644.aspx).
[27]. The Center for Internet Security assumed responsibility for the SANS Top 20 - https://www.sans.org/critical-security-controls/history.

Our colleagues in accounting typically maintain fixed asset accounts on the general ledger. This ledger can provide important details on the hardware being used within the organization. Similarly, procurement cards are a great tool for finding shadow IT – applications and services that are being used but that have not been fully vetted or sanctioned by IT. Basic inventorying practices are a CISO's best friend. These inventories can be cross-referenced with data flow diagrams, master vendor lists, and other inventories to ensure that critical information assets are captured and documented.

Reducing the Organization's Cyber Risk Exposure

Another basic set of security techniques can be summarized with the term "limit the blast radius." These techniques offer a great way to visualize the footprint of a given system within the organization. This footprint can be thought of in expansive terms to include locations, networks, users, hardware, protocols, vendors, etc. Understanding how pervasively a given application or technology is deployed will provide valuable context for the potential security impacts. Limiting the blast radius can help an organization reduce the operational footprint (and hence negative impact) of a given system should that system be compromised or suffer a service interruption.

Another way to describe this technique is: limit systems, services, and infrastructure to their minimal purpose with their minimal number of variables (be they users, interfaces, data sets, etc.). This is similar to the concept of least privilege, where access or information is purposely limited (controlled) to the minimum necessary to fulfill a job function. Within applications, using roles-based access controls to limit elevated privileges to only those very few roles and only during those very few times when they are required can help facilitate this effort. Application access controls are extraordinarily important given that most of the organization's crown jewels are found within applications – notably the application's database. Employing and enabling multi-factor authentication to access high-value applications should always be a top priority. Similarly, encrypting sensitive and proprietary data both in transit and at rest should also be part of the overall application control set.

On the network side, the use of access control lists (ACLs) to refine who or what has access to a given network should be a widely-deployed technique. Again, consistent with the concept of limiting the blast radius, segmenting networks to provide better control and restricting access are extremely import controls or security techniques. Employing a "default deny" for both access and egress is another technique that will reduce the threat surface of the system at hand. Protocols and ports should only be opened when there is a legitimate requirement for this access. Complementing the default deny and least privilege controls should be the white listing of specific networks (and by extension the exclusion of all others). Most organizational communication is far too promiscuous. With a bit of discovery, many of these unnecessary and risky communication channels can be reduced or eliminated.

Too frequently, these controls are employed only at the *perimeter* of the organization with the assumption that this boundary is actually that, a boundary. It's important to employ these techniques not only for north-south traffic (communications into and out of the organization) but, arguably more importantly, for east-west traffic (communications within the organization) as well. Organizational boundaries today are semi-permeable...well, permeable. Knowing which traffic patterns are legitimate and which need to be stopped is a critical part of any CISO's role.

Why Anomalous Behavior Is So Critical

Finding and evaluating anomalous behavior is another critical detective control for CISOs today. We are seeing some really innovative tools enter the market that help detect anomalous user and network behaviors – behaviors that would not necessarily be captured in standard signatures or heuristics. Effectively, they help find the unknown unknowns within user populations and networks.

These tools provide a great detective capability for CISOs and can be used to verify that policy compliance and required configurations are indeed in place. What's more, many of these tools integrate into security incident and event management (SIEM) platforms, allowing security personnel to quickly investigate deviations from normal or authorized behavior without necessarily having to sift through thousands of logs. Good anomaly detection tools use multiple models to machine learn normal behavior and surface anomalous activity in an intuitive visualization layer allowing for quick triaging. Network and user anomaly detection capabilities are quickly becoming a must-have tool, especially for larger organizations.

Whether an organization is large or small, good threat intelligence cannot be underestimated. Organizations should proactively sign up for their vendors' news and update feeds (where applicable), threat and vulnerability feeds such as US-CERT[28], as well as proactively liaise with local fusion centers (aggregation points between local law enforcement and federal cyber teams)[29], the FBI[30], and industry-

---

[28]. https://www.us-cert.gov/
[29]. https://www.dhs.gov/fusion-center-locations-and-contact-information
[30]. https://www.fbi.gov/about-us/investigate/cyber

specific Multi-State Information Sharing and Analysis Centers (MS-ISACs)[31]. Collectively, these resources provide access to timely information, the sharing of best practices, and a wealth of actionable intelligence that can be leveraged within the organization. There are also CISO round table and other organizations that are providing a vetted audience for CISOs to share best practices and insights.

As CISOs, we would love to have large security budgets, teams of fully-trained security architects, and access to the latest and greatest security tools and technology. The reality for most of us is far from this ideal. Our budgets are too small, our staff is poached from other organizations, and we are using older tools simply because they've already been purchased and the willingness to procure something new is a lost battle. In spite of these challenges, we are still expected to ensure the security and availability of the organization's assets.

The techniques that have been described above are designed to reflect this reality. Knowing our organizations in depth can help overcome these challenges, and the basic tools and techniques that are required can be implemented with most existing technologies. As noted earlier, the return on time invested to deeply understand the organization cannot be overstated. This knowledge, and frankly the political value of working closely with non-IT colleagues, can ultimately translate into the resources we need for our security program. The early heavy lifting of documenting BIAs, performing vendor risk analyses, creating data flow diagrams, and drafting policies will translate into greater organizational gravitas.

---

[31]. https://msisac.cisecurity.org/

> "...your job as the CISO is to assist the executive team in achieving its strategic objectives. Your job is to deploy cybersecurity as a service and reduce the organization's risk exposure for its current technology portfolio."

Organizations across the globe suffered nearly 43 million security incidents in 2014, a 48% increase according to the 2014 AT&T Cyber Security Insights report (AT&T Network Security 2014). That statistic is frightening when you think about it. It reflects known security incidents that were reported. By best estimates, organizations only report about a third of their security incidents to authorities – which means this number could actually be over 100 million incidents. This report also contained statistics that reflect the increasing assault on the connected technologies used by today's global economies.

Some data points I found extremely troubling were that even though companies are being subjected to a high rate of data breaches, nearly 75% report that the CISO or security team does not fully engage all of the executive leadership team in addressing cybersecurity concerns. This statistic amazed me because, if there is one thing I have learned as a CISO, it's that if you want to be effective you must collaborate and work with the company's leadership team. You must work to build trust with the organization's stakeholders and make the case that cybersecurity is a value proposition, a service that all business channels should leverage to be competitive. However, I am realistic and understand that many organizations don't understand why they need cybersecurity. They either don't notice or are afraid of the fact that today's business environment is heavily digitized and has become the playing field for many cyber-criminal entities.

To combat this rise in data breaches and cyber incidents, companies will need to implement and fund a mature cybersecurity and risk management program. They will need to change their corporate culture and accept cybersecurity as a valuable practice that will enable them to be competitive. However, the AT&T report found that even when companies fund a corporate cybersecurity program, almost 51% of them fail to review and keep their information security policies current. The report also estimated that approximately 78% of all employees don't follow their organization's security policies or procedures. These are the kind of numbers that can be daunting to a CISO. To spend your time building a security program and then have it ignored or bypassed for expediency can be frustrating. From experience, I have had this happen before and at first I was furious. However, on reflection, I realized that I had missed some important best practices in establishing my teams, which led to my organization not understanding my purpose as CISO or what value my security program could provide to their business operations. This leads us to the questions we will discuss in this chapter on the tools and techniques a CISO can use to implement his/her cybersecurity program so that it reflects the unique needs of their organization. The questions under consideration are:

1. What best practices would I recommend that new CISOs implement to reduce risk and provide value to their business?
2. What actions or techniques can the security program proactively take to protect organizational assets and preempt threats?
3. What are some core tools/solutions that I would recommend to a new CISO to support cybersecurity operations?

CISO Truisms to Manage Risk

As we begin our first discussion, remember that your job as the CISO for your organization is to assist the executive leadership team in achieving its strategic objectives. Whether these objectives are business oriented or service oriented, your job is to deploy cybersecurity as a service and reduce the organization's risk exposure to its current technology portfolio. To do this effectively, you will need to set in motion processes and policies for the company and your security teams to follow. These security techniques should be based on sound cybersecurity and IT best practices. However, do not be afraid to reach out to your peers and ask for assistance. As I have said, security doesn't exist in a vacuum. It is impossible to know everything about cyber. But in a cooperative community of peers, I have been amazed to watch a security program thrive and the knowledge you gain as a CISO in this kind of collaborative environment is truly significant.

So to begin our first discussion, we will talk about best practices and techniques that a CISO can implement to manage the risks faced by his/her organization. We will also discuss how the organization itself can employ specific directives to assist the CISO for the betterment of the cybersecurity program and the company's overall strategic business health. So let's discuss how I believe you as CISO should approach this first question and look for actionable answers: *"What best practices would I recommend that new CISOs implement to reduce risk and provide value to their business?"*

Data breaches are currently the most common and costliest security concern that all organizations face. Two of the main causes of this expensive issue are either misconfigured systems or applications, followed by user error. Both of these misjudgments (technical and human) can cost your organization far more in fines, lost revenue, brand damage, and missed business opportunities than it could have invested in building a resilient cybersecurity and risk management program. This leads us to our first discussion. To answer our selected question, we first need to understand how the business views cybersecurity. Do they truly understand that cybersecurity is not a concern that should be managed by the IT Department? Cybersecurity is a strategic asset for the business if done correctly and leveraged for excellence.

Cybersecurity ensures that the organization's business operations are healthy, the company's reputation and brand remains unscathed, and the organization's strategic plans, finances and data stay protected. In essence, when working properly cybersecurity directly supports the organization's business practices and corporate culture. For a CISO to have this type of impact with his/her security program, they must continuously evaluate their strategic cybersecurity program and make the necessary changes to enhance protection and account for new assets, processes, plans and data types. To conduct this evaluation, there are multiple best practices and/or techniques that I try to follow. There are several best practices that I would recommend to a new CISO. These processes should be deployed and periodically assessed to ensure the security program is on its path to maturity. My recommended best practices are as follows:

1. Speak with the executive leadership team. Collaborate with your own IT management team to determine/prioritize areas of concern.
   a. As a CISO you need to be visible. You need to be speaking with your executive team and educating them on the value of cybersecurity. If you are never invited to speak with senior leadership, it is extremely hard for you to answer their questions on the risk associated with technology-based decisions. I have found that starting with my department first, and then requesting to brief and answer questions for senior leadership in 1-to-1 meetings helps build credibility for my security program. The key point is this will take time. Be patient and build your relationships so you are considered to be

part of the strategic team.

2. Continuously monitor and inventory critical assets.
   a. Organizations are in a constant state of technological change. Do your security team and key stakeholders understand what assets are critical to the organization, where they are located, and who has access? Is this list periodically updated to reflect the addition of new technologies or the decommissioning of legacy systems? Is this list periodically vetted by those individuals in the organization that are deemed critical for the company's success?

3. Review and update company IT and cybersecurity policies and procedures.
   a. One of the first policies that I verify with this step is my cybersecurity policy. This policy is critical for your teams; it provides the guidelines for them to follow as it pertains to how cybersecurity is performed in your organization. It is considered industry standard for security professionals to review the organization's standing cybersecurity policies at least annually. I like to have my team members review the sub-policies, such as Acceptable Use, Social Media, Privacy, Remote Access, etc. at least every six months. This ensures they are educated on what is expected of them, and I get another viewpoint on policies that I have written to verify that they are still valid.

4. Make sure you periodically review and understand your budget and your department's budget. Make sure the projected costs and resource requirements in your 3-year project plan are accurate.
   a. As CISO, your organization faces a dynamic threat environment that is constantly evolving. This will require you to continually evaluate new threats and at times make changes to security controls and the technology you use in your security suite to protect the organization. These changes will at times have an impact on your budget and will influence projects that you have in your production pipeline. You need to be continually evaluating the risks to your organization and stay nimble enough to make changes to your project plans where required.

      In many organizations the budget for the cybersecurity program will be a component of the overall IT department budget. Because of this I would recommend that as a senior member of the IT department leadership team you need to be aware of your department's overall budget. You should know what departmental projects, outside of your division, have high visibility in the organization and understand which ones may impact any of your project timelines. This information will help you be more realistic about project funding and give you a more thorough understanding of what the business priorities are for the IT department. With this knowledge you can tailor your projects and ensure that the projected outcomes are described in business terms that meet your departments strategic goals.

5. Make sure your cyber incident response plan is current.
    a. This response plan is an essential component of your cybersecurity program. It is the guide to help the organization survive a data breach. There are six categories of costs associated with data breaches:
        i.   Reputation/brand damage
        ii. Lost productivity due to downtime/system performance
        iii. Lost revenue due to system availability issues.
        iv. Forensic costs to triage the event
        v.   Technical support costs to restore systems/data
        vi. Compliance/regulatory costs and fines

The incident response plan should be designed to help mitigate many of these costs through the execution of response procedures that team members can take to respond to an incident and reduce its impact to the organization. It should be reviewed for updates at least semi-annually and tested annually to verify that all parties who are part of the response team understand their parts in using the plan to protect the organization and its assets during a breach event.

6. Verify the company's back-up procedures. Periodically test the back-ups to ensure data is retrievable and accurate.
    a. A general rule for you as a CISO is if the data is deemed important to the organization it should be backed up. You never want to find out after the fact that the R&D data required by the organization for a new business venture has been lost because the backups were never verified. You need to verify that there is a regular backup procedure in place with people identified who are responsible for it. You need to verify that the backups are happening automatically, understand the backup schedule, and request sight verification that the backups work and can be replicated.

7. Make sure you have initiated a cybersecurity awareness training program for company employees.
   a. If you say "what program?" you know you have an issue. You should have a training program to educate employees on cybersecurity policies, best practices, and current threats, and you need to keep it relevant. By relevant I mean that it needs to be up to date and the training should reflect issues that are currently facing the organization. Remember, employees are the first line of defense for the organization. Educate them so they are cyber aware and your organization will be more resilient to the threats it faces.

8. Make sure your patch management program updates desktops, servers and applications.
   a. As any security professional knows, missing patches are one of the easiest ways for a digital asset to be compromised. As the CISO, you should ensure your organization has a mature patch management program and that it uses an automatic software solution that pushes updates out when they are available. Obviously, your patch management program will have guidelines for how patches are tested before deployment and you should have a set schedule for when to deploy critical updates versus a nice-to-have add-on package. Your job as CISO will be to monitor this program and verify that patches are being installed. One way I test to ensure patches were deployed is to scan with a remediation tool before the patch management cycle and then scan again afterward to verify that deployed patches were installed correctly.

9. Verify that the anti-virus solution installed on servers and desktops is current.
   a. I understand that the end-point security solution is quickly changing and there are many products that could be purchased to protect your assets. With that said, anti-virus is still a vital tool required by every organization that uses technology connected to the Internet. This is a solution designed to be preventive and react to threats that are trying to enter your networks. Anti-virus provides you time to counter the threats that have been contained, so they can be remediated. It is incumbent upon you as a CISO to ensure your security teams manage this tool appropriately and that its threat database and software is current.

10. Periodically perform vulnerability scans on all networks, servers and desktops in the organization.

a. Organizational enterprise networks are dynamic entities that are constantly changing and because of this I would recommend that you create a program and use a solution to periodically scan for vulnerabilities. This will ensure that your assets are patched, configured correctly and security controls are in place. For my cybersecurity program, I use NIST SP 800-137, "Information Security Continuous Monitoring (ISCM)" (Johnston, et al. 2011), as a guideline for how I set up my vulnerability scanning, monitoring and remediation program. I use the ISCM methodology for my teams and I maintain an ongoing awareness of cybersecurity controls, asset vulnerabilities and threats to my organization. Information we discover through this process is provided to the organization's executive leadership team to assist in making strategic risk management decisions.

11. Use a local encryption solution for computer workstation within the organization?
    a. Consider which business requirements will dictate the need to have laptops, desktops or servers encrypted. Previous experience has shown that this requirement was implemented on laptops for personnel who traveled with sensitive data or servers that contained critical proprietary information that they organization couldn't risk being compromised. This basic level of security that should be deployed to these types of critical assets, it will provide you with the assurance that even if hackers access these assets they will not be able to access company data.

12. Periodically test the wireless networks to verify they are secure.
    a. If your organization uses wireless access points, do you have an updated inventory with a current network map? Do you have a copy of the current configurations used on these wireless access devices? Do you have a standard policy on how these devices are managed, how they are periodically scanned for vulnerabilities, the level of encryption they use, and whether guest access is allowed for third party vendors and contractors? As the CISO for the organization, another issue you will need to periodically audit is what devices are being connected to the corporate wireless network and do any of them have a regulatory/compliance mandate such as PCI or HIPAA? If so, you will need to look at your wireless architecture and verify that it meets the security requirements of these regulatory frameworks. As you can see, the use of wireless in an organization's network

architecture requires answers to many questions and continuous monitoring due to the risks associated with the hacking of these network access points.

13. Use email filtering and Internet traffic filtering software.
    a. Web-based attacks and targeted email phishing attacks against organizations are on the rise. Due to this increase, I feel this technique is one cyber hygiene process that a CISO must deploy to protect his/her first line of defense – the organization's employees. There are multiple tools that can be used to provide these critical services. I have in the past used next-generation firewalls that provided Internet content filtering in both inbound and outbound modes. I have also deployed multiple email solutions, both on premise and cloud, that provide mechanisms to scan email and attachments for malware, viruses and questionable web links. This best practice won't prevent all attacks from this threat vector, however it will reduce the risk and make enough noise to provide time for other mechanisms to react and remediate any issues.

14. Employ a malware scanning/remediation solution and have it actively scanning all networked assets within the organization.
    a. Your anti-virus tool works reactively; it works after an asset has been infected. This tool, however, seeks to identify possible threats and protect assets by preventing the malware's ability to communicate outbound from the organization to hacker-controlled assets. Many of these solutions will also provide the ability to continuously scan, alert when malware is discovered and remediate the compromised computer. As CISO, you will need this solution because it is inevitable that you will get some type of malware in the corporate environment. You must have the ability to hunt it down and eradicate it as soon as possible. As with your anti-virus solution, ensure that it is kept up to date, fully patched, and document how it should be used to protect the company.

This is by no means a complete list of best practices for a CISO to follow. These are just several that I would recommend to make sure your security program has the capabilities it requires to get a healthy start and enable you to demonstrate that cybersecurity is valuable to the business. As I mentioned above, you and your team should have well thought out criteria for tool selection, as well as implementation and performance management goals to ensure you are meeting your risk reduction goals. Having these written criteria and performance objectives is critical. They can be used for audit purposes and they will become the standard reference guides for you and your teams to consult when there are procedural questions.

Techniques and More Techniques

There are many aspects of an organization's security program that will determine how well it detects and responds to cyber incidents. If the program lacks critical components such as the correct mix of talent, support from executive management, or the correct security resources, the program in my mind might actually expose the organization to more risk than it prevents. With this in mind, understand that even the best cybersecurity strategy will typically fail if it falls short on these types of critical factors. So in our next topic for discussion, let's look at some techniques a CISO can use to proactively deploy cyber and improve his/her security program. Our next question is: *"What actions or techniques can the security program proactively take to better protect organizational assets and preempt threats?"*

One of the first questions I like to ask my teams and stakeholders is, "Do we know the ways in which our company is susceptible to cyber-attacks?" This is one of the first techniques I recommend to new CISOs. Get out into your departments and talk to your stakeholders. Educate them on the risks facing the organization and then ask them questions. Some questions that I would recommend you ask are centered around how they work, what data they use, who has access to it and what applications are critical for them to be successful. This information will provide you with some insight into the information your company, employees, and partners have that criminals may target. The biggest motivator for cybercriminals is still money and data is an international currency. So my first recommended technique is: *"Educate yourself and your stakeholders on what is valuable to the criminal and what methods they may use to access it, and use that information to focus your security program and reduce the organization's exposure to risk."*

The next technique I recommend is one of healthy paranoia, born from working in the field of cybersecurity for over 20 years. I never assume that my security controls are working. I always assume something will eventually fail, so I am constantly looking for that failure.

Many organizations look at security as an issue that needs to be fixed; they put security controls in place and then assume that they're working. Unfortunately, with this line of thinking if the security controls aren't working correctly then the organization is unprepared for a breach because they don't know that the controls are no longer functioning. What I advise is to assume that not all of your controls work as advertised. I have seen many instances where new technologies or changes to workflows for an application have a negative effect on a security program's installed controls.

I would advise you to continually assess the effectiveness of your controls and build into your program an assumption that they will fail. Plan for it, continually assess for it, and when found, remediate it. This mindset, *"Assume your security controls are going to fail,"* will allow you and your teams to keep your security control portfolio flexible, and over time you will gain a better understanding of their impact on the organization's business operations.

The next technique that I would recommend to you as a CISO revolves around your security teams and your personnel. In every organization that I have worked at, I truly believe that it was my teams that enabled me to be successful. Part of this success was understanding the skillsets of my personnel, the skillsets required to manage the security suite, and the training that would be required to manage any future changes to the security program and its suite of tools. This technique addresses a major operational issue that is currently impacting all organizations, which is the shortage of trained, knowledgeable security professionals. The technique I recommend is to assess the education, certifications and experience of your staff members. Then proceed to build a training program for each staff member and share it with them so they see that the organization plans to invest in them.

I would then proceed to lay out your plan to your manager to gain funding for building a training program for your teams. Start small, possibly one class at a time, and eventually build to a program where you might offer access to online training and attending an annual security conference to keep your personnel up to date on the latest threats to the organization. I believe this technique, *"Invest in your people,"* will provide you with dedicated staff members who are interested in the work they are performing. You will also reduce the risk exposure to your organization of having a security team that is understaffed, ill trained and not motivated.

The next technique I recommend revolves around the fact that in most organizations, the cybersecurity program typically lacks full visibility into the organization's enterprise landscape. This typically results in some security processes having to be completed manually to compensate for the lack of visibility. Unfortunately, hackers don't have this barrier and will leverage any issue, including time consuming, manual processes, to compromise a network. The technique I would recommend is *"When in doubt, upgrade and automate it."*

As a CISO, you should seek to automate basic security processes that deal with low-level threats so you can focus your resources and staff on tougher challenges. You will find that as the cyber threats we face are ever increasing, so is the volume of security data they generate. For the organization to respond appropriately to the strategic cyber threats it faces, it will need to scale and use automation to analyze the collected security data. As the CISO, you should champion the use of techniques such as scripting and automation tools to remove the noise from your collected security data. This will provide you with the visibility you require to identify and remediate any residual threats, providing a valuable service to the business.

My final technique is, *"Security doesn't exist in a vacuum – so go get some help!"* In cybersecurity you will never know everything. You will need to collaborate and get information from time to time to assist you with strategic planning, emergency operations, and sometimes just a different point of view even if just to verify you're not going crazy. So as we conclude this topic, what is important for you to understand is that these techniques are all part of different leadership styles that I have found particularly useful for a CISO in a dynamic, fast-changing environment. Picture each of these techniques as an extra push – a push for you to focus on your security program, the threats the organization faces, educating your organization on the value of cybersecurity, investing in your teams – and be willing to collaborate and understand that you will never know everything about cyber, so ask for help.

Some Tools for the Tool Box

As I previously stated, the rise of cyber incidents and the increasing threat to organizations has moved the topic of cybersecurity to the agenda in many corporate boardrooms. It has also encouraged many venture capitalists to pour money into the growing sectors of cybersecurity and data analytics, hoping to address security issues on traditional networks, as well as for cloud and IoT (Internet of Things) deployments. However, the security tools developed in these new companies are currently fragmented at best. This is due in part to the fact that many are created to deal with threats that are often difficult to describe. To make matters worse, they are being created and marketed in ways that make it extremely frustrating to categorize them and compare their effectiveness. Over the last 20-plus years working in IT and cybersecurity, I have come to view security solutions in three broad categories:

1. *Preventive* – they protect the enterprise, they attempt to identify an attack and stop it (e.g., anti-virus).
2. *Detective* – detect incidents that have bypassed protection, focused on shortening the time for discovery (e.g., SIEM).

3. _Corrective_ - investigate/remediate issues found by detective tools. Sometimes this capability is built into detective tools (vulnerability scanner, packet capture).

This brings us to our final discussion. We will talk about tools that fit within these categories and how they should be used as effective assets for the corporate cybersecurity team. Our final question is, _"What are some core tools/solutions that I would recommend to a new CISO to support cybersecurity operations?"_

To begin our discussion, I think it is best that we first understand that as the CISO for an organization, you will be the expert for selecting the hardware, appliances, and software solutions required for the corporate security program. Part of selecting the right security solutions is understanding the _"cybersecurity inherent risk"_ of the organization. This is the risk posed by an organization's business activities, its connections to third party vendors and partners, and finally, any active risk-mitigating controls. Understanding your organization's risks provides insight into what is important to the business leadership team. It can help you select the level of technology you will need to deploy and where in the business' technology portfolio it will need to be connected.

To me, a technology portfolio is very similar to the old TCP/IP stack. It is really centered around how data flows in an organization and can provide you with a more strategic view of where you would plug in security controls to minimize risk to the organization's business operations. Within aa organization's technology portfolio, there are basically four domains where I believe security controls and solutions should be incorporated to manage the organizations exposure to cyber risk. These four domains are _"Application, Network, Endpoint/Desktop, and Cloud/Virtual."_

- _Application_ – this is the domain within enterprise networks where applications interface with the Internet, networks and users. Here data is manipulated, stored, accessed and at times erased. There are many types of security technologies designed to test data in applications at this level, the applications themselves and who has access to them. Some tools that I have used within this domain are code testing and review, application penetration testing, web application firewalls, identity/authentication management and intrusion detection systems designed specifically for application scanning and review. _Many of the tools here are detective in nature._

- _Network_ – this domain is extremely wide ranging and is the largest portion of an organization's technology portfolio.

This domain contains everything from tools for network and malware analysis, vulnerability scanning and remediation, firewalls, network intrusion/prevention systems, security information and event management systems (SIEM), threat intelligence feeds and security analytic solutions. Many of the tools here are both detective and corrective in nature.

- Endpoint/Desktop – this domain is focused down to the lowest denominator in a corporate network, the individual desktop/server. Many of the security tools you can select to deploy here are technologies such as anti-virus, personal firewalls, patch and configuration management, data loss prevention, host intrusion detection technologies and endpoint anti-virus/malware technologies. *These solutions are primarily preventative and detective in nature*, and they are focused on the care and feeding of the individual asset.

- *Cloud/Virtual* – this domain is the newest of the four and is growing very fast. It is a dynamic domain that can be on premise, within company owned facilities, or within the facilities of a third party vendor. This domain has many of the same security tools you would find in the previous three domains, except they are designed to operate in cloud / virtual environments. You will also find that many of the tools in the first three domains actually operate and store data in this domain – yes, it can get very confusing at times. This confusion is why many CISOs hire companies that specialize in providing security, integration services, and network/data management services within cloud / virtual environments. They find that it is a more effective use of resources to work with a specialized vendor until they can grow the required skillsets or build a team to manage it. *This domain has security solutions from all three categories – preventative, detective and corrective.* I will not list specific solutions here because many of them are already listed above. Again, this is a very new domain with a large number of security startup companies active in this space.

So in closing this last discussion, I explained how I view security tools fitting three categories that are based on the "purpose" they provide to an enterprise environment. I also explained how I view where these tools fit within the company's technology portfolio – their "domain," and how understanding your company's strategic risks will help you select the correct solutions and integrate them within the domains where they will be most effective. With that said, I still want to provide a list of tools because I am sure that as a CISO you want a list of resources you can use for your teams and yourself. As fate would have it, I have written two recent articles, "Good

Resources for the CISO" and "Good Resources for the CISO & Team" (Hayslip 2015). Both have extensive links to tools, recommendations for Linux operating systems, and books for the thoughtful, strategic CISO.

Chapter 8 Key Point and Action Item 5

CISOs have more tools at their disposal than ever before. Look for tools that offer economies of scope, skills, and budget. You want your security toolset to be readily available to address a number of workloads and platforms. You also want your tools to be easy for your security team to use. Tools that are overly complex, require too much training, or have a number of dependencies face inherent adoption risks. CISOs must ensure that their security budgets are aligned with their organization's risk appetite and that the tools they have available reflect this risk profile. Make sure your tools and techniques help you achieve your objectives. Force rank your tools based on their extensibility, affordability, and applicability.

You should compile a list of your security tools, force rank them, and validate the findings with your security team as well as with your colleagues in IT.

In many ways cybersecurity is a contact sport. When it is not done correctly it can have devastating consequences for a company and its business environment. When an organization follows best practices, when the CISO uses techniques to prepare his/her security teams and fine tune the corporate security program, when tools are leveraged and installed in the correct domains for maximum effectiveness then cybersecurity becomes a strategic asset. It is in this environment, where an organization values their cybersecurity program and empowers their CISO to innovate and be a valued business partner that I believe all security professionals want to exist.

I hope I have provided some insight as you establish your security program. Remember, you do not have to do it alone. To be effective in the role of CISO, you will need to collaborate. Security doesn't exist in a vacuum, but it does well in a community. So please reach out to your peers within your region or professional organizations, and build the relationships you will need to be an effective CISO for your organization.

Summary

In Chapter 8, we began our discussion by asking these three questions:

- If the CISO were a board member, what would the data the he/she would most want to see? What would he dashboard look like?
- What does the CISO want from the board in support of their information security responsibilities?
- What are recommended practices for reporting cybersecurity requirements to the board?
- How should the information be presented?
- What important aspects of cybersecurity and risk should the CISO ensure are conveyed to the board?

We are witnessing a watershed moment in cybersecurity that reflects a confluence of issues, including the significant increase in the volume and sophistication of attacks, the associated increase in cybersecurity risk awareness by key stakeholders, as well as a shift from largely preventative security techniques to a more expansive focus on detection capabilities that move beyond signatures and heuristics. We are entering an era of anomaly detection and the automation of much of our cybersecurity practices. There's significant work ahead driving innovation in our industry. What's clear is that the tools and techniques we used as CISOs in the past need to be updated to address our changing threat landscape.

In closing, we would like to leave you with these five key points and next steps:

1. Leverage frameworks and standards such as the NIST Cybersecurity Framework and/or the Center for Internet Security's Critical Security Controls to establish a roadmap to baseline your current security practices and controls. **You should formally select an information security framework that reflects your organization's industry and is best suited to baseline your process maturity.**

2. Organizational size, complexity, and maturity have significant and material impact on the organization's techniques. As we note throughout, "security doesn't exist in a vacuum." This situational awareness of the organization's capabilities has a profound influence on how cybersecurity programs are

implemented within organizations. It is important that your organization clearly understands the maturity and capabilities of the cybersecurity program. **You should create a maturity model to baseline your current practices vis-à-vis your organization's size, complexity, and industry and review this baseline analysis with senior leadership and the board of directors.**

3. Not all tools need to be complicated and expensive. A common thread throughout this book is the need to think beyond traditional IT and tie cybersecurity to organizational processes and systems. **You should work with senior leadership to compile a list of processes, locations, vendors, departments, and applications used within the organization and know their organizational value.**

4. Tie tools and techniques to processes and business objectives. A business impact assessment (BIA) can be the CISO's best friend in aligning cybersecurity objectives with those of the rest of the organization. It is critical to know the linkages between processes, applications, their data, and the value to the organization with the security practices at hand. **You should draft a BIA and validate with your colleagues throughout the organization that they agree with the organizational value and recovery point and recovery time objectives.**

5. CISOs have more tools at their disposal than ever before. Look for tools that offer economies of scope, skills, and budget. You want your security toolset to be readily available to address a number of workloads and platforms. You also want your tools to be easy for your security team to use. Tools that are overly complex face inherent adoption risks. CISOs must ensure that their security budgets are aligned with their organization's risk appetite and that their tools reflect this risk profile. Make sure your tools and techniques help you achieve your objectives. Force rank your tools based on their extensibility, affordability, and applicability. **You should compile a list of your security tools, force rank them, and validate the findings with your security team as well as with your colleagues in IT.**

Arguably, CISOs have one of the most challenging roles in industry. We are expected to know technology down to the bit and byte level, pivot to vendor management, and know enterprise risk from both a business and a technical perspective. The demands on the CISO have never been greater. As a consequence, our tools and the techniques we use to deploy them have never been more important. We invite you to think strategically about how you baseline your techniques in the context of recognized standards and frameworks as well as the specific context (industry, budget, and maturity) of your organization.

Chapter 9 – Security Policy

Introduction

In our final chapter we will review one of the core topics that all security and risk mitigation operations revolve around and that is the organization's cybersecurity program policies. Policies are the foundation for a security program. They explain how a program will execute specific processes, who has responsibility, and the resources required for mature operations. For many organizations, not having the correct policies can significantly impact their ability to defend itself against cyber criminals and degrade their ability to recover from a cyber incident. It is the responsibility of the CISO and executive management to have the correct policies in place, follow the policies, and periodically update them as the business/technology environment changes.

In this chapter our authors will provide their insight into the recommended policies an organization should have in its portfolio and will describe in detail the components of a corporate information security policy. Our authors approach this subject from different viewpoints, but it should be noted that their wealth of experience on this subject demonstrates the importance of the CISO understanding this process and accepting it as one of their core responsibilities.

Bill Bonney provides his viewpoint that information security policies are foundational to an organization. He discusses the relationship between policy, standards, guidelines, and procedures. Throughout, he notes how important it is to maintain the connection between business objectives and the organization's policies. Finally, Bill asserts that "policy has a purpose," that it is written for action, and proceeds to elaborate on the principles and steps for establishing an effective cybersecurity policy.

Matt Stamper states that CISOs use security policies to be effective in fulfilling the requirements of their position. He discusses the balance between creating a policy that has a specific objective and that is actually used in the organization. Matt then articulates the core elements of a well-structured policy and provides recommendations for specific policies that he deems crucial for an organization and its cybersecurity/risk management programs.

Gary Hayslip provides insight into the essential components of an organization's information security policy. He then walks the reader through a step-by-step process for creating an incident response

9.6 mandates that there is a policy to control the distribution of media.

In addition, the testing procedures for multiple requirements specifically instruct the QSA (Qualified Security Assessor) to verify that the organization's information security policies conform to minimum standards in domains such as cryptographic standards, data retention, access controls, firewall rules, and others.

PCI DSS Requirements	Testing Procedures
	3.1.c For a sample of system components that store cardholder data: • Examine files and system records to verify that the data stored does not exceed the requirements defined in the data retention policy • Observe the deletion mechanism to verify data is deleted securely.

There are also examples where minimum guidance is not given, but adherence to policy might still be a specific topic of audit. This is especially true for financial institutions, which may have a Statement on Standards for Attestation Engagements (SSAE) 16 in place for certain services they provide for their customers. It is extremely common to audit adherence to an organization's own internal security policy as part of the test of the effectiveness of internal controls. Because of these requirements, some organizations fall into the trap of asking the auditors or the QSA to "just tell us what the policy is supposed to say."

It's important to note that this is a particularly bad approach. Abdicating responsibility in this manner separates decision makers in the organization from policy setting and that has the immediate effect of disconnecting execution from principles. Further, "the auditor told us to do it" does not help anyone understand why a policy is written one way and not another and therefore creates a hesitancy to make needed changes. People become helpless to make needed changes because they lack the backstory and don't know what other problems they might cause by doing so.

There are a number of ways to provide guidance at various levels of detail and in various settings. These include guidelines, best practices, procedures, processes, standards, specifications, and policies.

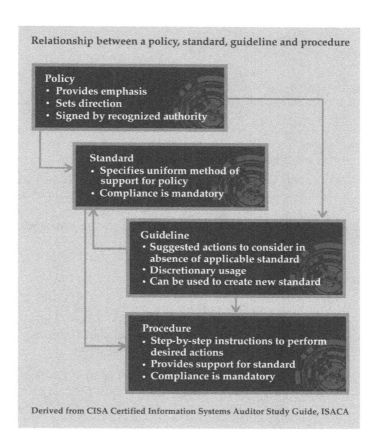

Relationship between a policy, standard, guideline and procedure

Policy
• Provides emphasis
• Sets direction
• Signed by recognized authority

Standard
• Specifies uniform method of support for policy
• Compliance is mandatory

Guideline
• Suggested actions to consider in absence of applicable standard
• Discretionary usage
• Can be used to create new standard

Procedure
• Step-by-step instructions to perform desired actions
• Provides support for standard
• Compliance is mandatory

Derived from CISA Certified Information Systems Auditor Study Guide, ISACA

When I say policies are foundational, I mean that if an organization wanted to give direction to its development team, it would want to set its policy first, then work with product architects to choose standards compatible with its environment that will allow it to adhere to its policy, and then allow the development organization to create specifications derived from those standards. Similarly, if an organization wanted to give direction to an operations team, it would set policy first, then as needed issue guidelines or cite best practices and then allow the operations team to develop procedures that adhered to policy and took into consideration the guidelines and best practices provided.

Don't blur the lines between policy and procedure. Policies set the tone at the top and establish organizational expectations. Procedures define operational activities. You don't need a large, encompassing mandate that would confuse everyone and result in a policy that is never followed. Keep the security policy reasonable in length and incorporate by reference more detailed procedural documentation. Procedures will change more frequently than the higher-level objectives established by the policy.

You should draft a list of the requisite components of your organization's security policy and inventory existing security procedures to reference.

Unintended Consequences

While information security policies do serve many purposes, it's important to not overload policies to include the guidelines, best practices, procedures, processes, standards and specifications. Doing so can have several unintended negative consequences.

One unintended negative consequence is an overly restrictive development or operational environment. Procedures and standards are by nature more detailed than policy. Policy is directional and constitutional. It lays out high-level parameters such as establishing a requirement for stepped up or more restrictive authentication mechanisms for establishing access rights for handling data at a certain sensitivity level to meet a regulatory or contractual obligation. Policy is typically drafted, recommended and approved according to governance rules that tie publication and adoption directly to senior management or the board of directors.

Standards are measures or models. The standard might indicate that one-time password (OTP) tokens or use of SMS is acceptable provided passwords rotate no less than every sixty seconds or SMS codes are valid for at most 120 seconds. Standards are typically drafted, recommended and approved according to rules imposed by architectural groups within the organization.

It would be a mistake to build the standard into the policy as the group developing the standard is usually closer to operations and is more intimately familiar with operational goals, problems and limitations.

Another potential unintended negative consequence is an over-burdened policy writing function that is hopelessly behind, producing policy that is out of date and irrelevant. This can create significant friction for any development or operations team. In the above example of OTP and SMS options for two-factor authentication, by the time these standards were baked into the policy and the policy was published, authentication apps on mobile phones might have become available that would meet the standard of 60 to 120 second password rotation but would not be usable within the organization because the policy was explicit about using OTP and SMS only and did not mention authentication apps.

While certainly there are examples where the specific type of two-factor authentication might need to be specified, the larger point is there are often many ways to solve a problem. Leaving as much flexibility as possible to the teams that are close to the issues is often a good strategy, and that strategy also applies to writing policy.

A final unintended negative consequence worth mentioning is that, as noted above, policy is often tested as part of the audit process. It is also reviewed as part of investigations associated with regulatory enforcement, contract enforcement, breach investigation, whistleblower investigation, or for other corporate governance related reasons. Findings of failure to follow internal policy can be construed as indicative of systemic wrongdoing, lax oversight, or careless behavior.

It bears repeating that except where the requirements are specific, such as with cryptographic standards for PCI-DSS, policy should be as high-level as it can be while still providing the necessary guidance to the organization. That leaves more room for variation in implementation and less likelihood of audit findings for a failure to follow policy given that real-world standards and procedures often change more rapidly than policy can be approved and issued.

Recognize that policy comes with liability at the audit and regulatory and prosecutorial level when not followed – don't just write it and forget it.

Policy Has a Purpose

One more abstract concept before we turn to the practical. When we think about what we want to get from setting and publishing policy, we should focus on two fundamental things: risk mitigation, and education and awareness.

As we identify risks and obligations we set policy for the behavior we believe will allow us to manage those risks and obligations. The policy helps us draw a direct line from senior management, with whom the identification and management of these risks and obligations sits, to every line employee who carries out the wishes of management to the customer's or shareholder's benefit. This direct line also serves as an educational vehicle to inform all employees, and state publically for customers, auditors, and shareholders, how the organization discharges its responsibilities.

Establishing Policies

Now that we have explored information security policy in the abstract, including that policy should be at the foundational level and some of the consequences of failing to acknowledge that, let's talk about how we would establish these policies and for what basic activities we should have information security policy in place.

Principles for establishing information security policy:

- Understand, document and communicate the relationship in your organization between policies,
  standards, specifications, guidelines, best practices, procedures, processes, contractual language, service level agreements, non-disclosure agreements, contract addendums and other ways you codify and communicate behaviors within your organization and with other organizations with whom you share data handling responsibility.

- Understand, document and communicate how to request changes for each of these, including who approves changes. Publish this information and routinely communicate outcomes of requests (accepted, rejected, redirected to a different governing body for consideration, etc.). Establish governing bodies as needed and record requests and outcomes. Be prepared to provide this documentation as requested by auditors and investigators.

- Write policy to provide foundational guidance. Avoid the temptation to endorse policy that institutionalizes activities that drive internal agendas. This often applies to customer advocates such as sales or product support teams, who are sometimes tempted to codify customer outcomes (whether for data handling or coding standards or response times, etc.) into internal compliance requirements via policy. When considering a policy change that enforces customer-facing behaviors, ask whether policy, procedure or contractual language (such as a service level agreement) would best address the concern.

- Fully explore and document how your information security policy should extend outside of your organization, through third-party agreements and contracts. At a minimum, understand where you are bound by regulation or obligated through contract to extend policy to third parties by reviewing the regulations you are subject to and the contracts you currently have in place.

  Beyond that, evaluate when policies you have in place for employee behavior should apply to contractors and consultants who might have identical or very similar data handling requirements. Make sure this is enforced through contract review, security addendums, non-disclosure agreements and periodic audit for compliance. As with policy for internal use, policy that extends contractually cannot be written (or signed) and then forgotten, it must be enforced.

- Consider using a well-known security authority as a source for templates, wording, and a starter list of policies for your organization. An excellent source that I recommend is the SANS institute. They make their policy templates for general, network security, server security and application security available for free. Suggested sections for the security policy template include:

  - Overview
  - Purpose
  - Scope
  - Policy
  - Policy Compliance
  - Related Standards, Policies, and Processes

A sample set for general security policies might include the following:

SANS General Policy Set

- Acceptable Encryption Policy
- Acceptable Use Policy
- Clean Desk Policy
- Disaster Recovery Plan Policy
- Digital Signature Acceptance Policy
- Email Policy
- Ethics Policy
- Pandemic Response Policy
- Security Response Policy
- End User Encryption Key Protection Policy

The full set of templates is available on the SANS website[32], and a sample (for email) policy follows in the appendix of this chapter.

Many of the words we use in information security, like "insurance," "risk," "breach," and "control," come with baggage. This applies to "policy" more than all the others. The dictionary tells us that policy is "a course or principle of action, adopted or proposed by a government, party, business or individual." The key words here as I've mentioned above, are principle and action. Policy is deliberate, it guides decisions, and once decisions are made the expectation is that action will be taken to ensure the policy is implemented. Keep policy at the institutional level and leave the "how" to the people closest to the operations and you can take away some of the baggage.

---

[32] https://www.sans.org/security-resources/policies/

> "One reason why so many policies are ineffective is that the actual structure of the policy has never been standardized within the organization."

Many CISOs may feel that our titles don't reflect what we actually do on a daily basis. It may seem that we are actually the CPO (Chief Policy Officer) of the organization and not the CISO. Our days are filled with writing, reviewing, and updating policies rather than deploying next-generation security tools, the fun stuff. Indeed, it can seem that there is no end to the number of new policies that we need to draft and disseminate within the organization. Too many policies, however, results in policy overload and policy fatigue among our colleagues. Too few policies, and the commensurate gap in procedures and practices could lead to operational blind spots that put our organizations at risk. There has to be a reasonable balance to ensure that the objectives of the policies, procedures, and practices are addressed without generating security apathy among our colleagues.

Just as important as the right balance and number of policies is how they should be enforced. A policy that is shelfware only should never be written. Policies should be operationally translated into documented procedures and practices – to wit, the notion of P-cubed (policy, procedure, and practice). Policies without the associated guidance on the procedures and practices are incomplete. It's easy to say that we should employ a least privilege methodology, that critical data should be encrypted, that we should have strong passwords, and on and on. However, without specific guidance on how these end states are achieved, there is too much room for ambiguity. Procedural guidance should indicate how the practices should be performed, how review and approval of activities is conducted and evidenced, as well as the documentation and systems used to complete a given procedure. Although often maligned as stifling and/or trivial, checklists can help validate that routine practices are accurately and completely addressed.

Structure Counts: Consistent Policy Design

One reason why so many policies are ineffective is that the actual structure of the policy has never been standardized within the organization. The consequence of this is that policies are incomplete and omit key elements required for their successful implementation, notably management authorization and employee acknowledgement. A well-structured policy should at a minimum include the following core elements:

- Policy ownership – in the context of a RACI matrix, a policy requires someone to be accountable for the policy's required procedures and practices. This individual or role should be noted as the policy's owner.

- Review and approval – policies should be reviewed and approved by executive management. This authorization should be formalized and include those executives that are impacted by the policy's scope. Stated differently, policies should capture the review, approval, and formal authorization of executives beyond traditional IT roles such as the CIO or CISO.

- Employee acknowledgement and sanctions – for policies to be effective, they need to be read and acknowledged by employees and, in many cases, independent contractors and vendors. A policy should include a formal acknowledgement section where employees confirm that they have read the policy and understand that failure to comply with the policy, unless duly authorized by management (and this would be an exception), could lead to disciplinary action up to and including employee dismissal. Ideally, once the policy has been signed by employees, these acknowledgement forms should be kept by human resources and maintained in each employee's HR file.

- Effective date – policies should have a clearly stated effective date. This formally conveys that the policy is in force and is part of the organization's overall governance practices.

- Review date – policies should be subject to review. Ideally, policies should be subject to an annual review where there may be updates to procedures and practices, scope, or policy ownership. Language indicating that the policy may be reviewed and updated from time to time based on changes to the organization, technology, or other changes should be incorporated to offer flexibility.

- Version – policies should be version controlled. The versions should be changed following each annual review (or during an interim review if required).

- Scope – policies should have a defined scope or boundary for their required procedures and practices. The policy's scope will define where applicability to required procedures starts and ends within the organization. As a case in point, there may be a policy to require encryption of data in transit and at rest. The scope of the policy would specify which types of information should be encrypted (e.g. PII or ePHI).

- Procedures and practices – Policies should reference the specific procedures and practices required to ensure that the policy objectives are being met. Good procedural documentation leaves little space for ambiguity. Procedures should include a basic RACI (RASCI for those so inclined) to note who is Responsible (the individuals or departments doing the actual work), Accountable (the specific role or individual that effectively owns the result of the procedure), Consulted (individuals with expertise and knowledge of a given domain that can help validate and inform procedures and practices), and Informed (those departments, individuals, clients, regulators, boards, etc. that should know about the existence of procedures and the outcomes of its activities). Procedural documentation should also capture the system(s) of record used to carry out the activities, the types of documentation created relating to the procedure, and where this documentation is stored. Validation and verification activities should also be clearly captured and understood. The documentation related to procedures and practices should operate with a basic premise to "declare war on ambiguity." There should be no doubt what's required, who is doing the work, and how it is measured and validated.

Collectively, these elements become requisite constituent parts of a well-structured policy. Clearly, there is also the actual content of the policy delineating the specific outcomes desired by the policy's enforcement.

other approaches to effectively restrict access should be incorporated into core security policies. In the aggregate, they impart an important tone-at-the-top validation that management is focused on limiting access to only those roles and individuals required to fulfill a function. Auditors, both internal and external, will often look to see that this language is part of the organization's overall security program and its documented policies.

Application Access – Within the core security policy, there should be a section that speaks to application access and associated controls. This section should overtly reference the acceptable use policy (described below) and state that access to the organization's applications is for official use only and that access rights reflect a least-privilege methodology. The policy should also outline the frequency or events that would trigger a substantive review of the access rights for specified material applications (defined as those applications that contain PII, cardholder data, ePHI, or other organizationally-sensitive data). Ideally, as sometimes found in larger and more mature organizations, access rights to specific applications and the roles that are enabled tie directly to specific job functions in documented and approved job descriptions. Access policies should also favor the use of multi-factor authentication (MFA), at a minimum for roles that have elevated privileges. The goal is to have documented authorization for application use and non-repudiation for any transactions that are associated with the application. Procedures should be established to ensure that access logs are maintained and reviewed for subsequent assessment.

Physical Access – Controls related to physical access should build upon those stated in the least privilege section noted above. Access to the organization's facilities, especially critical operational rooms, computer rooms and/or data center locations, and areas where sensitive information is maintained should be locked and access should only be granted to those individuals with a documented justification for that access. Good physical access policies and their corresponding procedures will ensure that critical access and egress points employ biometrics and other mechanisms to enhance physical security. The policy should also ensure that access logs are maintained and that there is a requirement to validate a government-issued ID to gain physical access for specific areas within the organization.

Acceptable Use – Similar to the privacy notice and policy, the acceptable use policy should ideally be reviewed by the organization's legal counsel as well as human resources. An acceptable use policy (AUP) needs to convey in no uncertain terms that the use of the organization's assets, including laptops, phone systems, servers, applications, networks, etc., is only for official organizational purposes. The AUP should explicitly prohibit the use of the organization's assets for illegal activities, the viewing of pornography (beyond being a poor use of organizational resources, these sites are typically filled with weaponized URLs and other malicious code), the e-mailing of unsolicited messages (spam), and the sending of proprietary or confidential information that is not protected by non-disclosure agreement, among other restrictions. The utopian goal of this section's language should result in employees agreeing to use the organization's assets only for authorized organizational activities. Clearly this is rarely feasible so the ultimate approach will reflect the organization's risk tolerance and organizational culture. An organization that precludes social media applications and online shopping may be in a permanent staffing crisis. There is nuance and balance as to the right level of "acceptable use" for the organization. Our goal as CISOs is to mitigate as much risk as is possible given the dynamics above.

Vendor Management – While vendor management policies have been the norm for large defense contractors and multi-national organizations concerned with supply chain risk, they have recently become part of the policy arsenal for small and medium sized businesses and organizations (collectively SMBs). The recent emphasis on vendor risk stems in part from the overt legal statutes requiring vendor risk assessments (e.g. HIPAA-HITECH[33] and GLBA[34]) as well as from well-publicized breaches that resulted from a compromised vendor (e.g., the Target breach[35]). Vendor management policies should outline organizational expectations with respect to privacy and security, authorization approvals to contract third-party services, how vendor risk is assessed and categorized, legal review practices for vendor or organization-supplied contracts (I strongly advocate requesting a right to audit clause), data flow documentation to show which information is shared with the vendor and how this is controlled, and standards for vendor operational reviews.

Change Management – A change management policy should be incorporated by reference into the core security policy. Managing change is never easy, so it's important to ensure that the organization is establishing clear expectations regarding how change should be addressed across the entire change-management lifecycle. Here the realm of IT Service Management (ITSM), as described in detail in the ISO 20000 standard, is extremely helpful in that it looks at change management practices holistically, incorporating configuration management and risk management associated with

---

[33]. Cornell's Law School has a great reference to quickly look up Code of Federal Regulation (CFR) references: https://www.law.cornell.edu/cfr/text/45/164.308.

[34]. http://www.occ.treas.gov/news-issuances/bulletins/2001/bulletin-2001-35a.pdf

[35]. http://krebsonsecurity.com/2014/02/target-hackers-broke-in-via-hvac-company/

changes. The policy should clearly indicate who is authorized to approve changes, the request process, how change is triaged for risk, including privacy and security risks, what the rollback procedures would be should the change fail, notification procedures, and expectations related to documenting changes to configuration items (CIs) or high-level infrastructure.

Incident Management – Let's face it, there will be an incident and there will be a need to quickly and efficiently address the situation at hand. The incident management policy (and plan) is critical. The policy should have clearly-defined response times and escalation procedures indicating who should be notified and by when. This policy absolutely requires the engagement of other C-suite executives as well as the organization's legal counsel. There is a school of thought suggesting that should an incident occur, external counsel should be notified first to invoke attorney client privilege. External counsel would then contract forensic teams and other vendors required to support the crisis-management activities associated with the incident. Regardless of whether this is your organization's approach, the incident policy should provide overt references to contractual obligations for notification, legal obligations for notification, and other prescribed activities. The procedures related to incident management should also be thoroughly documented, including how to best maintain forensic evidence.

Password Policy – No security policy would be complete without guidance and expectations related to passwords. We all know that passwords are the proverbial weak link in our security chain. That being said, there are some basic practices that can mitigate some of these inherent weaknesses. Password policies (and their associated procedural deployments with tools like Active Directory) should address password complexity (numbers, symbols, and spaces), the prohibition of using common names or other items that would make a dictionary attack easier, password aging, password length (the longer the better and ideally at least 12 characters), as well as overt prohibitions on sharing passwords. The procedures should also work to validate security practices regarding how passwords are stored (yes, clear text is bad), and special considerations for system administrator accounts.

Bring Your Own Device (BYOD) – There are few polices that are more organizationally challenging than a BYOD policy. Clearly, there is a requirement to engage human resources and legal counsel to ensure that the policy is enforceable in circumstances where an employee uses their own device for work-related activities (not an ideal scenario, but a very common scenario none-the-less). BYOD has significant procedural challenges, including enforcement of passwords, patching, and encryption practices as well as the use of non-sanctioned applications. Co-mingling is rarely a good idea. Even more operationally challenging is how to leverage mobile device management (MDM) tools with remote wiping capabilities. Given the costs of a breach and the risks associated with employee-owned devices, the incremental cost of providing the necessary tools to employees appears to be justifiable. Again, this is a policy that requires collaboration with colleagues across the organization and where risk-mitigating activities and risk exposure should be fully reviewed by the team.

Workstation Security – Depending on the organization's work environment, specific policy requirements for workstation security may be required by statute (notably in healthcare). A workstation policy should have standards related to user system timeouts, standards related to physical documents containing PII and/or ePHI at the workstation, and other controls such as anti-malware being deployed on the workstation. Newer anti-malware tools can help enforce the requirements of the AUP and white list only sanctioned applications while blocking applications and URLs that are either a distraction or security risk or both. Procedures may also be established to indicate which, if any, applications can be deployed to a workstation or other device by employees. There is a generational issue, similar to the BYOD policy above, in that younger employees may not welcome such controls and restrictions, the absence of which can create significant security challenges.

Clearly, there is an almost never-ending supply of security policy topics to address. How extensive an organization's policy environment is should reflect the size and complexity of the organization and the industry in which it operates. Structuring policies consistently, reducing ambiguity related to procedures and practices, and gathering the insights of colleagues will help ensure that the time invested in writing and reviewing policies will be time well spent.

> "I truly believe that when an organization follows best practices, and the CISO mentors his/her security teams, when tools are installed, tuned and leveraged for maximum effectiveness, cybersecurity becomes a strategic asset."

In the almost three decades that I have worked in the field of Information Technology and Cybersecurity, I have been with some good organizations and some that didn't meet my expectations. Those that I found to be excellent were those that had documented policies and procedures that were supported by executive management and enforced. This is important to a CISO because building expanding and maturing a cybersecurity program is hard work. Often, the challenges facing senior security professionals such as a CISO, will revolve around being able to explain why something must be done and how it will benefit the organization.

Within the company there are departments (business development, finance, etc.) who will have annual plans with objectives that are tracked and updated throughout the year. Many of these objectives will be focused around business plans, revenue forecasts and profitability numbers. For cybersecurity, we lack these types of concrete guideposts that help navigate departments through their fiscal year to meet strategic objectives. For cybersecurity teams, the selected security and risk management frameworks are the guideposts that drive a corporate security program. For these frameworks to be developed, implemented and managed correctly the CISO must create specific policies that enable the organization, its departments and the security teams to understand how cybersecurity is implemented and what processes and procedures must be followed for it to be effective.

With that in mind, to fight cyber incidents companies must fund and create a mature cybersecurity and risk management ecosystem. As I have stated in previous discussions, for a CISO to change corporate culture to accept cyber as a valuable practice they must have mature policies in place that are accepted as ground truth. This will not be easy because most departments look at the CISO and their teams as the people who say "No" and are not interested in any policies they may create. However, remember that many of the policies that you, as a CISO, put together will be for your teams and for the organization overall. What is important is that you put these guideposts in place so your teams have a concrete path to follow to effectively perform their jobs. Then, as you mature the processes for your personnel and reduce the organization's exposure to risk, you slowly proceed to educate your executive management team and the organization's various business departments. I have found that even if it takes me several years to finally get a department to follow policy, it is worth it. Once one department looks at you and your program as partners and works with you to accomplish some projects (which you may have to help fund), others will start to reach out and ask you to come in and discuss risk and possibly present to their staffs. To achieve this type of growth and impact within a company, it all starts with the guideposts – the policies and procedures you put in place to effectively implement your selected frameworks. This leads us to the three questions we will discuss in this chapter on certain policies I believe a CISO must create and evangelize to help the cybersecurity program mature in the organization. The questions under consideration are:

1. In building the organization's information security policy, what components should the CISO consider essential?
2. Does the organization have a formal, documented, incident response policy and plan? If not, what best practices does the CISO need to consider to create them for the organization?
3. In developing a mature cybersecurity program, what recommended policies should the CISO develop to increase his/her security program's effectiveness?

You Will Be Judged by Your Policy

As a CISO, one of the first requirements you will need to develop and evangelize within the organization, from executive management to the hourly line worker, is the company's information security policy. This document will become the key reference for your security program and the business for any issues that relate to cybersecurity. It will be used by your stakeholders as a guide to assist them when they order technology services, purchase new IT assets or implement strategic technology projects. They will also use it as an executive template, a ruler to measure whether they are within its acceptable parameters in relation to cybersecurity and risk exposure to the organization. So as you can imagine, this document will have some serious impact on the organization and how it conducts business. This is why it should reflect the organization's objectives for security and the agreed-upon strategy for securing information. It is also why, for it to be effective, it must be formally chartered by executive management. So let's discuss what components make up this important document. The first question we will consider is, *"In building the organization's information security policy, what is the process and what components should the CISO consider essential?"*

As CISO, the information security policy you create is a foundational part of your information security program, hence it is critical that we develop it with an understanding of its strategic importance to the organization. The first step you will need to take in developing the information security policy is to meet with executive management. This policy will have an impact across the organization and you will need executive management to sponsor it, providing it the legitimacy of an executive mandate. To get this type of executive support, you will need to meet with executive leadership and get their input. In these meetings, which I usually do one-on-one, you will want to find out how they view security; what data, processes and applications they view as critical to the business; and what types of data, work processes, projects, etc. should be classified as sensitive and afforded enhanced protective measures.

One thing I would highly recommend is that when you conduct these interviews with executive management you remember that you are there as a listener. Listen and do not interrupt. Learn what's important to them, note their responses to your prepared questions, and then follow up with a document summarizing their answers and what you have learned. This will convey to them that you cared about their input and it will demonstrate that their insight has been correctly documented.

With this information collected, you can now start to review it for commonalities. What I have found in the past is that specific applications and data types will stand out as critical to multiple members of the leadership team and thus should be highlighted as business assets that will require a higher level of governance. In Chapter 2, I outlined the importance of using this collected information to create a data governance program. This program will enable you to classify the identified data types in accordance with their criticality to the organization's business operations. This program should also be used to designate which identified data types have compliance requirements that will dictate specific security and handling procedures with respect to the business processes that created them. With this data governance plan in place, you should now have greater insight into executive management's opinions with respect to security.

You should also have a more concrete understanding of what data assets are considered important, and with this information it's time to create a comprehensive organizational security strategy. To do this we will first select a security framework that is consistent with the criticality of the identified data types. This framework will be the foundational platform on which you will build your information security program and will serve as a guide for creating the company's Information Security Policy. Using an industry standard security framework (NIST, ISO, ISACA, etc.) will help ensure that the policy you create has a legitimacy that executive management can accept and it will provide a policy that external auditors and business partners can endorse.

In creating the information security policy, there are a couple of best practices that I would recommend. First, it is imperative that the policy you create reflects actual business practices. If it doesn't, then the policy will never be fully accepted. I once worked with a CISO who created his policy based on best practices he hoped his organization would someday follow. Obviously that policy was never really followed, and the end result was an organization with no true guidance on cybersecurity.

The second best practice I would recommend to a CISO is to keep it small. You don't need a large, encompassing mandate that would confuse everyone and result in a policy that is never followed. Instead, agree to a small number of principles that all of the business managers in the organization can accept and use these as guides to build your first policy. Once this policy is created, provide it to the organization's executive leadership team for their approval and request that it be published through them to the company as an executive policy to be observed by all personnel, partners and third party vendors.

Now you may be asking yourself, "If this is an information security policy for the organization, why don't we include everything in it? Why keep it small?" As mentioned above, you want something that will be manageable and can be accepted by your business stakeholders. When I'm asked this question, I reply "The information security policy is like the handle of an umbrella. The actual umbrella top, that protects the organization from the digital elements, is the company's information security standards and guidelines document. It is the standards and guidelines documents that definitively spell out how company employees would follow the security policy and its mandates." Basically, you don't have to go in depth. You can keep the policy and its components generalized, and as an employee reads the information security policy, they will find references to explicit sections of the standards and guidelines documents.

These standards and guidelines will act as a point of reference, providing definite information for implementing a specific policy component. So to sum this up, the CISO should speak with executive management and senior business stakeholders. The data collected from these discussions should be used to create an executive information security policy. Stakeholders, throughout the organization, will use the detailed steps found in the information security standards and guidelines to implement this policy.

The information collected to create the policy will also be used by the CISO for selecting an appropriate security framework. This framework will be the foundation for managing the risk exposure for the critical data assets identified by executive leadership. This selected framework in turn will drive the creation of an information security program, and as this program matures it will be the primary vehicle for the CISO to govern the organization's information security policy.

As you can see, we are looking at a life cycle. The CISO will periodically meet with executive management and over time changes will require policy and program updates. What this should mean to you as a CISO is that this process doesn't stop. It is continuous, and you need to own it as one of the core business processes for your cybersecurity program.

Chapter 9 Key Point and Action Item 4

There are certain requisite elements security policies should incorporate. While larger, more complex organizations may have a more expansive list of policy objectives, at a minimum a security policy should address the following topics: acceptable use of organizational assets and systems, password guidelines, data governance and classification, bring your own device (BYOD) policy, privacy notice and policy, establishment of a least privilege methodology, physical access, application access, and encryption·

You should validate the requisite elements of your organization's security policy and add the missing elements.

Some final notes that I believe we should talk about before you create your information security policy. *First*, don't forget that this document should be kept high level because you have other methods to provide in-depth information. *Second*, if you are with a large organization you will need to write your policy with the understanding that each business channel/department will probably have a departmental policy on how they will interpret the corporate policy so that it meets their business requirements. *Third*, if you decide to add sub-policies to the overall document, make sure they don't repeat a subject in the parent document. This will prevent confusion and general mistrust of the overall policy.

Now for the actual components of an information security policy. These are just some recommended components. You should choose the ones that fit your executive leadership team's requirements.

1. _Purpose_ – should address the strategic reasons for the document, and describe some of the processes the organization hopes to establish with it.

2. _Scope_ – should address all organizational assets the policy applies to.

3. _Information Classification_ – in this section, you should provide content-specific definition of data classification. Don't use generic terms such as "sensitive" or "confidential."

4. _Management Goals_ – this section is where executive management can provide the specific corporate reasons why this policy is mandatory, for example: "prevent loss of intellectual property."

5. _Definitions_ – provide the definitions of specific words so there is a clear understanding of their meaning as it pertains to this policy and the organization.

6. _General Policy_ – this is one of three major sections of the information security policy and it pertains to all departments, partners and third parties who do business with the organization.
   a. _Authority_ – addresses who has authority for information security within the organization and what actions go with that responsibility.
   b. _Rights of the Organization_ – addresses that the organization has rights to all computers, data, and assets created, stored, and owned by the organization.
   c. _Access to Information_ – will typically spell out the basics of authorized access, logon and password requirements, prohibiting the connecting unauthorized assets to corporate networks, etc.
   d. _Unauthorized Practices_ – addresses the installation of unauthorized software, the use of hacker-type tools by unauthorized personnel, and the use of software/hardware to obscure, hide or interfere with audit/logging mechanisms.

7. *Departmental Management Policy* – this is the second of the three major components of the information security policy and it is specifically orientated toward departments.
   a. *Responsibility* – addresses the fact that the departmental directors are ultimately responsible for departmental compliance with the provisions of this policy.
   b. *Training* – addresses the fact that management within the department must provide sufficient training for personnel so they can follow policy mandates.
   c. *Manage Sub-Policies* – each department will review and update its own sub-policies for how it will implement the mandated security standards.
   d. *Access Management* – addresses how the department will manage access for its personnel, how accounts and data will be managed for terminated employees, and requirements for personnel requesting specific types of supplemental access.
   e. *Incident Response* – addresses how department personnel will act if there is a cyber incident and who they should report suspicious issues to in their office.

8. *User Policy* – this is the last of the three major components of the information security policy. It contains specific requirements that all users must follow.
   a. *Responsibility* – addresses the overall responsibility of users who use organizational IT assets.
   b. *Consequences* – states that personnel will be disciplined if they violate the standards and guidelines spelled out in the appropriate use policy.
   c. *Cooperate with Investigations* – all employees are directed to fully cooperate with investigations.
   d. *User ID and Password* – states that all personnel will use a unique user ID and password, and that passwords will comply with information security standards and guidelines.
   e. *Acknowledgement Form* – when they are given their user accounts, all personnel will sign and acknowledge that they have read the information security policy.

9. *Security Manager/Administrator Policy* – specific requirements for administrators are delineated in this section of the policy.
   a. *Responsibility* – addresses the fact that if a computer system has been breached by an unauthorized party, or there is a reasonable suspicion of a breach or other system compromise, the administrator must immediately change the password on the involved system.
   b. *Management of Logs* – Logs of computer security related events must provide sufficient data to support

comprehensive audits of the effectiveness of, and compliance with, security measures.

    c.   *Implementation of Security Controls* – Mechanisms used to detect and record significant computer security events must be resistant to attacks. These attacks include attempts to deactivate, modify, or delete the logging software or the logs themselves.

    d.   *Protection of Sensitive Data* – Production application systems which access financial or sensitive information must generate logs that show every addition, modification, and deletion to such information.

    e.   *Access Management* – addresses how the CISO will manage access for his/her administrators, how accounts and data will be managed for terminated employees, and specifies requirements for personnel requesting specific types of supplemental access.

10. *Roles and Responsibilities* – need to be specific from CEO to department heads to CISO to service providers and users.

11. *Appendixes* – typically list references that direct the policy requirements.

    a.   *Legal References* – compliance regulations, organizational policies, laws, etc.

    b.   *Required Forms* – forms personnel typically will fill out as related to this policy.

    c.   *Distribution* – who will receive and distribute the policy.

    d.   *Administrative Department* – the department that will manage the policy, update it, and when required, decommission it.

As we finish our first discussion, I hope you have gained some insight into how, as CISO, you would create an information security policy. I also hope that I conveyed the criticality of getting your executive management involved in this process. I have found, over the 20-plus years I have been working in this field, that organizations do not like change. Especially change that may come on an enterprise wide scale. So understand that you need to get management involved. With their input, you can craft an information security policy and program that aligns with the business' strategic goals and in the process get management buy-in to employ your program as a mandate for everyone to follow.

Now as we transition to the next section, I will state that even with this executive backing, it is still incumbent on you as the CISO to talk with your stakeholders. Don't be afraid to go on a road show to answer their questions, send out "How To…" documents to help their personnel, and evangelize the importance to the organization of not only accepting but embracing cybersecurity as part of its culture for it to succeed.

Incident Response, The Policy No One Wants to Use

So now I want to paint a picture for you. It's two o'clock in the morning and as CISO you receive a phone call informing you that everything is not right at the organization's primary datacenter. The company's network team and security liaison, who work the night shift, are both reporting that they see suspicious traffic and upon investigation have found evidence of a malware outbreak in several production servers. As you wake up and shift into troubleshooting mode, you receive more information. This isn't just a few servers; the issue has multiplied to several of the organization's datacenters. It is at this time that you transition into your role as the incident response team manager and you activate the organization's incident response plan. The next issue we will discuss is centered around incident response, the best practices for building an incident response policy and recommendations for creating and managing an incident response plan. So our next question is as follows: *"Does the company have a formal, documented incident response policy and plan? If not, what best practices does the CISO need to consider to create them for the organization?"*

IT leaders today know that they must align their departments with the business and support its strategic goals to be successful. However, one area many companies still need to work on is incident response. That is because enterprises plan for and spend ample amounts of time and resources developing security processes and policies to secure their networks and critical assets. Yet when there is a security incident, it is often found they are lacking in how to lead a coordinated response to the event within the organization and with external partners.

I am sure there are many reasons why organizations are found lacking and do not have a formal incident response policy or a documented incident response plan. I personally have seen companies focus on their technology, believing that when the time comes the hardware and software will save the day. In that belief, they are missing a critical point – incident response isn't about technology, it is really about business.

At its core, incident response is about an organization's strategy and business processes, it is tactical in nature, and it will incorporate stakeholders from many departments within the company and its external partners. Incident response is an action plan for dealing with events like internal/external intrusions, cybercrime, disclosure of sensitive information, or denial-of-service attacks. As you can see from all four of the example events I provided, they definitely impact the organization and its ability to conduct business. In the discussion that follows, I will describe some best practices to embrace in developing an incident response policy and plan. So let's get started.

Chapter 9 Key Point and Action Item 5

Incident response is quickly becoming a required organizational competency, whether it is to address a security breach or another event that impacts operations. Incident response is ultimately about organizational resiliency. Incident response policy requires the input of and collaboration with other departments within the organization, especially as it relates to escalation and notification requirements that may be required by regulators, customers, or other key stakeholders.

You should review and update your incident response policy, including escalation and notification procedures, to make sure it's consistent with the organization's obligations.

The primary objective of incident response should be to guide the incident response team members in a methodical way to respond to and remediate an incident. This process should be focused on managing the cyber event in a methodical way to reduce its impact on the company, reduce the recovery time for full operations, and minimize the costs to triage the incident. There are several issues I have seen that can prevent an organization from implementing their incident response plan effectively. Some of these issues are:

1. The documentation for the incident response policy and its tactical plan is out of date or it is too generic. Both of these issues I believe can be tied to how the plan is managed and whether it is assigned to a specific team member (CISO, CIO, CRO, etc.). If it's not assigned to anyone specific, it becomes an orphaned process and thus a piece of paper that doesn't provide much benefit during the response to an incident.

2. Another issue I have seen is that incident response plans in large organizations tend to be developed in silos. Individual departments or businesses will create an incident response plan for how they will respond. Unfortunately, with the advanced threats we face today, these types of plans may work well for a targeted attack, but are not effective for an incident that spans across the business and involve multiple

business channels.

3. One last issue that I have observed: in times of emergency, many of the decision-making opportunities are based on the relationships and the organizational knowledge that team members have versus a well-defined process. This leads to decisions being managed by a few people who have institutional knowledge and may result in a "single point of failure" scenario if they are unavailable when an incident occurs.

For these reasons, organizations should create an incident response policy backed by executive management and a strategic incident response plan to execute the policy in detail. There are many advantages to having an incident response process that can significantly help organizations. Two advantages that I believe are critical to the organization are the improvement of decision making by team members and having a methodology that is followed by all stakeholders who respond to the event.

With an incident response plan, you will have a documented "decision/responsibility" matrix. This in essence helps team members understand who is making the decisions and at what level they are authorized to do so. It also provides clear delineation of specific incidents where escalation of the response from the organization is warranted, and who is authorized to make those decisions.

Another advantage, which I believe is crucial for the incident response team, is that with an effective incident response policy and plan, team members are empowered to coordinate and respond to each other across all business functions. Incident response has typically been thought of as an IT department process, but an effective incident response process will incorporate stakeholders from many departments within the enterprise, including communications, public affairs, legal, human resources, compliance and audit, and business operations. The response plan will also include response processes for external parties such as law enforcement, third party incident and forensics teams, and strategic partners. From these two lists, I think it's evident that incident response requires coordination with both dissimilar internal team members and external entities.

One last advantage I believe incident response plans provide to a company is they help ensure that minor incidents don't become major incidents. In the numerous plans I have created over the years, I have always had an escalation matrix that documented for my team members who is to respond, the processes/tools they should use, and what information/artifacts/actions they are allowed to take to remediate the issue. All of my plans are written to respond and remediate at the lowest level and communicate to executive management the end results. All of my plans use the incident response life cycle found in NIST's Computer Security Incident Handling Guide (Cichonski, Millar, Grance, & Scarfone, 2012). A picture of that life cycle is as follows:

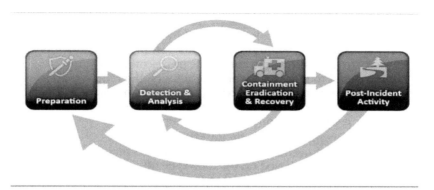

Incident Response Life Cycle

Now that we understand some of the issues with not having a plan and the advantages of having one, let's look at the basic building blocks that you should incorporate into your first incident response policy and incident response plan. The components that I consider best practice are taken from NIST SP 800-61 rev2, "Computer Security Incident Handling Guide" (Cichonski, Millar, Grance, & Scarfone, 2012). NIST recommends that you first create an incident response policy. The elements of this policy will be used to create a more in-depth incident response plan.

As we noted in the discussion above about creating an information security policy, you will create a policy to speak to the need for the process and then create a plan/program to actually execute and manage the process for the organization.

Before we get into the specifics, I do want to state that the selected components I list below for an *incident response policy* will vary from organization to organization. The components I have selected and used in previous policies are as follows:

- Statement of Management Commitment
  - o Highly recommended so stakeholders throughout the organization know this is a policy supported by executive leadership.

It is better to have an incident response framework to assist them and collaborate with your partners to make sure the incident response process is executed correctly the first time rather than you trying to manage everything on your own. Remember, *"security does not exist in a vacuum, but it does well in a community."*

In completing this question, remember that as the CISO for your organization you will probably be designated as one of the leaders for the company's incident response team. You will also probably be the person given the responsibility of keeping the program and all of its documentation updated, and researching what tools, training and best practices the team members will require to be effective.

I recommend that you reach out to your community and see what lessons learned your peers have to offer as you manage your program. Also, I highly stress using a framework like the NIST reference I provided or another framework such as ISO/IEC 27035-2. What is important is that you use these frameworks as your guidepost to assist you and your incident response team. This issue is critical for your organization, so don't try to design an all-inclusive incident response program from the ground up. Use a solid, vetted industry framework, talk to your community for best practices to fine tune the program, and train, train, train the team so that in the event of an incident your response will be like "muscle memory."

Policies and More Policies, Why Are They Important?

For the final question of this chapter I want to talk about what information security policies a CISO should include as part of his/her cybersecurity program. These policies form the foundation for how a CISO will incorporate cybersecurity throughout their company and strive to make it a standard process that is included in all business decisions. Without formal information security policies and standards, an organization cannot effectively secure its critical information assets and this will significantly impact its ability to succeed. Information security policies and standards establish executive leadership's commitment to securing critical information assets. They also provide guidance to managers and other employees regarding their information security responsibilities, set the *security tone* for the organization and, finally, provide standards for your team members and IT personnel to reference in the daily execution of their duties. It's with the importance of policies and standards in mind that we focus on our last question: *"In developing a mature cybersecurity program, what recommended policies should the CISO develop to increase his/her security program's effectiveness?"*

To begin, remember that the information security policies and the standards you create need to accurately reflect the organization and current business processes. If they do not, then you as the CISO will find yourself in conflict with the organization because your information security policies and standards do not support organizational realities. If you continue to write policy without taking the business into account, you risk damaging the organization's commitment to cybersecurity and you will diminish the effectiveness of the program you are trying to build.

In creating information security policies, I strongly recommend that you design them with the business and its operations in mind. Some helpful ideas that I believe you should consider as you write policy are as follows:

Policy Writing Guidelines

- What is the organization's strategic focus, where is it going?
- What type of data and applications does the organization use?
- Do you understand the different classes of information workers and the types of data they require?
- Are there unique needs for data sharing/access and protection requirements between different parts of the business?
- Do you understand the needs for data sharing/access and protection requirements between the business and its third party vendors and partners?
- Does the organization have unique data or industry compliance requirements, obligations and duties?
- How well does the organization and its culture embrace opportunities for change?
- How stable is the organization's current technology portfolio? Is it undergoing significant change?
- Are there previous information security policies and standards that can be leveraged?
- Are there other organizational policies and standards that can be used as references for the information security policy requirements?

I recommend that you seek answers to these questions before you put a significant amount of time into writing and implementing any information security policies. The answers to these questions will help you understand what's important to the organization, and as a result you will have more context on what needs to be protected.

Now that you have some ideas for writing policy, let's look at what policies you should include in your cybersecurity program. We have already discussed that you will need to write the organization's corporate information security policy because this policy will become the standard for why the corporation needs a security program.

We also just finished a discussion on why you will need an Incident Response Policy for managing how the organization and the incident response team will remediate cyber incidents. That still leaves a wide range of policies that you, as the CISO, will be required to create to manage the risk associated with all facets of how the organization and its third party vendors and strategic partners use the organization's critical information assets.

I am going to provide a list of policies that I recommend. This is by no means a comprehensive list, and some of these policies may not apply to your organization. As CISO, you will find that the policies you create will typically be dictated by the organization as it upgrades technology, changes business processes or acquires new assets. So with that in mind, the following are some policies I recommend that new CISO's create to manage their organization's risk exposure:

- *Acceptable Use Policy (AUP):* Defines the acceptable use of organizational assets and the appropriate security measures that employees should take to protect these corporate resources.

- *User Account Policy:* Formalizes the account and access request process within the organization.

- *Audit/Investigation Policy:* Addresses the requirement to conduct audits and risk assessments, investigate incidents, ensure compliance with security policies, and monitor user and system activity where appropriate.

- *Data Governance Policy:* Identifies the requirements for classifying and securing data in a manner appropriate to its sensitivity level.

- *Password Policy:* Provides the standards for creating, protecting, and changing strong passwords.

- *Risk-Assessment Policy:* Defines the requirements and provides the authority for your information security team to identify, assess, and remediate risks to the enterprise infrastructure that is required for conducting business.

- *Email Policy:* Provides the requirements for what email is to be used for within the confines of standard business operations. I have also used this policy to describe what email is not allowed to be used for, such as spam, political activities, sending inappropriate content or automatically forwarding business email outside the organization to commercial email providers.

- *Remote-Access Policy*: Defines the standards for connecting to the organization's network from any host or network external to the organization. You would also provide requirements for the security of any remote access technologies, for example the use of IP Security (IPsec) or Layer 2 Tunneling Protocol (L2TP) for VPN connections to the organization's network.

- *BYOD Policy*: Defines the information security requirements for organizational personnel to use their personal communication devices, such as voicemail, smartphones, tablets, and so on.

- *Acceptable Encryption Policy*: Defines the requirements for encryption algorithms that are used within the organization. As CISO, I have had to refer to this policy multiple times when discussing the purchase of a SaaS solution by one of my departments.

- *Extranet Policy*: Defines the requirements that third-party organizations need to implement if they require access to the organization's networks. I have had processes implemented that require partners or third party vendors to sign a third party connection agreement.

- *Network Access Policy*: Provides the requirements for any device that requires connectivity to the internal network. It should also discuss the standards for secure physical port access for all wired and wireless network data ports.

- *Wireless Communication Policy:* Defines standards for wireless systems that are used to connect to the organization's networks.

- *User Education and Awareness Policy*: Specifies that employees must be trained regarding corporate information security policies and practices.

- *Removable Media Policy*: Provides guidance on the use of removable media if the organization is a regulated entity or the organization uses data that has specific regulatory guidance against use of removable media.

- *Malware Protection Policy*: Defines standards for the use of industry standard anti-virus/malware software installed on organizational assets. May spell out requirements for assets that are standalone or BYOD.

- *Secure Configuration Policy*: Provides guidance on having a current inventory of all key information assets, subscribing to notification services for vendor updates on critical patches, and procedures for addressing secure configuration activities, such as changing default passwords in software and hardware or implementing recommended configuration settings to reduce risk exposure to organizational assets.

- *Social Media Policy*: Addresses how employees may use social media for company business and details when the use of social media on company IT assets is considered inappropriate.

As we conclude, many of the above policies can be incorporated into the information security standards and guidelines. Many times, as a CISO for an organization, rather than writing multiple independent policies I would instead detail within the information security standards and guidelines how to conduct some of the procedures listed above. I would do this because the standards and guidelines is a reference document, similar to the procedures documents used in incident response. As a reference document, it's a working checklist of processes that should be followed for a specific subject. I found it was much easier to include many of these sub-policies within this overarching reference than to create separate documents for each specific subject.

Understand that there will be times when for compliance or regulatory purposes you may be required to have a separate document. If this is the case, one reference I have used in the past to provide context when writing policy is the Foley & Lardner "*A Practical Guide for Officers and Directors*" (Foley & Lardner LLP, 2015). This is a good whitepaper to use as a checklist for many of the major policies you will have to write and it provides strategic information that you can use to educate executive leadership on why these policies should be championed by them and implemented.

As I complete our last question, I want to say that I have truly enjoyed our discussions over these last nine chapters. I hope that in

Medication Instructions

Name: MATTHEWS, EVAN   Date: 02-08-2019

You are being treated for: %Diagnoses%

Please take your medications as follows:

Name of Eye Medication	Dosage	Eye	Duration
Besivance	STOP	STOP	STOP
Prolensa	STOP	STOP	STOP
Lotemax	2-4x a day, one drop	Both	As needed for dry eyes and mild irritation
Artificial Tears	Up to 4x a day, one drop	Both	Until next visit
Preservative Free Artificial Tears	As many as needed, one drop	Both	As needed for dry eyes

Comments: If you are taking more than one eye drop, always wait at least **10 MINUTES** between each medication.

Please contact our office if you have any questions.

Jane A Semel MD

Semel Vision Care and Aesthetics

390 N Sepulveda Blvd., Suite 1100 El Segundo, CA 90245   P(310)641-1700 F(310)535-2155 E drsemel@semelvision.com

our discussions I have provided some valuable insight and experience into how a CISO can build his/her security program and in the process contribute value to the business. I truly believe that when an organization follows best practices, when the CISO uses techniques to mentor his/her security teams, and when tools are leveraged and installed in the correct domains for maximum effectiveness, cybersecurity becomes a strategic asset.

So in closing, please remember that to be an effective CISO you will need to partner with your organization, meet your stakeholders, and turn them into champions for your program. Always remember to collaborate because *"Security doesn't exist in a vacuum, but it does well in a community."* Build your community, mentor where you can, and partner with your peers. With that, good luck and welcome to the cyber community as a CISO.

Summary

in Chapter 9, we began our discussion by asking these three questions:

- If the CISO were a board member, what would the data the he/she would most want to see? What would he dashboard look like?
- What does the CISO want from the board in support of their information security responsibilities?
- What are recommended practices for reporting cybersecurity requirements to the board?
- How should the information be presented?
- What important aspects of cybersecurity and risk should the CISO ensure are conveyed to the board?

An organization's security policy functions as a foundational control, setting the tone for the organization's security program and practices. Security policies also become a focal point for audit and regulatory review. As Bill Bonney notes, "Recognize that policy comes with liability at the audit, regulatory, and prosecutorial level when not followed – don't just write it and forget it." You can be held to account for the content of your security policy, so make sure that it's consistent with your organization's capabilities and accurately reflects current organizational expectations. Take a collaborative approach to drafting and implementing security policies.

In closing, we would like to leave you with these five key points and next steps:

1. Don't blur the lines between policy and procedure. Policies set the tone at the top and establish organizational expectations. Procedures define operational activities. You don't need a large, encompassing mandate that would confuse everyone and result in a policy that is never followed. Keep the security policy reasonable in length and incorporate by reference more detailed procedural documentation. Procedures will change more frequently than the higher-level objectives established by the policy. **You should draft a list of the requisite components of your organization's security policy and inventory existing security procedures to reference.**

2. Policies should have a defined structure. Policies should incorporate basic structural elements including version, ownership, scheduled review dates, effective date, employee acknowledgement and sanction for non-compliance, scope, purpose, and evidence of management review and approval. **You should create a policy template that incorporates these minimum structural elements to ensure that policies are consistent in their format and execution.**

3. Know your data and your obligations related to this data explicitly. The data governance and classification policy should inform a number of tangential policies and procedures, including data retention periods (typically covered in a backup policy), encryption policy for certain data types such as cardholder data and electronic protected health information (ePHI), and privacy policies and notices. It is important that you know in intimate detail the types of information your organization creates and uses, how they should be controlled, how they are shared, and ultimately how they are destroyed. **You should create an inventory of data types noting their locations, ownership, controls, and security procedures.**

4. There are certain requisite elements security policies should incorporate. While larger, more complex organizations may have a more expansive list of policy objectives, at a minimum a security policy should address the following topics: acceptable use of organizational assets and systems, password guidelines, data governance and classification, bring your own device (BYOD) policy, privacy notice and policy, establishment of a least privilege methodology, physical access, application access, and encryption. **You should validate the requisite elements of your organization's security policy and add the missing elements.**

5. Incident response is quickly becoming a required organizational competency, whether it is to address a security breach or another event that impacts operations. Incident response is ultimately about organizational resiliency. Incident response policy requires the input of and collaboration with other departments within the organization, especially as it relates to escalation and notification requirements that may be required by regulators, customers, or other key stakeholders. **You should review and update your incident response policy, including escalation and notification procedures, to make sure it's consistent with the organization's obligations.**

We leave this chapter on security policy recognizing that CISOs are in extraordinarily demanding roles. Your position requires a level of operational excellence and domain knowledge rarely matched by other organizational roles. Use your security policy to enhance your knowledge of the organization's activities, stakeholders, and legal obligations. Leverage this insight to set the right tone for your organization, one that focuses on operational resiliency and the protection of the organization's critical assets.

Appendix
Sample Email Policy

Free Use Disclaimer: This policy was created by or for the SANS Institute for the Internet community. All or parts of this policy can be freely used for your organization. There is no prior approval required. If you would like to contribute a new policy or updated version of this policy, please send email to *policy-resources@sans.org*.

Things to Consider: Please consult the Things to Consider FAQ for additional guidelines and suggestions for personalizing the SANS policies for your organization.

Last Update Status: Updated

Overview
Electronic email is pervasively used in almost all industry verticals and is often the primary communication and awareness method within an organization. At the same time, misuse of email can pose many legal, privacy and security risks, thus it's important for users to understand the appropriate use of electronic communications.

Purpose
The purpose of this email policy is to ensure the proper use of <Company Name> email system and make users aware of what <Company Name> deems as acceptable and unacceptable use of its email system. This policy outlines the minimum requirements for use of email within <Company Name> Network.

Scope
This policy covers appropriate use of any email sent from a <Company Name> email address and applies to all employees, vendors, and agents operating on behalf of <Company Name>.

Conclusion

Throughout Volume 1 of the CISO Desk Reference Guide, we've sought to provide you with practical advice, grounded in best practice, that you can start to implement immediately. It is our hope that the questions we have used to frame our thoughts throughout this book served to stimulate your thinking and that the key points and actions in the summaries give you a starting point for improving your organization's cybersecurity program.

As Gary Hayslip is fond of saying, cybersecurity is a contact sport. We encourage you to immediately begin to build your human network by engaging with your peers within your organization and with your colleagues in the broader cybersecurity community. The San Diego model is highly collaborative and completely self-organized, but every region has ample opportunities to meet and form relationships with leaders and experts. Seek them out, it will be well worth your time.

With Volume 1, we've helped the CISO lay the foundation for an effective cybersecurity program. Volume 2 will help CISOs mature their program and address topics such as talent management and education to help you strengthen your team, approaches to monitoring, threat intelligence and backups and planning, and finally setting up programs for incident management, communications, recovery and forensics.

We welcome your feedback and invite you to visit our website: http://www.cisodrg.com or our LinkedIn company page: https://www.linkedin.com/company/ciso-desk-reference-guide.

Bibliography

Adler, Steven. 2007. "CIO Magazine." *CIO Magazine Website.* May 31. http://www.cio.com/article/2438861/enterprise-architecture/six-steps-to-data-governance-success.html.

Ambrose, Christopher. 2014. "Gartner Vendor Management." *Gartner.* October 31. https://www.gartner.com/doc/2894817/monitor-key-risk-criteria-mitigate.

AT&T Network Security. 2014. "Business Section: AT&T Security." *An AT&T Web site, Network Security.* December 12. https://www.business.att.com/content/src/csi/dec odingtheadversary.pdf.

Atkinson, Joyceline R. Davis and Tom. 2010. "Need Speed? Slow Down." *hbr.org.* Harvard Business Review. May. Accessed March 2016. https://hbr.org/2010/05/need-speed-slow-down.

BISSON, DAVID. 2015. *The State of Security.* September 23. http://www.tripwire.com/state-of-security/risk-based-security-for-executives/connecting-security-to-the-business/the-top-10-tips-for-building-an-effective-security-dashboard/.

Caldwell, French. 2009. "Assess Vendor Risks." *Gartner.* September 10. http://www.gartner.com/document/1175014/gart ners-simple-vendor-risk-management.

Chickowski, Ericka. 2016. "Dark Reading: Analytics." *Information Week, DarkReading website.* March 16. http://www.darkreading.com/analytics/10-ways-to-measure-it-security-program-effectiveness/d/d-id/1319494.

Cichonski, Paul, Tom Millar, Tim Grance, and Karen Scarfone. 2012. "Special Publications: NIST Pubs." *National Institute of Standards and Technology web site.* August 23.

http://nvlpubs.nist.gov/nistpubs/SpecialPublicatio
ns/NIST.SP.800-61r2.pdf.

CIS. 2010. "CIS Consensus Information Security Metrics."
Center for Internet Security. Center for Internet
Security. November 11. Accessed June 11, 2016.
https://benchmarks.cisecurity.org/downloads/metr
ics/#progress.

—. 2015. "CIS Controls for Effective Cyber Defense ver 6.0."
Center for Internet Security, CIS Critical Controls.
Center for Internet Security. October 15. Accessed
June 11, 2016. https://www.cisecurity.org/critical-
controls/.

—. 2000. *CIS Critical Security Controls.*
http://www.sans.org/critical-security-controls/.

CMMI Institute. 2002. *About CMMI Institute.* Accessed June
10, 2016. http://cmmiinstitute.com/about-cmmi-
institute.

Cooper, Price Waterhouse. 2014. *Price Waterhouse Cooper.*
12 31.
http://www.pwchk.com/home/eng/rcs_info_securit
y_2014.html.

Deloitte Development, LLC. 2015. "Cybersecurity and the
role of internal audit: An urgent call to action."
Deloitte University Press. Deloitte University Press.
Accessed March 2016.
http://www2.deloitte.com/content/dam/Deloitte/u
s/Documents/risk/us-risk-cyber-ia-urgent-call-to-
action.pdf.

Economic Espionage Act, 18 U.S.C. Ch. 90 § 1839. 1996.
*United States Code Title 18 Chapter 90 Section 1839,
Economic Espionage Act of 1996.* Edited by Office of
the Law Revision. Washington, DC: Government
Printing Office.

FDIC. 2008. *Guidance For Managing Third-Party Risk.* June
6. Accessed June 10, 2016.
https://www.fdic.gov/news/news/financial/2008/f
il08044a.html.

FFIEC. 2015. "Responsibility And Accountability." *FFIEC Online IT Examination Handbook.* FFIEC. November 10. Accessed June 8, 2016. http://ithandbook.ffiec.gov/it-booklets/information-security/security-process/governance/responsibility-and-accountability.aspx.

Foley & Lardner LLP. . 2015. "Intelligence: Taking Control of Cyber Security." *Foley & Lardner LLP .* March 11. Accessed June 11, 2016. https://www.foley.com/taking-control-of-cybersecurity-a-practical-guide-for-officers-and-directors-03-11-2015/.

Greenwald, Judy. 2014. *Home Depot has $105 million in cyber insurance to cover data breach.* September 14. http://www.businessinsurance.com/article/20140914/NEWS07/309149975.

Hayslip, Gary. 2015. "LinkedIn: Pulse "Good Resources for the CISO"." *LinkedIn.com for Professionals.* 12 15. https://app.box.com/v/CISO-Team-Resources .

IBM & Ponemon. 2015. "NH Learning Solutions Document Portal." *NH Learning Solutions Website.* March 15. https://nhlearningsolutions.com/Portals/0/Documents/2015-Cost-of-Data-Breach-Study.PDF.

Ide, R. William, and Amanda Leech. 2015. "tcbblogs.org." *The Conference Board Governance Center Blog.* July 27. http://tcbblogs.org/governance/2015/07/27/a-cybersecurity-guide-for-directors/.

ISACA. 1996. *COBIT 4.1: Framework for IT Governance and Control .* Accessed June 1, 2016. http://www.isaca.org/Knowledge-Center/COBIT/Pages/Overview.aspx.

—. 2007. *COBIT Mapping: Mapping of CMMI for Development V1.2 With COBIT.* Accessed 2016. http://www.isaca.org/Knowledge-Center/Research/ResearchDeliverables/Pages/COBIT-Mapping-Mapping-of-CMMI-for-Development-V1-2-With-COBIT.aspx.

—. 2015. "ISACA Knowledge Center, State of Cybersecurity 2016." *ISACA - CYBER.* December 31. http://www.isaca.org/cyber/Documents/state-of-cybersecurity_res_eng_0316.pdf.

ISO. 2015. "Information security management. Retrieved from International Organization for Standardization (ISO)." *ISO/IEC 27001 - Information security management.* ISO/IEC 27001. December 31. Accessed June 11, 2016. http://www.iso.org/iso/home/standards/managem ent-standards/iso27001.htm.

ISO/IEC. 2008. "Information Classification Policy (ISO/IEC 27001:2005 A.7.2.1)." *Information Security Standards.* July 9. Accessed June 11, 2016. http://iso27001security.com/ISO27k_Model_policy_ on_information_classification.pdf.

ITI. 1988. *ITIL Open Guide.* Accessed 2016. http://itlibrary.org/.

Johnston, Ronald, Alicia Jones, Kelley Dempsey, Nirali Chawla, Alicia Jones, Angela Orebaugh, Matthew Scholl, and Kevin Stine. 2011. "NIST: Special Publications ." *NIST, U.S. Department of Commerce Website.* September 30. http://nvlpubs.nist.gov/nistpubs/Legacy/SP/nistsp ecialpublication800-137.pdf.

KPMG. 2013. "KPMG ." *KPMG.* 12 31. https://www.kpmg.com/US/en/IssuesAndInsights/ ArticlesPublications/Documents/vendor-risk-management.pdf.

Lockton Affinity. 2015. "2015 MSPAlliance-Cyber-Coverage." *MSPAlliance Cloud Insurance Program.* March 20. http://mspalliance.com/wp-content/uploads/2008/11/2015-MSPAlliance-Cyber-Coverage-10-Reasons-White-Paper-3-15.pdf.

McMillian, Jeffrey Wheatman & Rob. 2015. "Business, Not Bytes - A Practical View of Security Metrics." *Gartner Security & Risk Management Summit.* Washington D.C.: Gartner. 22.

Mohamed, Arif. 2013. "Data classification: why it is important and how to do it." *ComputerWeekly.* http://www.computerweekly.com/feature/Data-classification-why-it-is-important-and-how-to-do-it.

National Institute of Standards and Technology. 2014. "Framework for Improving Critical Infrastructure Cybersecurity." *National Institute of Standards and Technology.* February 12. Accessed June 11, 2016. http://www.nist.gov/cyberframework/upload/cybersecurity-framework-021214.pdf.

NIST 800-30 r1. 2012. "Guide for Conducting Risk Assessments." *NVLPUBS.NIST.GOV.* September. Accessed June 2016. http://nvlpubs.nist.gov/nistpubs/Legacy/SP/nistspecialpublication800-30r1.pdf.

NIST. 2015. "Cybersecurity Framework Frequently Asked Questions." *National Institute of Science and Technology - Cybersecurity Framework.* National Institute of Science and Technology. December 31. Accessed June 11, 2016. http://www.nist.gov/cyberframework/cybersecurity-framework-faqs.cfm.

NIST. 2004. "FIPS PUB 199." *Standards for Security Categorization of Federal Information and Information Systems.* Prod. Information Technology Laboratory Computer Security Division. Gaithersburg, MD: National Institute of Standards and Technology, February.

—. 2014. *Framework for Improving Critical Infrastructure Cybersecurity.* February 12. http://www.nist.gov/cyberframework/upload/cybersecurity-framework-021214.pdf.

Paul E. Proctor, Jeffrey Wheatman, Rob McMillan. 2016. "How to Build an Effective Cybersecurity and Technology Risk Presentation for Your Board of Directors." *Gartner Website.* March 03. http://www.gartner.com/document/3238219.

PCI-DSS. 2006. *Payment Card Industry Data Security Standards.* Accessed June 2016. https://www.pcisecuritystandards.org/.

Raptis, Steve. 2015. "Cyber Risk: Analyzing Cyber Risk Coverage." *Risk and Insurance.* March 13. http://www.riskandinsurance.com/analyzing-cyber-risk-coverage/.

Scholtz, Tom, and Rob McMillan. 2014. "Tips and Guidelines for Sizing Your Information Security Organization." *Gartner.* April 24. http://www.gartner.com/document/2718319?ref=TypeAheadSearch&qid=c0a5b37bd85c58a1a5eafcc60c0fdce8.

Security, Center for Internet. 2016. *CIS CONSENSUS INFORMATION SECURITY METRICS.* March 01. https://benchmarks.cisecurity.org/downloads/metrics/.

Security, ThreatTrack. 2014. *ThreatTrack Whitepapers.* December 13. http://www.threattracksecurity.com/resources/white-papers/chief-information-security-officers-misunderstood.aspx.

Seiner, Robert S. 2014. *Non-Invasive Data Governance, The Path of Least Resistance and Great Sucess.* Basking Ridge, NJ: Technics Publications.

The Santa Fe Strategy Center LTD. 2016. *Standardized Information Gathering Questionnaire.* Accessed June 13, 2016. https://sharedassessments.org/.

Tucker Bailey, Josh Brandley, and James Kaplan. 2013. "Business Functions: McKinsey&Company." *McKinsey&Company Website.* December. http://www.mckinsey.com/business-functions/business-technology/our-insights/how-good-is-your-cyberincident-response-plan.

UCF. 2004. *Unified Compliance Framework.* Accessed 2016. https://www.unifiedcompliance.com/.

Wikipedia 2. 2016. *ITIL security management.* March 19. Accessed June 12, 2016.

https://en.wikipedia.org/wiki/ITIL_security_manag
ement.

Wikipedia. 2016. *Capability Maturity Model Integration.*
March 31. Accessed June 10, 2016.
https://en.wikipedia.org/wiki/Capability_Maturity_
Model_Integration.

—. 2016. *ITIL.* May 31. Accessed June 12, 2016.
https://en.wikipedia.org/wiki/ITIL.

Index

I

Incident Management 233, 239, 304
Incident Response   163, 174, 175,
  239, 312, 314, 322
  attorney-client privilege   304
  escalation 5, 115, 195, 233, 304,
    316, 327
Indicators of Compromise   12, 157
Insurance
  cyber liability insurance 210, 219,
    222, 223

L

Laws
  breach notification
    Massachusetts   36, 49, 78
    Nevada   36
    New Mexico   49
    North Dakota   49
Legal Requirements
  Contracts
    master service agreements 86,
      120
    non-disclosure agreement
      (NDA) 102, 104, 105, 294,
      295, 303
    service level agreement (SLA)
      86, 105, 121, 125, 131,
      138, 140, 168
    service level objectives (SLO)
      86, 121
    contractual obligations   33, 43,
      54, 70, 71, 75, 85, 123, 224,
      289, 304
    federal law 35, 50, 53, 148, 198,
      289
    lawsuits & litigation 48, 159, 192,
      214, 238, 242
    state laws   54, 85

M

Mandates
  regulatory   61
Media

news media   48, 215
physical   81, 239, 290, 324
social media   29, 239, 274, 324
Metrics
  KPIs   93, 138
  MTTD   162, 163

N

National Association of Corporate
  Directors   193
Networks
  corporate   29, 233, 311

O

Obligations
  regulatory   15, 105, 196
Organization   1, 11, 13, 24, 25, 219
Organizational Hierarchy   35
  Chief Compliance Officer   23
  Chief Executive Officer   v, 1, 4, 6,
    7, 12, 14, 23, 24, 25, 93, 154,
    182, 185, 192, 201, 204, 227,
    313
  Chief Financial Officer   1, 5, 12,
    14, 23, 35, 36, 37, 38, 190,
    192, 227
  Chief Information Officer   1, 4, 5,
    6, 7, 8, 9, 12, 23, 24, 25, 31,
    35, 58, 85, 154, 201, 204,
    217, 218, 227, 298, 315
  Chief Operating Officer   5, 7, 23,
    35
  Chief Privacy Officer 29, 36, 227,
    297
  Chief Resilience Officer   4, 36,
    102, 190, 201, 315
  Chief Risk Officer   36, 59, 244,
    252
  Chief Technology Officer 4, 7, 12,
    23, 31, 35, 85, 154, 201, 204
Organizational Structure
  centralized / decentralized   5
  embedded   5, 39, 214
  full time employees   27
  leadership team   13, 14, 22, 67,
    92, 142, 147, 152, 154, 165,

S

About the Authors

Bill Bonney (CISA) is a Principal Consulting Analyst at TechVision Research with specialties in information security, Internet of Things (IoT) security and identity management. Prior to joining TechVision Research, he held numerous senior information security roles in various industries, including financial services, software and manufacturing.

Bill is a member of the Board of Advisors for CyberTECH, a San Diego incubator, and in on the board of directors for the San Diego CISO Round Table, a professional group focused on building relationships and fostering collaboration in information security management. Bill is a highly regarded speaker and panelist addressing technology and security concerns. He holds a Bachelor of Science degree in Computer Science and Applied Mathematics from Albany University.

LinkedIn Profile: https://www.linkedin.com/in/billbonney

Matt Stamper, CISA, CIPP-US, brings a multi-disciplinary understanding to cybersecurity. His diverse domain knowledge spans IT service management (ITSM), cloud services, control design and assessment (Sarbanes-Oxley, HIPAA/HITECH), privacy, governance, enterprise risk management (ERM), as well as international experience in both Latin America and China. His executive-level experience with

managed services, cybersecurity, data centers, networks services, and ITSM provides a unique perspective on the fast-changing world of enterprise IT, IoT, and cloud services.

Matt received a Bachelor of Arts from the University of California at San Diego, where he graduated Cum Laude and with Honors and Distinction in Political Science. His graduate studies include a Master of Arts in Pacific International Affairs from the University of California at San Diego and a Master of Science degree in

Telecommunications sponsored by AT&T.

LinkedIn Profile: https://www.linkedin.com/in/stamper

Gary R. Hayslip, Deputy Director, Chief Information Security Officer, City of San Diego, CA

As Chief Information Security Officer for the City of San Diego, Gary advises the City of San Diego's executive leadership (consisting of Mayoral, City Council, and 40+ city departments and agencies) on protecting city government information resources. Gary oversees citywide cybersecurity strategy and the enterprise cybersecurity program, cyber operations, compliance and risk assessment services. His mission includes creating a "risk aware" culture that places high value on securing city information resources and protecting personal information entrusted to the City of San Diego.

Gary is a proven cybersecurity professional, with a record of establishing enterprise information security programs and managing multiple cross-functional network and security teams. Gary has established a reputation as a highly skilled communicator and presenter. He has demonstrated ability to work within all business channels of an organization and is extremely effective in communicating the nuances of cyber security in business/risk terms for executive management. He has strong business acumen and problem solving abilities and solid critical thinking skills.

LinkedIn Profile: http://www.linkedin.com/in/ghayslip
Twitter: @ghayslip